FOLSOM'S 93

The Lives and Crimes of Folsom Prison's Executed Men

April Moore

CRAVEN STREET BOOKS

Fresno, California

Published by Craven Street Books
An imprint of Linden Publishing
2006 South Mary Street, Fresno, California 93721
(559) 233-6633 / (800) 345-4447
CravenStreetBooks.com

Craven Street Books and Colophon are trademarks of
Linden Publishing, Inc.

ISBN 978-1-61035-172-0

135798642

Printed in the United States of America
on acid-free paper.

Library of Congress Cataloging-in-Publication Data

Moore, April

Folsom's 93 : the lives and crimes of Folsom Prison's executed men / by April Moore.

    pages cm

Includes bibliographical references and index.

ISBN 978-1-61035-172-0 (pbk. : alk. paper)

1. Prisoners--California--Biography. 2. Executions and executioners--California. 3. Folsom Prison. 4. Murderers--California--Biography. 5. Prisons--California. I. Title. II. Title: Folsom's ninety-three.

HV9467.8.M66 2013

364.66092'279453--dc23

                        2013002868

Contents

Introduction

Growing up, I had a fascination with my great-great aunt. Betty was distinctive for both her six-foot height and her fiery red hair. She also possessed impeccable taste, invariably sporting the latest fashions. She could often be found lounging on her patio, wearing large sunglasses, a silk kimono, and smoking a cigarette. Her passion for Chinese art filled her home with Asian antiques—jade dragons, embellished screens, and ginger jars of every size and pattern.

Betty lived in Los Angeles, a fact that only added to my infatuation. Stories of Betty's work in L.A. clubs shimmered with exciting details I'd never imagined during my Colorado upbringing. Betty had married Tom, a self-proclaimed professional gambler who ran a bookie business from their home, and this situation made our visits to Betty's even more intriguing. Betty never divulged much of her secretive past, but several family members enjoyed dishing up the gossip they were privy to.

Not one to pass up an opportunity to impress and awe, on one occasion, Betty brought out a small, flat box during one of our visits. We never knew what treasure Betty would show us next. Sometimes it was a piece of art or an antique brooch. Her hats and costume jewelry always provided my sister and me with plenty of entertainment.

Expecting to see an antique Chinese sketch or a string of crushed pearls, we received a shock. From inside the box, an assortment of black-and-white mug shots—images of men with austere expressions and old-fashioned hairstyles—stared back at us. Betty had a flair for drama, so as a twelve-year-old I relished hearing the story behind this disturbing, yet fascinating, find.

"The Folsom warden gave these to him," she told us.

Betty met Tom in 1937 when she was 17. He was 46 and married. Tom's wife refused to grant him a divorce, but he and Betty carried on a relationship anyway. They finally married in 1968, after Tom's wife passed away. He made a living as a gambler and by investing in real estate deals. According to my grandmother, Tom entered a silent partnership with Anthony Cornero, an organized-crime figure, to build the Stardust Hotel in Las Vegas. Cornero died before construction was complete, and Tom apparently pulled out of the deal. Tom supposedly had more ties to the mob than just his relationship with Cornero. His inner circle of friends and associates included the notorious gangster Benjamin "Bugsy" Siegel. Betty and other family members insisted Tom never "crossed that line" into the "business," and preferred to remain only a social acquaintance to these men. People described Tom as kind and gentle, characteristics which he often disguised with a gruff exterior. He died in 1979.

When Betty eventually went through his belongings, she came across the box of mug shots. Other photos included twentieth century inmates lining up outside a prison, as well as images of what appeared to be the early construction of a cellblock and other surrounding buildings.

Stashed beneath the pictures was a stack of papers. On forty pages of onionskin, someone had typed a chronology of Folsom Prison, detailing its initial planning stages in 1858 through 1943, when, presumably, the text was written.

The text found with the photos documented important events, along with the prison population and daily per-capita costs. It also listed the number of parolees and how many had violated parole and returned to the prison. The text's author remains unknown, but according to Jim Brown, former Folsom guard and curator of the Folsom Prison Museum, an inmate entrusted with secretarial duties likely compiled the information from another source. The text serves as an entertaining read, describing in detail several escape attempts and other amusing anecdotes.

Tom acquired the photos when he visited the prison some time during the 1930s or 1940s to collect money from an indebted inmate. Betty said that Tom never intended to keep the pictures, but he didn't know who to give them to. They remained tucked in a closet for the next thirty to forty years until Betty rediscovered them. She showed them to me and my family in the late 1980s.

We warily looked through the pictures, fearing that somehow the fiendishness of the subject would rub off on us. Some men in the photos wore bowler hats, others bowties. A few had their hair smoothly slicked back, while others appeared disheveled and unkempt. The pictures spanned a number of years, as evidenced by the men's evolving fashions and mustache styles. Some mug shots depicted a friendly, neighborly-looking kind of guy, or even a schoolteacher type of person. Others fit the criminal stereotype, with shifty eyes and a menacing stare. Many looked downright surprised or stunned, not unlike a typical driver's license photo.

Ninety-three men were executed at Folsom prison from 1895 to 1937. All had been convicted of first-degree murder, except one, and all were hanged to death.

Typed on the back of each picture is the man's name, along with information such as his crime, the county in which his particular crime occurred, and his date of execution. At the top right corner was a number—the order in which he was executed. A few of the pictures had a piece of paper attached to the photo with a rusty paperclip, providing more information about the condemned man and his crime.

The pictures and the original document remained with Betty, but she supplied us with copies of the text. As I grew older, I stored Betty's unusual treasure in the back of mind, recalling every so often that my great-great uncle had visited Folsom prison once and brought back creepy photos of inmates.

In 2008, I found a copy of the text among my father's own writings. I had forgotten he planned to write about the photographs, but he passed away the previous year. I spent the next hour reading the pages, something I hadn't bothered to do until then. As a writer and history enthusiast, I was enthralled. I needed to see the pictures again, but Betty had since died. Fortunately, my grandfather, Betty's nephew had kept them. "I don't know why you'd want to look at these ugly mugs, but you're free to have them," he said. Frankly, I didn't know either, but if there were stories behind those mug shots, I wanted to tell them.

Within a week, I had the photos and original text. Perhaps it was because of their particularly sad, vacant eyes or their sinister glares that I recognized certain faces from when I first laid eyes on them nearly twenty years earlier. After I had exhausted online resources, my ensuing research led to two trips to California's State Archives and a tour of Folsom Prison in 2011. After four years, the project that began with a return trip down an unlikely memory lane turned into a book detailing the eerily fascinating lives of ninety-three condemned men and their victims. The stories that unfolded made me cringe, laugh, and cry. Regardless of my personal reactions to these men and their lives, I knew these were stories that deserved to be told.

> "Strap the man's hands straight down his sides, so his elbows will not strike against the sides of the trap as he drops through. Strap him on the trap. One man places the noose over his head, the knot behind his left ear. Another places the black cap on. Another buckles a strap below his knees. The noose is drawn with a quick pull as tight as possible, and the trap is sprung."
> —James A. Johnston, one-time warden of Folsom, San Quentin, and Alcatraz prisons, April 16, 1916

Death by Hanging

James Johnston saw forty-seven men die on the gallows. He attended the executions only because the law required it of him. "Every execution upset me," he wrote in his 1937 book, *Prison Life Is Different*. "I could not get used to them. I could not get hardened to the idea of seeing a man swing to everlasting destiny on the end of a rope; not even when it seemed the logical ending to a lawless life or the proper penalty for a monstrous murder of extreme abhorrence."

Folsom's Condemned Row, or "Back Alley," as it was called, was a long narrow room of grey granite. Two rows of solitary cells lined the room. At the end of the room, thirteen steps led upward to the gallows. Some historians say each step represented the convicting jury and judge and that above the loop of the noose, the rope wrapped around thirteen times. Others scoffed at this assertion, saying it was just an instance of the unlucky number. Either way, the prisoner climbed these steps to stand on the trapdoor. After a given prisoner was duly executed, each man awaiting the same fate was moved from his current stone cell to the next stone cell, located closer to the stairs that led to the scaffold, until eventually he occupied the last cell next to the gallows. Thus, each condemned man knew when he was next to die.

Executions were performed on Fridays. On Wednesdays, the Captain of the Guard selected two guards to act as the "death watch." He also determined who would carry out the execution itself.

In the early years, Folsom's wardens sent invitations printed on white cards to those they deemed would be interested in witnessing the execution. "Strange that anyone should actually like to see a hanging," wrote Johnston, "but soon after the newspapers printed details of a scheduled event, I would get letters asking me to put the writers on the list."

Usually, the condemned man spent his final hours writing letters, listening to records played on a phonograph the warden provided, and partaking in his last meal. "From the way he eats they know how he is going to take it—whether he will hope on, or give up," Johnston wrote. "Most of them hope. They look for last minute reprieves. Frequently, condemned men sent for me a few minutes after they got upstairs. They would want me to telephone lawyers and telegraph the governor. It was easy enough to send messages, but difficult to tell them the truth about their chances and at the same time keep hope and courage alive. When they sent for me the second night, it meant entrusting me with last words to be delivered to nearest and dearest after ten o'clock Friday morning."

The customary death suit was all black, with a collarless white shirt that left room for the noose. Minutes before the time of execution, which typically took place at ten in the morning, the warden and two guards arrived at the death cell. A guard then slipped a leather belt around the prisoner's waist, strapping his wrists to his sides. The condemned man and his guards then began their short, grim march. It wasn't uncommon for the condemned man to have his last cigarette perched between his lips during his walk to the gallows. The prison chaplain led the way, saying a prayer. Once on the trap, an officer placed the black cap over the prisoner's head, while another looped the noose over his neck. A third guard arrived and strapped the man's ankles together. The men worked quickly.

A guard pulled the rope tight, securing it behind the prisoner's left ear. Then the guard raised his right hand and three others cut the cords, releasing the trap and sending the inmate to his death with a violent wrench. Spectators would clearly hear the drop of the trap. Someone usually fainted. "It's all over—not before they realize what has happened, but too quickly for them to take in the details," observed Johnston. Marked by an obviously broken neck, the man's head hung limply toward the right.

The prison physician climbed a small stepladder and steadied the still twitching body. He monitored the slowing heartbeat, which oftentimes took up to fifteen minutes to completely stop. Finally, he would make his declaration: "Dead! Officially dead!"

Other convicts would then carry in a coffin and place it under the suspended figure. While one man cut down the body, others would lower him into the plain pine box for transportation to the morgue. If the body wasn't claimed within twenty-four hours, the dead man would be buried in the prison cemetery, identified only by his prison number.

PART I: 1895–1900

Folsom Wardens: **Thomas Pockman, appointed July 15, 1880**

        John McComb, appointed November 1, 1881

        Charles Aull, appointed December 26, 1887

        Thomas Wilkinson, October 18, 1889–December 1, 1903

California Governors: **James Budd, January 11, 1895–January 4, 1889**

        Henry Gage, January 4, 1889–January 6, 1903

Approaching the turn of the twentieth century, Californians had reason to be optimistic. The advent of electricity illuminated San Francisco as early as 1879, and by 1900 smaller communities and business districts benefited from this technology. In 1895, a long-distance power line connected Folsom Prison to downtown Sacramento, home to the Grand Electric Carnival. Even the concept of solar energy was advanced in California during this time, promising to provide farmers with power to increase productivity and eliminate payments to the water-power companies for the same services.

The newly invented automobile presented Californians with opportunities to expand their businesses, increase productivity, and, of course, travel freely without the limitations of train schedules. During the earliest years of automobile production, only the wealthy could afford such luxury, but by the early 1900s, this innovative machine began to make its way to residents across the state.

In addition to the significant mining industry, the Southern Pacific railroad ruled California's economy, much to the chagrin of most residents. In 1900, the railroad monopoly had grown into the state's largest employer and landowner and enjoyed a seemingly insurmountable stronghold in California politics, which the company used to protect and increase its interests. Owning the bulk of the state's ferry services, local transit companies, and wharf facilities, the railroad crushed any competition, with average California citizens bearing the brunt of the railroad's greed. Californians were also losing patience with the corrupt, boss-ruled municipal governments which controlled water, power, and transportation. Change would not come until the 1911 election of Governor Hiram Johnson, who ushered in the "Era of Reform."

California's population exploded to one and a half million residents in 1900. This population growth helped San Francisco become a major industrial player, attracting migrants from around the United States and other countries. Anti-Chinese sentiments rose when Chinese began performing jobs for lower wages and when diseases and problems with drugs, such as opium, spread from the Chinese communities to the general population.

Starting in the 1870s, the Chinese community had formed various "societies" or "companies," based mainly on trade guilds. A paid-membership promised not only hospital care and housing, but also protection in the form of the highbinders. Likened to gangs, highbinders were hit men who offered services to those who may have been offended by another company. The highbinder regarded his job as being as legitimate as any other profession and considered his position honorable.

During the 1890s, two major highbinder gangs, the Chee Hong Tong and the Bing Hong Tong, wreaked havoc in Sacramento and San Francisco. The hub for these rival gangs, downtown Sacramento, also served as the venue for numerous "wars" between them. These brutal battles escalated in the early years of the 1890s. A cigar merchant who was gunned down in his Sacramento shop led to Folsom Prison's first execution in 1895.

"I do not know the man. I never see him. How can I shoot him?"
—Chin Hane, 1893

1. Chin Hane, December 13, 1895

During the spring and summer of 1892, downtown Sacramento suffered through multiple Chinese gang wars between the Bing Hong Tong and Chee Hong Tong societies. On May 31, a gunman killed forty-five-year-old cigar store merchant Lee Gong. Called a "well-behaved, industrious Chinaman" by the *Sacramento Record-Union*, Gong lived in an apartment above his shop with his wife, Ah Wah, and their two young daughters. Gong took a bullet through his chest and died in his wife's arms, his daughters looking on. The same newspaper remarked, "she [one of the daughters] was exhibiting as much feeling and agony as any white child would have manifested under the circumstances."

Rumors quickly circulated that the Bing Hong Tong society had marked Gong for death. Gong allegedly supported its rival tong society. According to Ah Wah and Lee Sam, the cook, the man who killed her husband bore a scar on the side of his head. Ah Wah claimed that two men entered the store. When she turned to retrieve a cigar for one of them, his scar-faced companion shot Gong through a window which led to an adjoining room. Lee Sam chased after the fleeing men and fired his own gun into the air. The gunshots apparently ignited a cacophony of gunfire that erupted throughout the city, sparking a late night riot.

At 11:30 that night, a Chinese man named Yesso Jim led officers to a home where Chin Hane relaxed on a bed, smoking opium. According to later reports, officers initially attempted to arrest another man in the home, but Yesso Jim clearly identified Hane, and so the officers arrested Hane for Gong's murder.

A scar ran down the right side of Hane's head. It matched the critical identifying detail that Ah Wah had provided. When asked about the riot, Hane and

3

others, including the houseowner and her young son, said they thought they had heard firecrackers, not gunfire.

Soon, police also arrested one Hoey Yen Sing as he slept, recovering from a bullet wound in his leg he had suffered during a previous riot. Officers dragged him to the police station. There, Hane waited in a large cell, surrounded by nearly twenty other suspects. Ah Wah came to identify her husband's killer and immediately focused on Hane. "She sprang at him with flashing eyes and in great excitement, fairly dragging him from the farthest corner behind the crowd," wrote the *Sacramento Record-Union*. The next day, Lee Sam identified Hane as Gong's killer, yet according to the newspaper, several onlookers stated, "That is not the one; that is the wrong man."

A city newspaper described Hane as a "villainous-looking fellow" who "maintained a stubborn silence and did not look his accusers in the face. Hane is a harder-looking customer than the average highbinder and appears to be a few shades darker in color and more dogged in demeanor." The newspaper expressed its opinion of Gong's wife, too: "So far, Ah Wah has shown herself to be, unlike most Chinese, possessed of the ordinary human emotions, and her grief over Gong's sudden taking off is fairly pitiful."

Police accused Hane of being a member of the Bing Hong Tong, which had ordered him to kill Gong. Hane denied any involvement with the gang and claimed that he only arrived in Sacramento from San Francisco the day before the shooting.

Hane told authorities that he was a doctor, a trade he learned from his father. Hane said he specialized in venereal diseases and he was tending to a patient during the riot—a story later corroborated by others in the patient's home. Hane also told authorities he did not know the other suspect, Sing, or Yesso Jim, the man who fingered him.

The trial began a year later. Describing the two defendants, the *Record-Union* wrote, "The Chinamen are very unprepossessing specimens of a race which is not very prepossessing at its best. Hane especially has a cruel face and cold, ferocious eyes. He has an ugly scar on the right side of his temple and looks as if he was cut out specially for his profession of highbinder. Hoey Yen Sing is not quite so repulsive-looking, but is far from being a beauty." The reporter then described Ah Wah as "not uncomely for a Chinawoman and is evidently possessed of much finer feelings than the average of her race."

Ah Wah testified seeing Hane, whom she had never met before the incident. Her story at trial did not vary from that of the night of the murder. However, Lee Sam, the other principle witness, was missing and never testified at the trial. The defense attempted to show that Gong died from random riot-related gunfire, but the jury found Sing and Hane guilty of murder. Sing received a life sentence and Hane received the death penalty. He was incarcerated in Folsom Prison.

The defense immediately filed an appeal, sporting affidavits from several Chinese locals who swore that prosecution witnesses were paid fifty dollars each to testify against Hane. For nearly two years, Hane and Sing awaited the outcome of their appeal. In September of 1895, the California Supreme Court affirmed the judgment. Hane would become the subject of Folsom Prison's first execution.

A crowd of witnesses came to appeal to Governor Budd's private secretary, E. C. McCabe, proclaiming that Hane did not murder Gong. They asserted that key witnesses were bribed, including Ah Wah, who reportedly received $400 and passage to China. Several of the Chinese told of how Lee Sam, who conveniently disappeared before the trial, was in love with Ah Wah, and together the two planned Gong's murder. After interviewing each person, McCabe determined the information to be inconsistent and contradictory. Governor Budd refused to interfere with Hane's execution.

Many witnesses maintained that Lee Sam killed Gong and accused Hane of the crime. He admitted to willingly firing his gun at the scene and his was the only gun found in the vicinity of the crime. Yet Hane's visible scar proved the linchpin in his conviction.

Folsom Prison conducted its first execution on December 13, 1895, sending the alleged highbinder to his death.

"If I am guilty, then let them find out."
—Ivan Kovalev, 1895

2. Ivan Kovalev, February 21, 1896

Seventy miles southwest of Cape Sirotoko in the Okhotsk Sea, the captain of the *Chas W. Morgan*, an American whaling ship, spotted something in the water. It was an open boat containing ten Russian men, nearly frozen and starved. It was September of 1893; the men had escaped from Saghalien Prison in Siberia ten days earlier. For weeks, they had planned the break. They hid an iron kettle, a tin pan, handfuls of rice, and a keg of water in the woods. Then they stole a boat moored near the guard camp and rowed it with rough-hewn timber oars. The men didn't speak of other details, although one did remark that he would not be surprised if a couple of the guards turned up missing.

Transported to the *Cape Horn Pigeon* via another whaler, the Russians arrived in San Francisco in November. They were immediately jailed while awaiting official word on their situation from the U.S. government. A newly enacted treaty between the United States and Russia contained extradition clauses that made even political offenses extraditable crimes.

Months earlier, a St. Petersburg journalist visited Saghalien Prison and reported the severe isolation, abuse, and even cannibalism that allegedly occurred. His article, which ran in American papers for several months, explained that a majority of the inmates were political prisoners. When the ten Russian escapees adamantly claimed to be political prisoners, they received public sympathy and support despite the Russian minister's contention that they were indeed criminals, and that three of them were murderers.

Russian professor and lawyer J. A. Hourwich, of the University of Chicago, came to San Francisco to represent the men. "I have in my possession a list of five hundred Siberian political refugees. Should the names of these ten men now held in San Francisco appear in this list, the case will be settled." He also presented the affidavits of numerous other Russians in the United States who were "familiar with the circumstances under which [the escapees] were sent to Siberia."

Based on Saghalien Prison's reputation, Hourwich's findings, and the sympathies of the Americans, U. S. Secretary of the Treasury John Carlile made his decision—he released the men. He then sent a message to the Russians: "The United States will not be bullied." American newspapers praised their government for saving these "poor refugees" from the sufferings of their homeland, which they called unscrupulous and undiplomatic. Liberated, the men were put on "display" as martyrs at a five-and-dime museum in San Francisco; then they mysteriously disappeared—but not for long.

Within two years, several of the ten Russian prison escapees were serving time in Folsom and San Quentin for various offenses, including burglary and embezzlement. However, one of the men made it all the way to the gallows of Folsom Prison. His name was Ivan Kovalev.

Between the Chinese gang wars and constant robberies, Sacramento experienced a "carnival of crime" in 1894. On December 29, a double murder sent the city over the edge, and committees were formed, joining with the Citizens' Protective Association to rid the city of all "criminal and tramp elements." The association forced the closing of numerous saloons—mostly those considered dives—and broke up hobo camps. Detectives pored over lists of ex-convicts they could target to drive from the city. However, despite all efforts, police could not find the one responsible for murdering fifty-nine-year-old Francis Weber and his wife, Lizzie, who owned the Temperance Family Grocery and Goods store. The disturbing crime scene made it difficult for police to fathom such violence.

Luther, the couple's twenty-five-year-old son, had entered his parents' store late in the morning of December 30 and discovered the gruesome scene. Drenched in blood, the floor revealed both bare and shoed footprints. Two killers had obviously waded through the gore as they ransacked the store and the upstairs apartment. Luther noticed a pool of blood dripping from the ceiling. In the apartment above, he found his father. He had been struck with an ax twenty-six times and was unrecognizable. His mother suffered the same grisly fate and her body lay in the hallway. The apparent killers, who would later be named as Ivan Kovalev and Matthew Stcherbakov, had made off with jewelry, cash, a revolver, and clothing.

Two days later, on New Year's Eve, Kovalev shared a San Francisco jail cell with several other men arrested for intoxication. Following their release the next morning, jailers found a woman's gold watch under the toilet seat. It belonged to Lizzie Weber.

"Someone in the San Francisco police department is evidently unfit to be prison keeper," wrote the *Oakland Tribune*. Jailors hadn't searched Kovalev or the others because they assumed them harmless, holiday revelers. Most likely, Kovalev stashed the watch, with its engraving partially scratched off, to avoid being found with it.

Kovalev and his cohort Stcherbakov continued their crime spree. On March 31 in San Jose, the men were joined by another Russian footpad and together they attempted to rob business owner William Dowdigan as he walked home.

A struggle ensued. Stcherbakov suffered a knife wound to his neck, inflicted in self-defense by Dowdigan, who fled unharmed. Fearing a deathbed confession, Kovalev and his new companion-in-crime stabbed Stcherbakov in the heart and stripped his body of money, valuables, and clothing. They buried the body in an empty lot several blocks away. Meanwhile, San Francisco police continued to run down their list of New Year's Eve "guests," but hadn't yet identified Kovalev—or John Koboloff, his alias. By the end of June, however, they had made more progress.

Vladislav Zabrewski had been the *Cape Horn Pigeon's* ship carpenter. He told police that Kovalev had come to his home drunk and confessed that he and Stcherbakov killed Francis and Lizzie Weber. Kovalev's roommate, Arnold Levin, corroborated the claims and Kovalev was soon in custody. Acting on Zabrewski's word, authorities exhumed Stcherbakov's body and identified the vest and coat he was wearing when buried as Mr. Weber's. Stcherbakov's trousers were missing.

Although at the time of his questioning he was wearing suspenders Mr. Weber's daughter had made for her father, Kovalev claimed he had not been in Sacramento at the time of the murders. However, a witness named George Jost stated at the preliminary hearing that he had seen Kovalev outside the Webers' store on the night of the crime.

Unable to speak or understand English, Kovalev pleaded not guilty, but said in Russian, "If I am guilty, let them find out." Trial was set for November. By October, Kovalev had grown despondent and county jailers described him as "crazy." Unable to converse with English-speaking prisoners, he became frantic, destroying his cot and breaking anything he could get his hands on. He also complained constantly of head pain.

His court-appointed attorneys, Major W. A. Anderson and Senator E. C. Hart, acknowledged that their client's circumstances appeared "exceedingly black." Their defense was that Kovalev had fallen victim to a well-planned conspiracy. Supposedly, certain Russians in San Francisco wanted him out of the way.

By the time the trial began on November 4, Kovalev claimed to have no memory of the crime, and oftentimes he didn't seem to understand anything said to him, even through an interpreter. Anderson and Hart requested an insanity hearing to show that Kovalev's emaciated and listless appearance indicated insanity. Newspapers referred to him as "Crazy Kovalev," but the three examining doctors concluded that he suffered from melancholia. At one point, when pressed further about the murders, Kovalev replied flippantly, "Ah, that's a question. That's for you to find out."

Finally, Kovalev told the jury what they wanted to hear. The *Oakland Tribune* summed it up for its readers: "Ivan Kovalev, rioter, thief, and murderer, standing in the shadows of the gallows, and manacled with a chain of proof not one link of which is imperfect or unbroken, had confessed. . ." It came even as a shock to his attorneys, whom he also confessed to during a court recess. However, Kovalev only admitted to being at the crime scene—not to killing Mr. and Mrs. Weber. That he lay upon his companion, Matthew Stcherbakov, who Kovalev claimed used "hypnotic influence" over him while he watched Stcherbakov butcher the elderly couple.

Against his attorneys' protests, Kovalev took the stand. The judge told him that he need not testify, but Kovalev replied, "I was present and participated in the murder." The courtroom erupted, and the judge ordered Kovalev's remark stricken from record, as it was not what the judge had asked. Kovalev proceeded to confess on the stand, describing how he and Stcherbakov climbed the back fence and killed Mr. Weber in the entrance of the store, dragging his body to the upstairs apartment. There they encountered Mrs. Weber, subsequently killing her in the hallway.

The jury wasted no time in reaching a guilty verdict. Kovalev was sentenced to hang on February 21. Newspapers no longer supported him as a Russian refugee. "A sentimental sympathy for bad men has seldom gone so far as it did for these escaped criminals," they wrote, adding, "A great deal of sympathy was wasted on these diabolical criminals."

While confined for two months at Folsom Prison, Kovalev was described as a "walking dead man," and he was quoted as saying he'd rather be hanged than go insane from the mental torture he was experiencing. It was rumored that the former shoemaker also confessed to a guard that he had been sentenced to Saghalien Prison for life after poisoning a man in Russia.

On the morning of his execution, Kovalev refused an offer of whiskey, opting for a glass of milk instead. Called a "cringing coward" on the scaffold, Kovalev was weak and trembly. He could barely walk up the scaffold. Without a word, Ivan Kovalev fell through the trap to his fate, less than a minute after leaving his cell.

"I thought that if I did attempt to go away, I would get shot in the back, and I thought I would stand and take it in the front . . ."
—John Craig, 1894

3. John Craig, June 12, 1896

Through the kitchen window, two-year-old Edna Craig giggled at her father's silly faces. John Craig stood outside his in-law's ranch a few miles outside Los Angeles, hoping to see his estranged wife Emily and their three young children. He walked to the screen door and opened it, but the glassed door remained locked. Emily moved aside the curtain covering the glass and peered through.

"What do you want?"

Craig replied that he only wanted to see his children, that he had a right to see them. Albertina Jensen, the house servant, attempted to herd the children away from the brewing confrontation between the couple, but they refused to leave. Craig pleaded with his wife. George Hunter, one of Emily's brothers, approached from one end of the porch. Craig backed away as Emily unlocked the door and let George in. Craig watched through the screen as George walked down the hall into the dining room. He emerged seconds later and walked toward his brother-in-law.

Craig eyed a glint of something shiny in Hunter's right hand. Hunter swung the screen door closed and whirled around to face Craig. Two quick shots rang out and Hunter fell to the porch, a bullet in his cheek. Emily Craig's body lay in the doorway behind him.

Emily married twenty-nine-year-old John Craig on her nineteenth birthday on December 8, 1884. Nearly ten years later, Emily filed for divorce, citing cruelty at the hands of her husband. She moved to her parents' ranch with her three young children. William and Mary Hunter then moved into their daughter's former home on Buena Vista Street in Los Angeles and evicted their estranged son-in-law.

By this time, Craig had lost his position as a police officer with the city of Los Angeles, although he served a short stint as a United States deputy marshal. His reputation varied widely, ranging from "quarrelsome and aggressive" to a "devoted and loving husband and father." The disdain his in-laws felt for him, however, was indisputable. Mary often threatened to "horsewhip" Craig if he ever visited the ranch.

Once, after being refused visitation with his children, Craig told his wife, "It is awful bad when a fellow comes out here to see his children, to be treated this way." During an argument with George Hunter, Craig accused George of destroying his marriage, saying, "You have coaxed my wife from me, you have taken my children by force, and taken them out there, and deny me, and refuse me by force to see my children, and now you are going to kick me out of my house and home where I have got no place to live, and no money or work, and you are trying to drive me from the city."

Craig also accused George Hunter of "abusing" him with profanity and threats when Craig tried to see the children, claiming that Hunter had said, "If you ever come out to the ranch I will fill you so full of holes that you will never be able to carry them [the children] home." Despite the threat, Craig would try to visit the ranch again.

At Craig's trial, Albertina Jensen, the house servant at the Hunter ranch, testified that on July 25 John Craig held a revolver in each hand, stepped over his wife's prone body, and said, "I've got revolvers enough for the whole family." She recounted that the Craig children, crying hysterically, gathered around their mother's body. Jensen herself escaped to one of the other Hunter homes on the property where Willie, the Craig's eight-year-old, had also fled. In the meantime, Craig unhitched his horse and buggy from a tree and rode to 727 Buena Vista Street, where his in-laws sat on the porch. Craig shot William and Mary Hunter, killing them both. He then turned the gun on himself, inflicting only a superficial wound.

Prosecutors predicted they would easily win a conviction for the murder of Emily alone. They charged Craig with the single count of homicide and decided not to "complicate" the case with further charges. Craig maintained that he shot George Hunter in self-defense and that Emily died accidentally as she stood behind her brother.

One witness, Peter Castoreno, testified that weeks prior to the killing, Craig confided that he loved his wife and children, but the "old folks" were against him and Craig would "put an end to all of them." Craig emphatically denied Castoreno's testimony. He claimed that he hardly knew Castoreno and would never speak of private affairs with a stranger.

While on the stand, Craig explained the testimony of three Hispanics from whom he borrowed guns on the day of the murder(s). Craig said he ran into an old friend who wanted to ride to Pasadena, and the friend had asked Craig to procure guns for self-protection. The friend later decided to go to San Francisco with another companion, leaving Craig with two loaded guns. Efforts to locate and subpoena this traveling friend were unsuccessful.

Craig described borrowing the horse and buggy from an acquaintance, with the intention of riding to the ranch to see his children. On the way, he stopped at George Paine's house to ask him to accompany him to the Hunter ranch. Paine's daughter informed Craig her father was working in the fields, so Craig went on alone to the ranch.

The defense argued that Craig's inquiry at the Paine farm showed he wanted to bring a witness and, therefore, had no intention of killing anyone.

Albertina Jensen's testimony proved most damaging to Craig's defense. Not only did she testify that Craig threatened to kill her, she swore that no one ever found a gun on George Hunter. During the trial, Craig, who insisted he feared for his life when Hunter approached him that night, stated, "I thought that if I did attempt to go away, I would get shot in the back, and I thought I would stand and take it in the front." Craig told the Court, "I'm sorry. If I killed my wife, I did it accidentally."

It didn't take the jury long to convict Craig of first degree murder. Craig's attorneys immediately filed an appeal, but the California Supreme Court deemed that Craig "unlawfully, feloniously, and with malice aforethought" shot George Hunter and Emily Craig.

A month before his execution, Craig received hopeful news: Several affidavits filed in court supported Craig's claim of accidental death. Adele McCarn, unacquainted with either Craig or the Hunters, had information regarding Jensen's testimony. She claimed Jensen told her she loved Jesse Hunter, Emily's brother, and that Jesse wanted Craig to be hanged. Jensen perjured herself to keep her job with the Hunters. McCarn also claimed that Jensen felt wracked with guilt and attempted to poison herself shortly before testifying, but the druggist gave her "some drug instead to quiet her nerves." Jensen reportedly told McCarn the drug "had such an effect on her physical and mental system that she hardly knew what she said or did for several days."

Susie Hunter, one of Emily's sisters-in-law, believed Craig unintentionally killed his wife. She swore in an affidavit that Mary Hunter constantly tormented Craig with threats, but that Craig "was always a kind, devoted, and loving husband and father." Susie's statement continued: "...on the 25th day of July, 1894, about an hour before she was killed, Emily Craig said to me, 'I wonder if Jack [Craig] has had anything to eat today. He gave me all he had, except fifteen cents last night.'" Susie went on to say, "The children were affectionate, at all times, towards their father and he was to them."

Jailors and sheriff's deputies deemed Craig a "model prisoner," who protested his innocence and showered his children with love and affection during monthly visits to the jail.

The Court refused to re-evaluate the case. The day before mounting the gallows, Craig made his second suicide attempt by driving a wire through his chest, just missing his heart. The *Oakland Tribune* assured its readers the condemned man would not escape the noose: "The wound is not fatal and it will not interfere with tomorrow's necktie party."

The following day, the *Tribune* described Craig's final moments:

> There could not have been a more perfect execution. The condemned man was completely resigned to his fate and walked to the gallows as coolly as though going to a wedding. As he stood on the gallows waiting for the attendants to strap his feet, he looked down at the faces upturned at him from the floor below and his eyes fell on Joseph Hunter, one of the sons of the old couple whom [sic] Craig so cruelly butchered two years ago. No sooner did Craig see Hunter, than he gave a sudden start and riveted his eyes full upon him and slowly shook his head. He then said in a voice that could be heard throughout the room: "Oh, Joe! I love you." He then raised his eyes to heaven and closing them remained in that position until the trap was sprung.

"I comitted [sic] this crime of murder under the influence of liquor; had it not
been for liquor I certainly never would have done it."
—Paulo Kamaunu, 1894

4. Paulo Kamauna, June 19, 1896

Paulo Kamaunu left his native homeland of the Sandwich Islands (present-day Hawaii), leaving behind a servant position in the Queen's home, to travel to California in the 1890s. By May of 1894, Kamaunu and his companion, Le Loi, were making a living working as woodchoppers. One job took them to Latrobe, California, near the remote home of sixty-three-year-old widow Ellen Robinson. Kamaunu purchased a chicken from her and later noted to Loi that the elderly woman readily made change for a five-dollar gold coin. As she lived alone, Kamaunu saw her as an easy target.

The next morning, a neighbor found Ellen Robinson's crushed and battered body lying near the entrance to her home. Her lower jaw was broken, as were each of her ribs, and her face bore the unmistakable imprint of a boot heel. Robinson's home had been ransacked, furniture overturned, and drawers and cabinets hung open.

Soon afterward, police arrested Kamaunu and Loi as they boarded a train to Sacramento. Each man pointed his finger at the other, but Kamaunu happened to be wearing boots with mismatched heels, as if one heel had recently been replaced. Kamaunu then confessed to the County Clerk, claiming his intoxication had led to the murder. At trial, however, the confession proved to have been involuntary and, therefore, was inadmissible in court; Kamaunu denied all guilt. Despite all circumstantial evidence, Kamaunu, the man labeled by one newspaper as "a handsome specimen of physical manhood," received a guilty verdict. The Hawaiian government pleaded with Governor James Budd for a commutation of sentence, but no evidence supported it. On June 19, 1896, without any final words, Paulo Kamaunu fell through the trap.

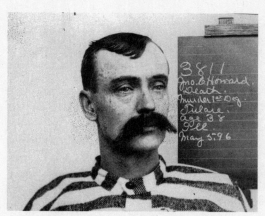

"Well boys, the hide goes with the tallow..."
—John Howard, on the scaffold, 1896

5. John E. Howard, July 17, 1896

John Howard claimed he had been acting in his capacity as deputy marshal when he went to the Tulare, California, home of Martanani Del Nini and his mistress Susana Del Gardo on June 16, 1894. Howard initially insisted he held a warrant for Del Nini's arrest for beating Del Gardo. However, upon his arrival at Del Nini's house, he decided Del Nini "was not the man I am after."

At Howard's suggestion, the two men set out for the Europa Hotel. Del Nini went to the hotel dining room, while Howard continued on to a bordello, where he remained for some time. Witnesses later reported that Howard eventually returned to the hotel dining room and argued with Del Nini. The two men moved outside to the back of the hotel, where Howard drew a pistol from his pocket. As Del Nini turned to go back inside, Howard called Del Nini "a son of a bitch" and shot him in the back of the head.

Howard acted as his own attorney at his trial. He claimed Susana Del Gardo sought help from him the day before the shooting, saying Del Nini was physically abusive. The following day, Howard said he ran into Del Nini at the Europa Hotel. Del Nini said, "You son of a bitch, you want my woman to have me arrested." Howard asserted that Del Nini pulled a knife, forcing Howard to shoot him in self-defense. During trial, Del Gardo testified that Howard had made threatening remarks toward Del Nini, and she claimed she had never contacted police for help. Moreover, no evidence existed of a warrant issued for Del Nini's arrest. Finally, Del Nini's knife never surfaced, although Howard swore he saw another man grab the knife and flee. This evidence, combined with the fact that Del Nini was shot in the back of the head, resulted in a guilty verdict. The Appellate Court affirmed the verdict and Howard hanged on July 17, 1896.

15

"Am I hurt much?" "My good man, you are dead already."
—Roberts's victim's final conversation with a doctor, 1896

6. George Washington Roberts, September 4, 1896

On April 14, 1896, George Roberts and Walter Freeman, a twenty-four-year-old hotel owner and the son of former California Senator J. H. Miller, sat drinking in a saloon in Latrobe, California, twenty miles outside Placerville. The men discussed wrestling, a subject Roberts enjoyed debating. According to witnesses, fifty-seven-year-old Roberts tried to engage Freeman in a wresting match of their own, but the young athlete replied, "You are too old a man for me." Roberts insisted and, finally, Freeman quickly "floored" his opponent.

Dusting himself off, Roberts bought a round of drinks and left the saloon. Within thirty minutes, Roberts returned, brandishing a pistol that bystanders promptly took from him. Later, with a calm and friendly demeanor, he joined Freeman at the bar. Then, in an unexpected rage, Roberts drew a jackknife from his pocket and sliced Freeman's throat, severing his jugular vein. Lying in the arms of a doctor, Freeman reportedly asked, "Am I hurt much?" to which the doctor replied, "My good man, you are dead already." Indeed, Freeman died within minutes. Other bar patrons held Roberts until the sheriff arrived.

At his trial, Roberts blamed excessive drinking for the attack on Freeman. "Well, I can recollect eight or ten drinks I had in me . . . before I stopped counting." Roberts insisted he didn't remember the attack, but somehow he recalled that Freeman challenged him to a wresting match and Roberts claimed he had replied, "I am too old to wrestle." Roberts also told the jury that Freeman wanted him to pay for two rounds of drinks in a row. On June 3, 1896, after deliberating for three hours, the jury returned a guilty verdict of murder in the first degree.

While awaiting his execution at Folsom, Roberts earned a reputation for considerable bravado. One newspaper called him "one of the jolliest prisoners here." He even joked he would dance a jig on the scaffold. Freeman's father and brothers watched Roberts swing from the noose on September 4, 1896.

"I want nothing to do with you."
—Benito Lopez to his victim before killing him, 1896

7. Benito Lopez, May 21, 1897

When April of 1896 arrived, George Washburn had been a resident of San Andreas in Calaveras County for forty-one years. He and his long-time neighbor, Benito Lopez, rarely got along. Washburn's backyard sat across the road from the front of Lopez's home. A major source of angst between the men stemmed from a spring on Lopez's property that constantly overflowed, flooding Washburn's garden and damaging his well.

The sixty-eight-year-old Washburn had grown weary of his neighbor's negligence and decided to remedy the problem himself. Washburn grabbed a hoe, walked to the road, and began to dig a small trench to divert the water from his yard. Lopez stormed out of his house and demanded that Washburn stop. At sixty-nine years, Lopez had a long history of violent behavior. He had recently been issued a peace bond after stabbing one of his tenants.

Washburn continued working, while exchanging heated words with Lopez and calling him a thief. Washburn's wife watched the scene unfold from near the house. At one point, her husband raised the hoe and waved it at Lopez, but the men stood too far apart for Washburn to harm his neighbor.

Lopez retreated to his home and returned with a .45 caliber Colt. He told Washburn, "I want nothing to do with you," and then he shot Washburn twice, once in the back of the head and once in the shoulder. Lopez quietly went back into his cabin and placed the gun under his mattress. He then went to town to tell Constable Masterson what he had done.

"What did you shoot him with?" asked Masterson.

"A pistol, and a big one—I meant to kill," replied Lopez.

After he was found guilty and sentenced to death, Lopez's children pleaded with Governor James Budd, emphasizing their father's age and ill health. His daughter, Louise, claimed her father suffered from partial paralysis and was "out of his head at times." Budd refused to grant clemency and Lopez—the oldest of Folsom Prison's ninety-three—was executed on May 21, 1897.

"The secret why I killed her, that will go to the grave between me and my God."
—James Berry, 1897

8. James Berry, August 13, 1897

Alice Berry feared her husband James would kill her one day. People knew James Berry as controlling and abusive, and Alice as having survived many episodes of domestic violence. Respected by the community, Alice worked as a servant for a prominent family in Modesto, California. After he noticed the results of one of Berry's beatings, Alice reluctantly told her employer, J. F. Tucker, of the constant abuse inflicted upon her by her husband. When Berry came looking for his wife, Tucker called the sheriff. The sheriff told Berry to go home. Alice stayed at her friend Belle Campbell's house that evening.

Around 6:30 the next morning, on May 19, 1897, Berry arrived at the Campbell home, shouting and banging on doors, demanding his wife come out. Campbell refused to produce Alice or to open the door, but Berry crawled through an open window. He spied his wife, still dressed in her night clothes, sneaking out a back door. Alice ran toward a nearby home, but James tackled and beat her. He then shot her, sending a .38 caliber bullet into her heart.

Berry left the home and headed to town. Along the way, he seemed delighted to tell all he met, including blacksmith Felix Anaya, what he had accomplished: "I just killed my wife a few minutes ago, Mr. Anaya. Deader than hell, and I'm going downtown; I'm afraid they'll have the rope around my neck; I'm going downtown to give myself up."

Berry did, in fact, turn himself over to the town marshal, who had already been looking for him. Later, during his trial, Berry shocked his court-appointed attorney by demanding the judge put him to death, saying, "All I ask of you is not to worry my life out in the penitentiary, but I would truly say I would be the happiest man in the state of California if you would signed [sic] the warrant for my execution tomorrow and take me and lay me by her side out there."

Berry lacked remorse for his crime, and he told the court, "If I was to do over and she was in sight I would blow her up if God Almighty would strengthen me with power enough to pull the trigger." Berry anxiously awaited execution at Folsom Prison. Often heard laughing and cracking jokes, he consistently displayed good spirits and, on August 13, 1897, he went to his death with a smile.

"God pays me."
—C.H. Raymond, when asked
how he made a living, 1897

"Gentlemen of the jury, I don't
blame you for what you have
done, but I do blame these liars,
perjurers, bribers, and murderers."
—Harry Winters, 1898

9. C. H. Raymond, May 8, 1898,
12. Harry Winters, December 8, 1899

The Grand Hotel in Baden (now southern San Francisco) housed approximately thirty boarders, mostly workers at the Western Meat Company. The meat packers received their paychecks on Tuesdays. Most owed the majority of their checks, nearly three hundred dollars, to the hotel owner, Patrick Ferrier.

At two A.M. on Wednesday, November 17, 1897, Ferrier awoke to the sound of his dog's vociferous barking. He found a stranger near the hallway stairs who wanted whiskey for himself and a friend who were going clam digging. Ferrier told him to go to the bar and "gave him a push" toward the steps. When Ferrier returned to his room at the end of the hall, he nearly ran into another man, who pointed a gun at his head. "Throw up your hands," the gunman ordered.

Ferrier had no intention of handing over his earnings, and he later remarked, "I made a quick jump for him and grabbed the weapon, yelling for help at the same time." Ferrier's brother John, his brother-in-law Richard Connelly, and boarders Gus Andrews and James McNamara rushed to Ferrier's aid. Three of them wrestled the gunman to the floor while Patrick Ferrier plucked the pin from the gun's cylinder, rendering it useless. The hallway was dark and Andrews ran to his room for a candle. Upon Andrew's return, the man who Ferrier had met just earlier at the top of the stairs (later identified as C.H. Raymond) yelled, "Let my pal go or if you don't, I will riddle you all with bullets!"

Raymond fired four shots. One struck Connelly's leg and two lodged in Andrews's abdomen. The ensuing chaos provided the opportunity for the two assailants to escape from the hotel. Connelly survived, but Andrews died from peritonitis three days later.

Within hours, police had arrested Raymond as he walked the road toward San Francisco. The .38 caliber revolver that he was found carrying smelled as if it had been recently discharged. Raymond told police that he worked for the Salvation Army, but he couldn't produce credentials. Arresting officer Eugene Herve asked him how he made a living. Raymond replied, "God pays me." The officers transported Raymond to the county jail, where Ferrier and the others identified him as the shooter.

As for Raymond's companion, Ferrier said he'd be recognizable: ". . .the fellow will undoubtedly have some marks or bruises about his head and face." Meanwhile, Raymond accused fellow ex-con James Willet of being the other robber and masterminding the holdup. "It is like getting money from home," Willet purportedly had said to Raymond. "All we have to do is tell them to throw up their hands and they will do the rest."

Ten days after the murder and attempted robbery, police arrested Harry Winters at a waterfront saloon. "They will find that they arrested an innocent man," Winters protested. "I was not in Baden at the time of the holdup and I can prove it." Winters insisted he had an alibi, but before he could produce it, Raymond broke down, confessing that both Winters and Willet were involved.

Willet remained at large while Raymond and Winters faced separate trials, both pleading not guilty. Ferrier and the other boarders positively identified Raymond as the shooter and Winters as the other assailant, even though the hallway's light came from a single candle. Constable Frank Desirello testified that he had seen Winters and Raymond together the day before the incident, and Ferrier claimed Winters had a beer in the hotel's bar that day.

Winters's defense team called Charles George to the stand, claiming he could provide an alibi for Winters. Winters insisted George saw him at a saloon in San Francisco, but George couldn't remember whether it was on the night in question. Another defense witness testified he met with Winters on the 17th and noticed nothing unusual about his appearance—no bruises or marks of any kind on his head or face.

Both Raymond's and Winters's juries found their respective defendants guilty. Raymond appeared "wholly indifferent" to his fate, according to the *San Francisco Call*, whereas Winters "lost all control of himself and denounced the witnesses who appeared against him as perjurers, liars, and murderers."

Within weeks, Raymond made a full confession to Warden Charles Aull, admitting to firing the shots and proclaiming Winters's innocence. "Winters was not at the hotel on the night of the murder that I know of. James Willet was with me when the crime was committed." Raymond claimed the three men met at Holy Cross Cemetery, where Winters supplied the two men with guns, which was the extent of his involvement. Prison officials disregarded Raymond's confession, considering it an act of vainglory.

Authorities captured James Willet in Arizona in March 1898. Willet detailed the crime as it happened and insisted he and Raymond alone carried out the ill-fated robbery. While planning the heist, Willet called Winters a "tenderfoot" and a "bum" and objected to having him "in on the deal." Edward Gabriel, who employed Willet on his farm at the time of the crime, corroborated Willet's story. He said Willet told him of the attempted robbery and how he eluded police.

Raymond never filed an appeal or an application for pardon. He said nothing on the gallows, and after his execution on May 8, 1898, it was reported, "cool and collected, [he] died bravely." Willet pleaded guilty and received a life sentence. As for Winters, he hoped Willet's confession would exonerate him, but the California Supreme Court decided by a margin of four-to-three that Winters must hang. The combination of an insufficient alibi, positive witness identification, and a prior felony conviction, doomed Winters to the noose.

On December 8, 1899—over a year after the execution of his accomplice, C. H. Raymond—Harry Winters, whom the press called a German socialist, died without demonstration or outcry on the Folsom gallows.

FIRST INMATE KILLING AT FOLSOM

The first prisoner killed by a fellow inmate at Folsom prison was murdered on September 29, 1898. Jacob "The Human Tiger" Oppenheimer (see story #28) stabbed Charles Ross in the yard. Four years earlier, in an effort to shift blame, Ross had framed Oppenheimer for a robbery, yielding Oppenheimer a fifty-year sentence.

"I have not always done right myself, but few of us do."
—John Barthelman, 1896

10. John F. Barthelman, May 12, 1898

In the early evening of November 3, 1896, H.W. Holden had been at home, playing with his three-year old granddaughter, Dorothea, when he heard four gunshots. He knew immediately they had to do with his daughter, Mabel, and her ex-husband, John F. Barthelman. He raced down the narrow, windy path through a thick grove of eucalyptus trees and encountered Miss Angie Lord, his daughter's close friend and fellow co-worker. She confirmed Mr. Holden's worst fear: Barthelman had shot his daughter and was now escaping through the hills surrounding his Los Angeles home.

Mabel died later that evening from bullet wounds to her head and chest. A group of men who had been gathering down the street at a voting center came rushing to the scene after hearing the shots. They helped Holden carry his unconscious daughter to the home—the same home where Mabel had married John Barthelman, a German native, in December of 1892.

The couple had lived with her parents, but Barthelman did not get along with his in-laws and the pair, with their young daughter, moved out. An agent for the Singer Sewing Machine Company, Barthelman reportedly had an "ungovernable temper" and, even though he never physically abused his wife, he continually swore at her and called her "bad names." Holden told the press that he feared Barthelman and had grown wary of his son-in-law, but never imagined he'd kill anyone.

In March of 1896, Mabel had had enough and she left Barthelman, taking with her most of the home's furnishings and housewares, leaving him only with a blanket and pillow. She and Dorothea moved in with her parents on Emerald and Brook streets and she began working as a clerk in Sheward's dry good store.

In October, she secured a divorce from Barthelman on the grounds of extreme cruelty and received custody of Dorothea. Barthelman failed to appear for the court proceedings.

At five o'clock in the evening of November 3, Mabel received a note via messenger. Her ex-husband wished to speak with her. She agreed and at six o'clock she and Miss Lord left work and the women met up with Barthelman on Spring Street. Lord, noting that Barthelman appeared "calmer than usual," entered a grocery store, giving the pair privacy. She rejoined them a few moments later and she and Mabel boarded a street car. They were unaware that Barthelman, too, boarded the car, until he got off at the corner of First and Kern with them. The trio walked toward the Holden residence and up the winding path in a single file fashion, Barthelman leading and Lord trailing.

Lord listened as Barthelman repeatedly asked Mabel if he could take Dorothea, each time receiving the same answer of "No." He threatened Mabel, saying he could prove her unworthy of caring for the baby. She responded by daring him to produce the proof and that she would "willingly face any accuser he would bring against her." Barthelman then stopped, drew a revolver from his pocket and fired two shots at Mabel. She screamed and fell to the ground and her ex-husband fired two more shots into her. Lord fled toward the house in search of help and nearly ran into the arms of Holden. Barthelman in the meantime escaped.

While Mabel never regained consciousness and succumbed to her injuries, Barthelman spent the night wandering the city, stopping once to buy cigars and laudanum, a poison he planned to do himself away with. However, at ten the following morning, police arrested Barthelman at the home of his friend, John Vennum. Vennum described Barthelman as having a vacant stare when he arrived at the house and wouldn't respond to Vennum's questions. Reporting on the arrest, the *Los Angeles Herald* called Barthelman a coward who "lacked the moral courage to end his own miserable existence."

Barthelman said very little to reporters, only that he felt sorry for what he had done and that he had no intention of killing his former wife. He claimed he only had the revolver because he planned to be out late that evening to hear the election returns and needed the gun for protection.

When the trial commenced on January 18, hundreds of spectators packed the courtroom, anxious to get a look at the "cold-blooded brute." Barthelman presented himself with confidence and ease, "looking quite debonnair [sic], his round and rosy face the picture of health. No one would have selected him in a crowd as a wife-murderer or maniac."

A "maniac" was exactly what the defense hoped to portray their client as, presenting a number of depositions from Barthelman family members living in New York and Chicago, which depicted the defendant as insane. His sister, Mary Marseniak, said to have an "unsound mind," described the "crankiness of her whole family," which included their father. The defense also provided a long list of character witnesses who vouched for Barthelman's unstable mind and described a much different Barthelman than the cold blooded, dastardly murderer he appeared to be.

The prosecution responded with their own list of witnesses, who testified Barthelman showed no signs of insanity and opined that the defendant clearly knew right from wrong.

After an eight-day trial, the jury returned after forty minutes of deliberation, rendering a guilty verdict. The *Los Angeles Herald* reported that Barthelman "drew his legs up under his chair and gripped the arms with a tight grasp and that was all. He knew the worst." The defense motioned for a new trial based on various statutory grounds and misconduct on behalf of the district attorney and the jury. The court allowed the defense to prepare the documents, but eventually ruled against the defendant.

While awaiting the outcome of his appeal, Barthelman sent several letters to friends begging for help in "[breaking] up that combination in Los Angeles who are trying to wreck the life of my child." He went on to say that his little "Queen" Dorothea "has a wonderful future before her" and that there is a conspiracy to "ruin her the same as they did her mother." Barthelman's attorney, Frank Davis, described the letters as "strongly confirmatory of the fact that the terrible disease with which he has long been afflicted is rapidly reaching its culmination, and his complete insanity is a condition to be momentarily anticipated."

Contrary to Davis's belief, Barthelman remained stable and a year later, in March 1898, he appeared in court for resentencing after the state Supreme Court denied his appeal. The *Los Angeles Herald* noted the condemned man's appearance did not "indicate that he has undergone any mental suffering during his long detention." Called "fat and healthy," Barthelman "wore good clothing, was clean shaven, with the exception of a flowing mustache, and there was nothing about the cut of his hair to indicate his sojourn in a state prison." With no legal cause to postpone sentencing, the judge sentenced Barthelman to die on May 12, 1898.

When the fateful day arrived, Barthelman, seemingly resigned to his fate, said not a word on the gallows and fell through the trap.

**"I'm going to commit a terrible crime tomorrow. I'm going to commit a
tragedy that will shock the whole community."**
—Frank Belew, 1897

11. Frank Belew, June 16, 1898

Frank Belew watched quietly as his sister writhed in pain, slowly succumbing
to arsenic poisoning. She begged for help, but he only sat beside her and held
her hand. The tears rolling down his face were nothing more than a convincing
ability to cry on cue. He was, after all, the one who had poisoned her. The three
unsuspecting female caretakers, who were following doctor's orders, continued to
feed Susie the tainted water and soup broth. Frank looked on without any remorse.
Susie died the next morning at five; her brother, Louis, had met the same fate
hours earlier.

Two nights previous, on November 7, 1897, Susie invited Frank and her other
brothers to dinner. It was the first time in months Frank had spent time with his
siblings, as he had recently been caught forging checks using his brother Thomas's
name. Susie wanted to make peace and bring the family together. Frank had other
ideas.

Following a dinner marked by light conversation concerning the upcoming
marriages of both Susie and brother Louis, several guests departed. Susie sat in the
parlor, fixing her hair, as she waited for her fiancé Charley to arrive.

In the empty kitchen, Frank pulled a piece of folded newspaper from his pocket.
It contained rat poison from a box he purchased several years before. He poured
the poison into the teakettle and replaced the lid. Frank shoved the paper back
into his pocket and then joined Susie in the parlor where they talked about the
wedding and she showed him her wedding dress.

Frank left the ranch at about 8:30 that evening and slept soundly.

The next morning, Susie made a breakfast of eggs, mush, and coffee for herself, Louis, and Bruno Kline, the ranch hand. Later that afternoon, as she began preparing a stew for dinner, Susie fell violently ill, as did Louis and Bruno. Someone immediately summoned Dr. Trafton, who suggested they were suffering from simple indigestion. However, by evening, their conditions had worsened. Susie's and Louis's future mothers-in-law helped care for the ailing siblings and Mr. Kline. Having arrived at the farm, Frank Belew sat at the bedside of his dying sister, his tearful act seen as a genuine display of concern and grief.

When Susie's caretakers also took ill the next day, rumors of poisoning circulated. Tests on the food confirmed it contained arsenic and the search for the source began. Frank later admitted one of his biggest mistakes came when suggesting to District Attorney Frank Devlin that he check the teakettle—just in case. Sure enough, the teakettle contained enough arsenic to kill a stable full of horses, or in this case an entire family.

Following the deaths of Susie and Louis, Bruno remained in critical condition for several days. Doctors expected him to die at any moment, but after three days doctors transferred him to a hotel room where he eventually made a full recovery, as did the two caretakers.

The funerals took place on November 10, 1897, the day before Susie's ill-fated wedding was scheduled and only days from that of Louis. The small farming community of Dixon, California, came to a standstill that perfect autumn afternoon as it mourned the loss of two of its most esteemed citizens. Schools, businesses, and even saloons closed their doors so everyone could attend the service. No one showed more grief and anguish than Frank Belew. His performance earned genuine sympathy from fellow mourners, including his two other brothers, Arthur and Thomas.

The crime attracted newspaper reporters from San Francisco and surroundings towns and swarms of general spectators. Everyone proposed a theory as to the motive of the crime. Louis had been a witness in a perjury case months earlier. Susie had recently broken off an engagement to a different man, leaving her jilted lover incensed. However, Frank Belew didn't entirely escape suspicion. It was well known that Frank's deceased parents, who had run a successful livery business, left him the smallest portion of the sibling inheritance and that the other siblings, particularly Susie and Louis, received the bulk of the money. Frank, who separated from his wife and two young sons months earlier, lived in a rooming house in town and suffered financial hardship.

Suspicions swirled around town—the most vocal finger-pointer being Frank Belew. He immediately blamed Harry Allen, Susie's "discarded lover." Frank "unmistakably indicated that he does not believe Harry Allen too good [not] to commit such a deed." The *Woodland Daily Democrat* said of Allen, "…he is a good deal a blowhard, but many people take no stock in the charge that he is a murderer."

Hoping that one of the two men might voluntarily make damaging admissions, officers set up a private meeting between Belew and Allen. The event yielded only drama.

"One of the other of us has got to hang for this murder and I hope to God the guilty man will be hung," Allen exclaimed.

"So do I!" Belew cried.

"No, you don't," retorted Allen. "You are the guilty man and you don't want to hang."

That concluded the meeting.

Frank continued to play the part of a grieving brother and withstood a three-hour interrogation by Detective John Curtin and District Attorney Devlin without faltering. Allen, too, gave a statement and asserted that Frank killed his brother and sister over money.

Police needed to find the source of the arsenic. Law required drugstores to log all purchases of the poison, but Curtin and Constable Frank Newby found that local druggists routinely ignored the practice. It became a frustrating task for detectives and police officials, who knew arsenic showed up in large quantities on almost every ranch. Farmers used it for spraying fruit trees and on large vineyards. Authorities decided to abandon that direction of the investigation.

A few days later, at the coroner's inquest, Frank again proclaimed his innocence. "Could I have committed such a monstrous crime and stood there watching my sister suffer and see them feeding her more poison? No, sir, I could not be such a hardened monster." Brothers Arthur and Thomas sided with him.

Thomas said, "No matter what they say about Frank and no matter how black the storm may gather around my brother, there is just one picture that makes me know he is innocent. I can see him now at the deathbed of Susie, holding her hand when she died. No man can make me believe that my brother had the heart to poison those he loved this way. It is inhuman and unnatural. He has not that kind of heart."

During the inquest, Frank again proved a cool and intelligent witness, even admitting that several years earlier he had purchased Rough on Rats, a compound containing arsenic. During his testimony, he also revealed being angry about the inheritance and admitted that he and his siblings had not always been "on friendly terms," but that a reconciliation occurred. He claimed Susie and Louis were essentially broke and went so far as to say, "If my brother and sister have disposed their property, so there is nothing coming to me, all right; but if there is anything coming to me, I want it."

Mary Clark and the two others who cared for Susie the night before she died testified they became ill from drinking the same water and eating the same broth Susie drank. They testified that Frank never drank the water in question, and further stated that they believed Frank evidently had no qualms about poisoning not only Susie and Louis, but also a ranch hand and three other women.

The coroner's jury concluded Susie and Louis Belew were indeed poisoned, but by persons unknown. By the end of November, the prosecution team felt certain that Frank had murdered his siblings, but it failed to produce sufficient evidence to arrest him.

In spite of his cool demeanor and emphatic denials, suspicions aimed at Frank grew stronger. He had motive and opportunity, and his past was filled with incidents of fraud and thievery. Belew's father-in-law once accused Frank of stealing $400 from him. Not long afterward, Belew tried to shoot a farmhand to whom he owed money, although he pretended the gun discharged accidentally. Belew then attempted to poison the farmhand's food. The worker complained to authorities, but Belew successfully portrayed the laborer as insane and suicidal.

In January, Frank met with a San Francisco newspaper reporter to discuss the murders. His remarks to the reporter included the following:

> We would all contribute liberally to help hang the fiend who committed this dark crime. I don't think a worse murder was ever committed in the United States. It gave me lots of trouble, but I am glad they have let me alone now and are hunting elsewhere for the criminal. I do not believe there are many persons in this county who will believe that I could have poisoned my relatives and held my dying sister's hand while she was writhing in pain and slowly dying. Tommy will tell you that I did more for her and Louis while they were suffering than anybody else did, and that it broke me all up.

In February, authorities received the break they so desperately needed. John W. Bird, a Sacramento photographer married to the sister of Frank's wife, came forward with startling information. The day before the crime, Frank shared with Bird his bitterness about his siblings' upcoming nuptials. Introducing new people into the family would divide the hard-earned wealth of his parents. Frank told his brother-in-law, "They have not treated me right in regard to the estate, but I'll have some of it yet. They'll not live to enjoy it. Bird, I'm going to commit a terrible crime tomorrow. I'm going to commit a tragedy that will shock the whole community." The two men did not meet again until the funeral, where Belew admitted to Bird he had carried out his threat. Terrified of Belew, Bird consulted an attorney, who, in turn, spoke with Devlin in November at the coroner's inquest. Devlin, lacking the evidence to convict Belew at the time, sat on the information, although he began to formulate a plan to obtain a confession.

Bird agreed to keep Frank's admission secret, but when Frank persisted in trying to get Bird to accompany him out hunting to some lonely spot, or to pan for gold, Bird refused, having determined Frank wanted to murder him to "get him out of the way." Bird became paranoid, suspecting that every morsel he ate contained poison. These fears finally drove Bird directly to the authorities. "Frank has always admitted the crime," he told them. "He has never expressed remorse for the murder, but has often laughed at the way he eluded officers and perpetrated what he threatened. He said he did a good job and thought he was pretty smooth in getting away [from] the sleuths."

Devlin realized Bird could help him obtain the confession necessary to arrest Belew. An early-day "sting operation" ensued, but without tape recorders, wires, or any listening device other than a properly working ear and a curtain to hide behind. Belew and Bird met at Bird's photography studio. Constable Frank Newby hid in the room and listened as Belew confessed to buying the poison, which, he claimed, "did a good job." The *Woodland Daily Democrat* reported, "Nothing stranger than this iniquitous and soulless confession has ever characterized the dark story of human fiendishness."

Worried that Bird would tell others, Frank said, "You have always been my friend and I'll help you someday. I don't want anyone to know I did it but you and me."

"It's enough for you and me to know you poisoned them," Bird replied.

"Yes, and I am grateful to you for the friendship you have shown me and I would do anything for you."

Newby and Devlin were ecstatic, but to facilitate their investigation and allay suspicion, they told the press they had abandoned efforts to ferret out the murderer. The investigators had cloaked their movements so cunningly the public bought it.

At the appointed time, Newby, Sheriff J. Rush, and Undersheriff T. Robinson arrested a surprised Frank at a ranch eight miles beyond Elmira, California.

For two days, Frank sat in his narrow, dark, and damp cell, proclaiming that Newby and Bird lied and pursued "blood money." After a reporter asked Frank why he had told Bird about the murders, Frank answered, "He pumped me." Frank understood instantly what he had just done. He called an end to the interview and retreated to his bundle of damp blankets in the corner of the cell. His brothers implored him to tell them the truth. "I will not believe Frank is guilty until I hear him say so," said Arthur.

Later, in the presence of the reporter and Undersheriff Robinson, Frank crumbled. "I did it! Oh, I did it!" Frank cried. "I killed my brother and sister. I don't know why I did it." He proceeded to describe the night of November 7. "Some of the folk had gone out to the gate and I dropped [poison] in while they were out there." Belew insisted he used rat poison, not arsenic.

The next morning, Frank's attorney, Reece Clark, denied any such confession took place. "Belew will never hang unless he hangs himself, and this he will not do. What I mean is this alleged confession will not hang him." That night, a watchman at the jail said Belew tried to commit suicide by stuffing a handkerchief down his throat, although Belew denied it. In the morning, Belew made a full confession to

Devlin. At one point, he said he killed Susie and Louis because they had "slandered my wife. [Louis] said my wife had run away with another man."

Belew didn't want a trial. "I want to plead guilty and have it all over as soon as possible. I suppose there is no escape. I do want to escape as there is nothing in life for a man who has done what I have." Clark informed Belew the guilty plea would be a mistake and that he could do nothing more for him.

After a few nights in the desolate jail, Frank wasn't troubled by remorse, but by fear—fear of the noose. He decided to plead not guilty and rely upon a technical defense of insanity. Frank is reported to have remarked, "I do not feel as I did when I was arrested and have no desire to die. I think that imprisonment for life would suit me better."

Arthur stayed by his brother's side. "It seems to me impossible that he committed that crime while he was in the right mind, I think some strange emotion controlled him and he could not resist the idea to do what he did." Thomas, however, refused to speak to Frank again.

Frank continued to assert his motive as slander, not the issue of the family inheritance. As Frank explained in the ensuing days, "I conceived the idea that there ought to be some way to make them suffer. I do not think I had the idea of poisoning them in my mind for over three hours, but out on the ranch I suffered at the thought that my wife was not with me and that she was separated partly because of financial worries. I said to myself that it was not right for them to talk as they had done."

Judge Buckles set the trial for April 5. Frank's wife visited him twice during March. On both occasions, she begged him to plead guilty so his children could inherit his portion of the estate. The life sentence he sought would do nothing to provide for his two young boys. Perhaps Belew listened to his wife, for on March 30, when Buckles asked him for his plea, he responded, "Guilty, and I ask the mercy of the court." Despite the guilty plea, the trial proceeded in an effort to determine the degree of guilt. On April 9, Buckles informed the prisoner there were no mitigating circumstances to warrant life imprisonment. He would hang.

The judge fixed June 16 as the day of execution, and while Belew sat waiting in the "death cell" at Folsom, he offered another confession—"the whole truth" as he put it. He related a story to Sheriff Rush that for months, he and John Bird together planned the murder. Belew stated that "Our original intention was to murder Arthur and Tommy, also, but I did not get a good chance to do the job." He said that after he inherited the estate, he would make Bird administrator, "and [Bird] could have made a hand that way. If I got into trouble, Bird was to stand by me and do all in his power to save my life, but he went back on me and that is why I now want to tell the whole truth." Much to Belew's chagrin, law officers ignored his claim.

Defense Attorney Clark published a letter in the *Dixon Tribune* regarding his condemned client:

> Had not Frank plead guilty, I can say from any knowledge of the case, knowing all the facts as I know them, that the twelve men don't live that would have ever convicted him, and affixed the death penalty. They might have convicted him of something, but never would have given him the death penalty. In the eyes of the world he may be deserving of the death penalty, but I say and know that he is voluntarily going to his death against my protest and advice, impelled by a vain and hopeless love and confidence in people who like "Birds" of prey are perched in the distance whetting their beaks for the life blood [sic] of Frank Belew in the way of rewards and otherwise and praying for the 16th of June that he may be blotted out forever while they enjoy the pittance that his death may bring them. Even at this late day, if Frank Belew would permit me to do so, I could save his life and stand an even chance of acquitting him, strange as it may sound to those who are not fully acquainted with all the facts.

On June 16, 1898, Frank Belew stood calm and quiet on the scaffold. Ten minutes earlier, he talked with a reporter, inquiring after the welfare of his wife and children. A doctor finally declared Belew dead eleven-and-a-half minutes after the trap sprung.

In November 1898, a year after the murders, the case evoked another debate. Could a person acquire property as a direct result of his crime? Arthur Belew argued he could not, but Judge Buckles ruled against him, declaring that unless the court could change the Code of Civil Procedure, Frank's children would receive their father's portion of the inheritance. The case is often credited with the 1905 enactment of the California Probate Code sec. 258, which provided that a person convicted of the murder of a decedent could not inherit any portion of the decedent's estate.

As for J. W. Bird, he filed a claim with the Board of Examiners a month before Belew's execution, seeking to receive the $600 reward. As of November 1899, the last update on record, he still had not received it. The board refused to pay.

"To tell the truth, gentlemen of the jury, I know very little about this charge against
me. In fact, all I do know is from what I heard while the witnesses were testifying."
—George Putman, at trial, 1899

13. George Putman, November 19, 1900

George Putman had a score to settle. On May 15, 1899, Putman approached
fellow Folsom inmate John Showers, who stood in the doorway of a cell, and
stabbed him six times. Showers died quickly. The *San Francisco Call* reported,
"When questioned, [Putman] burst into tears, but would say nothing except cry
out: 'Oh, my boy! My boy!'" This "boy" was supposedly a childhood friend named
Abe Majors, whose father died at the noose after Showers turned state's evidence
against him. Majors was imprisoned under the death sentence in Utah for killing
a police captain. Majors said he knew of Putman only by sight and denied an intimate friendship.

Prison officials called Showers a hardworking, model prisoner who had "earned
the goodwill of all the officers and all the better class of convicts." On the other
hand, with fifteen reprimands in four years of incarceration, twenty-five-year-old
George Putman had garnered a reputation for trouble.[1]

Putman pleaded not guilty. He and his defense attorney applied to have thirteen
Folsom convicts, many on Death Row, transported to Sacramento for testimony.
Believing the convicts only desired a day's outing from the prison, the court
allowed the transportation of only six convicts. The other seven convicts refused to
give depositions at the prison. The defense appeared to be trying to prove Putman's
"emotional insanity," blaming an opium addiction as motive for the murder.

---

1. Incidentally, on the same day Jacob Oppenheimer (#28 in this book) attacked and
nearly killed a guard at San Quentin. The press claimed that Oppenheimer had a friendship
with Abe and his brother Archie, as well, and speculated the two attacks correlated in some
way. No information could be found to support that.

"To tell the truth, gentlemen of the jury, I know very little about this charge against me," Putman said. "In fact, all I do know is from what I heard while the witnesses were testifying. I swear to God that I had no knife. I remember a dispute, but with whom I do not remember, I recollect somebody calling me a vile name and then striking at me. I have a dim recollection of a struggle and of handing a knife to an officer."

After the jury reached a guilty verdict, Putman arrived for the subsequent sentencing with a bandage around his neck. Earlier that morning, while the prison barber shaved him, Putman grabbed the razor and ran it across his own throat. Although he inflicted a serious wound, Putman failed to sever the jugular vein.

The California Supreme Court rejected his appeal and Putman went to the gallows on November 19, 1900, and became what the *Oakland Tribune* called, "one of the most successful executions at the prison. Putman never twitched after the drop. His form remained perfectly rigid, the neck being broken by the fall."

PART II: 1901–1906

Folsom Wardens: Thomas Wilkinson, October 18, 1889–December 1, 1903

Archibald Yell, December 1, 1903–February 14, 1908

California Governors: Henry Gage, January 4, 1889–January 6, 1903

George Pardee, January 6, 1903–January 9, 1907

For Californians, the turn of the twentieth century brought the promise of wealth and prosperity. California could now boast having a new kind of gold: oil. After its discovery in California in the early 1890s, production had approached four million barrels by 1900, drawing a new batch of settlers from across the country. The new commodity lured not only families with dreams of striking it rich, but also gamblers, prostitutes, and con artists, who came to this exotic land looking for something other than the tranquil and Edenic life. Between 1890 and 1900, Los Angeles's population doubled, surpassing that of San Francisco and making it the largest city in the state. California had no fewer than two million residents, including many immigrants.

Anti-Chinese sentiment continued to run strong, with lawmakers barring Asians from residing in certain towns, owning land, or becoming citizens. The Chinese Exclusion Act restricted Chinese from entering the country, under threat of imprisonment and deportation, although the law excluded Chinese laborers. Congress finally repealed the act in 1943. The Gentleman's Agreement with Japan barred the Japanese from entering the United States; the agreement ended in 1924.

Rapid industrialization and expanding agricultural development changed the Golden State's landscape during the early 1900s. Factories and assembly lines, producing large quantities of products such as home goods, food, and machinery, employed both men and women, and changed the way Americans worked.

Widespread mass production also brought labor union disputes, strikes, and riots. In 1905, the Industrial Workers of the World began employing part-time migrant workers in California, turning the organization into one of the most hated labor unions in the United States.

The Southern Pacific Railway's political power continued to wreak havoc on the state, monopolizing branches of the often corrupt municipal governments and dominating local utilities, such as water, electricity, and transportation. Unscrupulous city bosses passed along bribes and favors to lawmakers, who signed legislative benefits to those with corporate interests. Reformers sought to solve these problems, but corruption continued until Governor Hiram Johnson ushered in the Progressive Era with his election in 1910.

Prisons in California needed their own reform. Allegations of cruelty at San Quentin and Folsom prompted investigations, which led to denials from prison officials and then, ultimately, to even harsher conditions out of retaliation. Folsom prisoners cited rampant abuse, condoned by prison officials, as the motivation for the infamous 1903 riot and breakout where thirteen prisoners escaped. Only five were recaptured.

Then, days after Folsom's twenty-second execution, San Francisco was shaken by an estimated 7.9 magnitude earthquake on April 18, 1906. Subsequent fires from ruptured gas lines destroyed 90 percent of the city, killing over 3,000 people. The tremors never reached Folsom, but the prison did experience a brief lull of incoming prisoners. One-time Folsom warden James Johnston (elected to the San Francisco Board of Supervisors in 1907) called the quake a "great purifier," saying:

> It scared the sin out of some people and tore masks off make-believers. Everybody cooked in the street and many slept in the parks, where fresh air and new thoughts could get at them. Button-pushers and bell-ringers took their turn with day laborers cleaning up the debris. There were no saloons to open or close, and nobody seemed to want a drink. The people had before them important business of planning and building a new city while the old still trembled and burned. There was little looting and pillaging.

The reprieve lasted only a brief time and, before long, the prisons had to make room for more inmates.

14. Frank Miller, September 26, 1902

While serving life at San Quentin for murder, Frank Miller killed fellow inmate Jerry Harris in the prison's jute mill on March 13, 1902. Harris and another convict had complained to the convict boss, Ernest Thompson, about Miller's poor work ethic. Miller confronted Thompson, demanding to know who ratted on him. When Thompson named Harris, Miller gave him a sharp blow to the head with an iron bar, pulled a sharp instrument from his jacket pocket, and sought after Harris.

Miller found Harris leaning back in a chair sewing jute mill sacks. Without warning, Miller rushed him and plunged the blade into Harris six times, killing him on the spot. After the murder, Miller exhibited no feeling of remorse; he called the act a justified killing.

At trial, Miller refused to enter a plea, so the judge entered "not guilty" on his behalf. The judge then assigned an attorney named Hawkins to represent Miller. Miller jumped up, shouting, "Mr. Hawkins will not dare touch the case and you shall not allow him to do so." Thereafter, acting as his own attorney, Miller declined to question any of the jurors or witnesses, and throughout the trial he appeared unconcerned, often showing no interest in the proceedings.

After being found guilty, Miller, also known as Frank Haines, bitterly awaited execution. Captain of the Guard R. J. Murphy described Miller to the press: "Since Haines's arrival at this prison, he had been very sullen, is abusive in his language to the prison officials, refuses spiritual consolation, and from present indications he will try to be troublesome at the time of execution, and, with that end view, all necessary precautions are being taken."

On the morning of his execution, Miller hid behind his cell door, wearing a pair of handcuffs. When Murphy entered, Miller tried to deliver a debilitating blow to the captain's head, but guards helped Murphy fight off the attack.

When asked on the gallows if he had anything to say, Miller made no reply. The *Oakland Tribune* said he "glared savagely" at witnesses as the black cap was placed over his head. The paper also reported that Miller made a feeble attempt to free himself from his bindings and seemed in a state of nervous collapse, but the effort could not save him from his fate, which he met on September 26, 1902.

THE GREYSTONE CHAPEL

In 1890, Chinese convicts began construction of Folsom's chapel, located on the north side of the prison yard. Completed in 1903, the granite chapel served as the venue for religious services, most often Catholic. In 1909, inmates enjoyed the prison's first showing of motion pictures in the chapel. Many convicts and visitors knew the chapel for its mural, a near-identical copy of the "Last Supper," painted by inmate Ralph Pecor in the late 1930s. Serving time for manslaughter, Pecor, an illustrator and Hollywood set designer, spent over a year painting the 12 x 21-foot mural. Some say the faces in Pecor's version are those of friends and fellow inmates. Today, the chapel caters to all faiths.

"I wish your mother was here and I would kill the whole family."
—William Glover to Agnes Nieroff, 1902

15. William Glover, February 6, 1904

According to fourteen-year-old Agnes Nieroff, William Glover aimed a rifle at her and said, "I have come to kill your father." The twenty-eight-year-old Glover was Agnes's supposed fiancé, and he later vehemently denied coming to the Nieroff property to kill Fredrick Nieroff. Rather, he claimed he had acted in self-defense.

William Glover and his brother, Oscar, had a mining claim on the American River. The only access to this claim was through the Nieroffs' property. Over the course of a year, Agnes's parents and sister became acquainted with the Glovers, even renting a room to William Glover. Then one day in June 1902, Nieroff ordered Glover off his property and told him never to return. The press said Nieroff disapproved of the relationship between his then thirteen-year-old daughter and Glover, but according to a Nieroff family descendant, Shelley Gaw, the age difference didn't really matter. In fact, Nieroff and his own wife, Minna, were nearly thirty years apart in age.

According to Gaw, Glover took advantage of Agnes's infatuation to gain access to his family's mining claim. When her father found out, he confronted Glover and revoked permission to cross his land. William Glover felt the only way he and his brother could regain access would be to kill Nieroff.

Whatever started the dispute, it ended on June 11. Only Agnes and her father were at home that day, and after Nieroff ate breakfast and went about his work outside, Agnes said she heard someone come up from the cellar entryway and enter the house. She discovered Glover in her bedroom, holding a rifle. After threatening to kill Agnes if she warned her father, Glover hid in the house most of the day until around four in the afternoon. Then he moved to a hiding place behind a tree in the yard. In the meantime, William's brother, Oscar, had come to retrieve a horse collar from Nieroff and the two men stood talking outside the barn. Agnes had come to the front door to call her father in for dinner and stood helplessly as she watched the scene unfold.

Glover stepped out from the tree and pointed the rifle at Nieroff. "Will, don't shoot," said Oscar. Nieroff also asked him to not shoot, and he stepped toward Glover to grab the gun, but Glover pulled the trigger and shot him. The brothers then got into Oscar's buggy and were starting to drive away when Agnes picked up the gun. Agnes claimed "[I] would have shot Will Glover if I had the strength. I did go to the door and pointed the gun at them, [and I] ordered them to bring father into the house." They obliged, laying him on the couch. According to Agnes, the men went outside, talked for a few minutes, and then returned. "Now," Oscar told Agnes, "when it comes into court, you say that your father had a club in his hand, and that it was accidental he was shot."

Oscar summoned a doctor to the home, where a direly injured Nieroff stated that the shooting was unprovoked. Afraid for her life, Agnes told authorities Glover shot her father in self-defense. Days later, at the coroner's inquest, she changed her story: "I went toward the room and met Will Glover coming out with a shotgun on his shoulder. He told me that he intended to kill the 'old man' and would kill me if I said anything. He watched every move that I made and I was terrified."

Claiming self-defense, both Glovers pleaded not guilty, but the jury ruled that William fired and killed Nieroff in cold blood. Oscar was tried on a count of complicity, but he was acquitted.

The California Supreme Court didn't buy Glover's claim of self-defense and denied his appeal. Glover, making no statement on the gallows, "died bravely," according to the *Oakland Tribune*. Oscar visited his brother that morning, but remained in the captain's office during the execution.

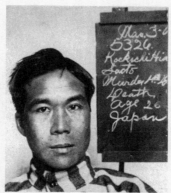

"[He was] so wrought upon by the long continued course of deceit and wrong practiced upon him by his sweetheart, his mind was unhinged . . ."
—defense attorney for Kokichi Hidaka, 1903

16. Kokichi Hidaka, June 10, 1904

While living in Seattle and working at a hotel, Kokichi Hidaka fell in love with Haro Yoshimoto, a waitress at the hotel's restaurant. Hidaka had saved nearly two thousand dollars from his job as a cook. Haro persuaded him to give her the money to save for their upcoming marriage. Within days, Haro disappeared and, according to Hidaka's defense lawyers, this "hard-working, industrious Japanese boy," who was "careful with his dealings, honest, and possessed of strict integrity," became unhinged and mentally destroyed. The woman left him heartbroken and bankrupt.

Months later, he read in a Japanese newspaper that Haro was in Sacramento and had a husband. Incensed, Hidaka set off for Sacramento, ". . . not for the purpose of doing her injury . . . but to recover some of his hard earnings . . .," according to his attorney. Hidaka confronted Haro at a restaurant, but she denied any knowledge of him or his money. On October 22, 1902, Hidaka returned to the restaurant, sat at the bar, and drank sake. He went downstairs and found Haro. Hidaka claimed not to remember what happened next.

With no witnesses, the prosecution later theorized that Hidaka shot Haro in the abdomen, killing her. When her husband came to her aid, Hidaka shot him in the shoulder. He died soon after in the hospital. As Hidaka fled, he also shot and killed M. Tokutomi, a waiter who tried to stop him. Revolver in hand, Hidaka escaped into the streets and spent the night walking to Florin, a town located ten miles away. Officers arrested him as he attempted to purchase a train ticket to Fresno. He not only confessed to the killings, but also told police he planned to murder a man in Fresno who "was his enemy," and then he intended to turn himself in to the authorities.

Hidaka's defense attorney attempted to argue that Hidaka was deranged at the time of the slayings, saying, "[Hidaka was] so wrought upon by the long continued course of deceit and wrong practiced upon him by his sweetheart, his mind was unhinged." However, Hidaka's insanity plea did not hold up in court and the judge sentenced him to death. After an unsuccessful appeal to the California Supreme Court, Hidaka died on the Folsom gallows on June 10, 1904.

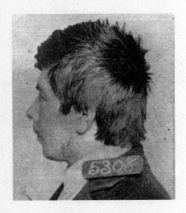

17. Charles Lawrence, October 7, 1904

Near the town of Elk Grove, in Sacramento County, hop farmers employed both Native Americans and whites to work their fields. Hop-pickers H. C. McCarty and Frederick Mize rode a cart into Elk Grove on September 4, 1902, to buy provisions, including wine. On their way back, the men encountered two Washoe Indian field workers, Augustine Morano and Charles Padilla. According to Mize, Morano and Padilla, both fifteen-year-old lads, had been drinking.

The boys asked McCarty and Mize for wine and they obliged. Charles Lawrence, Morano's half-brother, soon joined them. When the Indians demanded even more wine, Mize and McCarty refused. Padilla struck Mize in the head with a club, rendering him unconscious. Around midnight, Mize awoke to find his cart and belongings gone. McCarty lay dead in the road, severely beaten and with a bullet through his head.

The following day, an article in the *San Francisco Call* reported, "In some way, a crowd of the redskins got hold of liquor yesterday afternoon, although great care is usually taken to keep them away from it."

Based on witness accounts of the men boasting about the murder, police arrested Morano, Padilla, and Lawrence for the murder of McCarty. Witness Frank Blue said that the men claimed they had "kicked hell out of a couple of fellows down the road." Each defendant received a separate trial. None denied that the crime had taken place, although they argued over who actually shot McCarty. Lawrence and Morano blamed Padilla, while Padilla blamed Morano. The prosecution presented the theory that all three conspired together to commit the robbery when they earlier happened to overhear McCarty's and Mize's plan to purchase liquor. Lawrence rode into Elk Grove, confirmed the purchase, then rode back to inform his fellow conspirators.

Lawrence denied this story and insisted he tried to protect Mize from harm, stating further that he hadn't been near the cart when Padilla shot McCarty. Neither Morano nor Padilla testified at Lawrence's trial. Even though the jury heard much conflicting evidence, the members found Lawrence guilty of murder in the first degree.

After the Lawrence verdict, Morano tried to save his half-brother by claiming he, not Lawrence, shot McCarty. Instead, a judge sentenced Morano to seventeen years in prison. After receiving a death sentence himself for the murder, Padilla secured a new trial. Five days after Folsom executed Lawrence on October 7, 1904, Padilla was sentenced to life in prison.

18. Sing Yow, January 6, 1905

In the largely Asian-populated community of Walnut Grove in Sacramento County, Sing Yow and five other Chinese hid outside a restaurant on November 21, 1902. They waited for Jeong Him, who owed a gambling debt to Yow. After Jeong ate breakfast and emerged from the restaurant, Yow and two others shot at him and chased him to a nearby stable, where he died from seven gunshot wounds. Both white and Chinese witnesses testified to these actions on the part of Yow and the others.

Yow insisted he wasn't even in Walnut Grove at the time of the shooting, a claim supported by affidavits from two men. Charges were brought against four of the six men who had been identified by witnesses as participants in the shooting. Following an appeal of a first trial, Yow secured a new trial and provided more affidavits swearing he didn't participate in the shooting. However, the affidavits were suspect and authorities arrested a witness from the first trial on charges of perjury. Also, some Chinese were barred from the courtroom after court officials caught them coaching witnesses with hand signals. Other witnesses placed Yow at the scene, and despite contradictory evidence, a jury found Yow guilty of murder. One of his cohorts, Chin Non, received a life sentence. Yow was executed at Folsom on January 6, 1905.

"They will welcome me at
Folsom with a new hemp rope."

—Joseph Murphy, after his
capture in 1903

"I do not come before you as a red-
handed assassin begging you for that
mercy that I was not man enough to
extend to others, but simply for Justice."

—Harry Eldridge, in his appeal to
Governor Pardee, 1905

19. Joseph Murphy, July 14, 1905, 20. Harry Eldridge, December 1, 1905

At seven in the morning on July 27, 1903, Warden Thomas Wilkinson conducted business as usual by meeting with guards and convicts in the captain's office. For the previous three-and-a-half years, the meetings acted as a court hearing for inmates who had committed insubordinate acts, and punishments were meted out accordingly. The guards at these meetings/court hearings were always unarmed.

Prisoners waiting for court lined up after breakfast. Once inside the yard, they marched toward the captain's office. On this day, seven or eight inmates suddenly broke from the line, brandishing knives and razors. Storming the office, they took the warden and three or four guards by surprise. Other prisoners joined in the melee until thirteen inmates surrounded the officials.

"Blood began to fall in all directions," Warden Wilkinson later reported. "I saw it was hopeless to put up a fight against such odds." Guard P. J. Cochrane heard the commotion, rushed into the office, and joined the fight, swinging a chair at rebelling convicts. However, the severe stabs wounds he suffered stalled his efforts to defend his fellow officers. According to Wilkinson, an unidentified inmate approached him from behind and slashed his abdomen. Fortunately, his layers of clothing protected him from serious injury.

LIST OF ESCAPEES

Richard M. Gordon: serving 45 years for burglary, received at Folsom in February 1900; Harry Eldridge: serving 30 years for burglary, received in June 1903; Joseph Theron: serving life for robbery, received in June 1898; Ray Fahey: serving life for robbery, received in January 1891; Edward Davis: serving 33 years for robbery, received in January 1900; Frank Case: serving life for robbery, received in August 1900; John Woods: serving life for robbery, received in January 1902; Frank Miller: serving 12 years for burglary, received in April 1903; John Allison: serving 4 years for robbery, received in January 1903; Joseph Murphy: serving 14 years for bigamy, received in February 1903; Fred Howard: serving 15 years for robbery, received in April 1898; James Roberts: serving 20 years for robbery, received in April 1902; Albert Seavis: serving 25 years for robbery, received in August 1900.

Guard William Cotter lay on the floor, disemboweled by convicts Andy Myers and William Leverone. After killing Cotter[1], the two attacked gatekeeper W. C. Chalmers. Inmate Juan Martinez rushed to Chalmers's aid, disarming Myers. Martinez then sounded the alarm and carried Chalmers to the infirmary. Both guard Cochrane and gatekeeper Chalmers survived their wounds.

In the meantime, thirteen inmates took nine guards hostage, including Captain of the Guard R. J. Murphy, Warden Wilkinson, and the warden's grandson and stenographer, Harry. The officers were used by the inmates as human shields. Wilkinson and Murphy ordered the tower guards not to shoot. Helpless, sentinel guards watched the group gather at the armory, where Lieutenant of the Guard Henry Kipp handed over the key upon Wilkinson's direct order.

Stationed behind a Gatling gun overlooking the gate, guard Charles Gillice had a clear shot at Richard "Red Shirt" Gordon[2], who held Captain Murphy. However, Wilkinson ordered him to hold his fire. Meanwhile, as the riot progressed, convicts looted the armory, taking as many rifles and as much ammunition as possible and destroying what they didn't steal.

---

1. William Cotter, a fifty-five-year-old husband and father of two grown children, had recently announced his plan to retire from prison service within a few months, after seven years employed at Folsom. Cotter was the first prison official killed at Folsom.

2. Named for the red shirt he wore to identify him as an "incorrigible," the twenty-three-year-old Gordon was considered the ringleader of the escape plot. His forty-five-year sentence for burglary made it clear he'd probably never leave Folsom. After the escape, Captain of the Guard R. J. Murphy told the press, "It is possible that Gordon may get away, but he is such an ugly-looking fellow that anybody who has ever seen his picture would be sure to identify him." Authorities never found Gordon, and many other criminals admired him for the fact. Interestingly, in 1906, Adolph Julius Weber (story #23 in this book), unsuccessfully attempted to use Gordon's identity during a bank robbery.

GUARDS OF TORTURE

Corporal punishment at Folsom Prison ended in 1912. Before that time, inmates at Folsom feared the barbaric punishments, almost as much as those who dealt them out—namely guards P. J. Cochrane and R. J. Murphy. Called "Dirty Dick" by inmates, Murphy "believed in 'throwing the fear of God' into a prisoner the minute he arrived, by browbeating and bullying him, and every man went out of his office hating him," former Folsom inmate Jack Black wrote in his autobiography, *You Can't Win*. According the Black, Murphy developed the "perfect stool-pigeon system" during his twenty years at Folsom. "A visiting warden, surprised because there was no walls around Folsom, asked Murphy how he managed to keep the 'cons' there. 'That's simple,' he said. 'I've got one half of them watching the other half.'" Black wrote that Murphy's system of enlisting spies "caused many murders and assaults and at last it climaxed in the bloodiest prison break in the history of California."

P. J. Cochrane's job was to lace up the straitjackets insubordinate prisoners had to wear. He was "hated bitterly and every man that got near enough put a knife into him," said Black, describing the day of the break. After being stabbed and left for dead, "[Cochrane] recovered and later took his grudge out by brutalities to prisoners who had never harmed him," including Black. "You fellows tried to kill me," Cochrane said as he laced up Black, "now it's my turn." In 1924, Cochrane was killed by being slammed by the swaying masthead of a boon while inspecting the rock quarry.

Armed to the hilt, the band of inmates couldn't believe their luck. No wall surrounded the prison and armed tower guards could not shoot. The inmates easily escaped over the hills, using the hostage officials for shields.

The prison was left in chaos. However, things would have been worse if not for the efforts of convicted murderer Joseph Casey. As a trustee, Casey locked the inner gate that led into the yard, thus preventing a wholesale break.

When the group of escapees reached the Mormon Island bridge, located a mile from the prison, they forced their captives to undress and exchange clothing with them. The fugitives released Wilkinson, Captain Murphy, and the warden's grandson, Harry, who returned to the prison in their underwear. The warden immediately secured doctors and nurses to tend the injured, informed the sheriffs in surrounding counties of the break, and called in the National Guard.

Still holding six guards, the convicts continued northeast twenty miles to a hotel at Pilot Hill. There, they demanded food for themselves and their hostages. The escaped men surprised the hotel owners and staff with their polite and civil manner, especially when they thanked those they robbed. Guard John Klenzendorf later described the mood: "The convicts were in a jubilant frame of mind. They sang and danced and shouted with glee."

At approximately five o'clock that evening, everyone climbed aboard a horse-drawn wagon and forced the driver to take them south. A mile down the road, gunfire exploded from a posse of Folsom guards and sheriff's deputies. Both hostages and convicts scattered. John Allison, doing four years for robbery, sustained a bullet to his abdomen while taking refuge in the wagon. Fellow escapee Joseph Murphy watched Allison writhe in pain. "Allison, poor fellow," Murphy recalled, "died by his own hand. He asked us boys to kill him and put him out of his misery, as he had been badly wounded. We refused. Then he said 'Good-bye, pals,' shot himself, and died."

The posse shot and killed the four wagon horses, forcing the men to flee on foot into the forested hills, taking some of the guards with them. Two guards and the driver escaped by running back to the hotel. The remaining guards were released later that evening. All of the convicts eluded capture that night, but inmates Gordon and Frank Case were rumored to have been injured. They apparently broke away from the group, along with Joseph Theron, and set off on their own. Escapee Ray Fahey knew the area well and helped his fellow inmates navigate their way through the Sierra Mountains[3].

In addition to the National Guard and sheriff's posse members, Reno police officer Charles Ferrell and his renowned bloodhounds helped scour the Sierra Mountains. He tracked the escapees throughout the rough terrain with the aid of his two bloodhounds, Jumbo and Bess[4]. Ferrell stayed close behind the Folsom

3. The State Board of Prison Directors received a letter from Joseph Silvera asking for $700 to replace the horses prison guards and officers killed on Pilot Hill. The *San Francisco Call* wrote, "The directors thought that a thousand more bills of the same kind might appear and that it would be better not to establish a bad precedent by the payment of the first." Later, when Washoe County officials demanded the reward money for capturing two of the escapees, California officials promised to make the payment, but reneged once the fugitives were returned to California. Afterward, one Nevada official is said to have remarked, "Truly Californians are addicted to ways that are dark and tricks that are vain."

4. Ferrell, who became sheriff of Washoe County the following year, was considered one of the best "criminal catchers" in the region. Before the Folsom break, Ferrell and his hounds helped track down Harry Tracy, who escaped from Oregon State Penitentiary after killing Ferrell's brother, prison guard Frank Ferrell.

escapees for nine days, forcing the convicts to stay on the move. "That damned son of a bitch with the bloodhounds," one escapee remarked to a sheep herder the convicts robbed, "is close on us and if it wasn't for the dogs we could get away, but the hounds are giving a hot chase." In the end, Ferrell had to abandon the search. He and his dogs were exhausted.

Six days after the gun battle at Pilot Hill, a small group of pursuing National Guardsmen stumbled upon a group of escapees hiding in the brush twenty-five miles south near Placerville. Bullets flew and two guardsmen, Fetus Rutherford and Griffin Jones, were killed. The convicts eluded capture again. It was unclear at this point who was to blame for the guardsmen's deaths and exactly how the convicts separated. Authorities believed that lifer John Woods had been present at the time of the guardsmen's deaths after they found a pair of field glasses at the scene. According to Klenzendorf, Woods had stolen the glasses from the hotel and quoted Woods as saying, "I'll keep these glasses at all hazards."

Back at the prison, the returning warden and guards faced the scrutinization of the Board of Prison Directors and Governor George Pardee. One newspaper headline read, "Indicators Are That Those in Authority Lost Their Heads or Their Courage, Or Both." Prison Board Chairman R. M. Fitzgerald criticized Wilkinson's habit of meeting with prisoners in the office, calling it "most unwise and imprudent."

Although the board wouldn't censure the warden and his men for ordering a cease-fire, it denounced them for taking orders from the convicts. They reiterated, "...prison guards are to shoot escaping prisoners in the future, even if officers or other freemen are being used as shields by the felons." Many guards resigned or were dismissed as a result of the escape.

The Board of Prison Directors also blamed the state of California for failing to allocate supplies to build a wall around Folsom. Not only did the "invisible boundary" pose a threat of escape, it also presented accessibility to ex-cons who smuggled weapons onto the premise for their incarcerated pals—exactly what the board theorized happened.

After ten days, the various search parties had grown weary. Finally, however, their tenacity paid off. Escapee James Roberts, serving twenty years for robbery, was asleep under a tree when his captors found him in Davisville. Roberts insisted he wasn't part of the original conspiracy, but took the opportunity when it arose. He and Fred Howard, another robber, broke free from the group after Pilot Hill and actually backtracked to the prison. The following day, they went to Roseville where they split up and Roberts followed the railroad tracks to Davisville.

Next, Albert Seavis turned up. Sheriff's posse members shot the convict in the leg as he disembarked a train in Auburn. Called the "black brute" by the press, Seavis admitted defeat. "I'm up against it; this is my last break, but I will take my medicine like a man."

As the days stretched on, reports from all over Northern California came in describing encounters with the escapees. Bewildered ranchers and hotel owners told of the unexpectedly polite and well-mannered convicts who often left behind a five-dollar coin.

By mid-August, search teams from all over began to drop out—many having been on the hunt since the day of the escape. Then authorities learned that a small group of the escapees had eaten at a resort cabin at Lake Tahoe. Nevada lawmen decided to head off the convicts when they eventually emerged from the mountains. As expected, three convicts showed up in Carson City, Nevada.

On August 23, Washoe County sheriff John Sharkey and his men surprised Joseph Murphy and Frank Miller as they crossed a bridge heading toward Reno. Miller managed to elude the officers, jumping off the bridge and escaping into the darkened forest. Murphy struggled to remove his gun from his overalls, but he found himself wearing handcuffs before he could fully react. Bigamist Murphy didn't put up a fight. "It's all up with me now, I guess. I did not do this to get notoriety, but I wanted to get away from Folsom. They will welcome me at Folsom with a new hemp rope." Murphy had planned to hop an eastbound train to his home state of Pennsylvania, where he would have all of his teeth pulled and replaced with a new set in an attempt to conceal his identity. Murphy also said that while on the run and hiding in the brush near Lake Tahoe, his pursuers passed not more than two feet from him.

The next day, Washoe County officers got lucky again with the arrest of John Woods in a Carson City barbershop. Housed together in the county jail, Murphy and Woods awaited requisition papers to be shipped back to California. Fortunately for them, they'd enjoy nearly three weeks of humane treatment by Nevada authorities. Arresting officers refused to release the men before receiving the reward money. Murphy and Woods welcomed the reprieve: "If the prison

THE BOARD OF PRISON DIRECTORS

In 1880, the State of California formed a five-member Board of Prison Directors whose duties included appointing wardens for the two state prisons, creating prison industries, recommending prisoners for pardon, and generally supervising Folsom and San Quentin prisons. These men often took advantage of their power by taking favors, spending unauthorized money, and keeping poor records. By the late 1930s, inhumane conditions at San Quentin prompted a massive hunger strike at the prison. Governor Culbert Olson launched an investigation and concluded that the board's lack of leadership and control had caused the gross overcrowding and outbreaks of violence. Olson dismissed the entire board and appointed a new one. In 1944, the board was replaced by what is today known as the Department of Corrections.

guards would treat us like Sharkey and [Deputy] Maxwell [treat] the boys here, there would be fewer men in prison."

After California promised to pay the $1100 reward, Murphy and Woods arrived back in Sacramento on September 11. Murphy told the *San Francisco Call* that escaping from Folsom was the "easiest thing in the world. If the guards had been allowed to fire, it would have been a very different story. There was plenty of opportunity. There were times when a prisoner was twenty-five feet away from an officer and the guards could have opened fire without hurting an officer. Why, it would have been a hundred-to-one shot for the guards to have fired."

MURPHY'S POEM

The Washoe County Jail

It was on the 23rd of August, in the middle of the night,
While taking a walk through Reno we got into a fight,
The Sheriff and his deputies with their guns they did us assail,
And they gave us a hearty escort to the Washoe county jail.

They marched us up through Reno, and the people they did stare,
For they knew that we were convicts but little did we care
They marched us up to the Sheriff's office, and searched us through
And devil a thing they found on us except a "gat" or two.

They put us each in separate cells, upon the second floor
And when we wanted anything, we would rap upon the door
And when the Sheriff comes around shove out your little pail
And he will feed you bootleg coffee in the Washoe county jail.

Monday and Tuesday, they give you Irish stew,
Wednesday and Thursday beef and liver, too,
Friday and Saturday, 'murphies' we pare without finger nails
For they won't give a "con" a knife and fork, in the Washoe county jail.

Every Sunday morning as they open your cell door,
You listen to a preacher until your ears are sore
And if we were outside our cells, the walls we'd try to scale
For they teach us bum religion in the Washoe county jail.

The *Virginia Report* wrote: "To accuse the man, villain, convict or whatever you may call him of writing that 'poem' is downright persecution and little less than absolutely criminal. Murphy never wrote a line, a word, or letter of it and is very doubtful if he ever knew the effort was to appear in print . . . there are some things that should not be laid at the door of even the worst criminals."

District Attorney Arthur Seymour charged Murphy and Woods with the murder of William Cotter and the death of the militia men, as well as jail breaking. Even though convict Andy Myers actually killed Guard Cotter, Myers didn't escape from the prison with the others. Further, Murphy and Woods were the break's co-conspirators. Murphy admitted that Myers wasn't part of the original plot to escape, but he argued that Myers joined in once the break commenced. The jury discounted the argument and Murphy faced the noose.

John Woods, already serving a life sentence, received a second-degree murder conviction for Cotter's death, prompting Judge E. C. Hart to admonish the jury for their leniency. "Oh, I beg your pardon," he said with sarcasm. "I thought this was a case of disturbing the peace." He turned to Woods, saying "You may appear in this court one hundred years from today and receive your sentence." However, prosecutors succeeded in securing the death penalty for Woods when they charged him with the murders of Rutherford and Jones, despite purely circumstantial evidence.

In March of 1904, police arrested Harry Eldridge in Seattle. Guard P. J. Cochrane made the journey north to identify his one-time attacker. Upon seeing Eldridge, Cochrane exclaimed, "There's the man. You're the man who stabbed me as you escaped. I know you. You can't fool me." Eldridge merely smiled as the jailer led him back to his cell.

Accepting the same argument as for Murphy's conviction, the jury found Eldridge guilty for Cotter's death. After sentencing, Eldridge remarked, "Well, it's better than a life sentence." Curiously, the charges against Andy Myers were dropped after Eldridge's conviction. An obscure article in the *Oakland Tribune* in 1921 explained that prison officials feared bringing Myers's witnesses—"desperate criminals"—to Sacramento for trial.

In his appeal, Eldridge pointed out several instances during his trial where guards admitted Eldridge had prevented bloodshed. Captain Murphy explained how Eldridge refused to let convicts Fred Howard and Albert Seavis kill him. Guard Seavy also related an incident where Eldridge stood between him and another threatening escapee. The higher court found no merit in his case. Eldridge then pleaded with Governor Pardee to consider his "heroic" acts as well as Myers's involvement: "I do not come before you as a red-handed assassin begging you for that mercy that I was not man enough to extend to others, but simply for Justice." He also claimed he had nothing to do with the conspiracy, but when he saw an opportunity, he took it, saying, "I availed myself the opportunity and by so doing got mixed up in the break, but if I had any idea of the way that they intended to go out I would not have went."

Eldridge's cellmate, William Grider, sealed Eldridge's fate. Grider testified that Eldridge threatened him in order to enlist his participation in the break the night before. When Grider had an opportunity, he told a trustee of the plot, but the trustee didn't believe him. Serving a third term for burglary, Grider received a pardon. Joseph Casey and Juan Martinez were also pardoned for their efforts to quell the escape.

The embarrassing break left a bad taste in the mouths of the Board of Prison Directors. In November, the board replaced Wilkinson with Assistant District Attorney Archibald Yell. Within months, Yell dismissed several guards, including Captain R. J. Murphy. Murphy's dismissal was partly due to his having been taken hostage once again during a December riot, when he again ordered guards not to shoot.

On February 2, 1905, the same day as Captain Murphy's dismissal, John Woods hanged himself in his cell, denying the state the opportunity.

On July 14, 1905, Murphy mounted the gallows, following a restless night. He remained stoic, even as the officer placed the black cap over his head and the trap dropped. Eldridge met the same fate almost five months later on December 1. The *Reno Evening Gazette* said the condemned man "demanded that the death warrant

Rewards of the Day: Pardons and Commutations

Joseph Casey (pardoned) had served thirteen years of a life sentence when the inmates escaped. For twelve of those years, Casey manned the inner gate that allowed prisoners to pass through for work. When Casey heard the commotion, he immediately shut the inner gate, thus holding 500 men in confinement. Casey earned his sentence after killing a man over a disputed card game. He claimed self-defense. "...even if the Captain of the Guard did lose his trousers," wrote the *Oakland Tribune*, "one poor convict kept his head and grip on his nerve." Casey received a pardon in 1904 for his quick thinking and enjoyed his freedom until 1911, when he committed a felony and returned to Folsom to serve out his original sentence. Juan Martinez (pardoned) served nearly eight years of a 25-year sentence for rape and was considered a model prisoner. Martinez worked in the prison hospital and even lost an eye during his work in the infirmary. During the melee, Martinez assisted Cotter and dressed Cochrane's wounds, as well Guard Jolly's neck where Howard had stabbed him. After disarming a convict, Martinez helped injured guard W. C. Chalmers and then rang the alarm bell. Charles Abbott, 41, commuted, was serving a life sentence for killing a man in a drunken brawl. A former sailor, Abbott carried Cochrane to the infirmary. Incarcerated since 1883, he had become an expert stonemason and "never shirked any work assignment in ten years." William Grider (commuted) was serving five years for burglary—his third time behind bars—when Grider's cellmate, Harry Eldridge, told him about the break. Grider informed a trustee of the break, despite Eldridge's threats, but his warning went ignored. Just months after his release, Grider returned to Folsom, having committing another burglary. He attempted to hang himself in the county jail before his transfer to Folsom.

FAMILIES AT FOLSOM

Many of the guards and their families resided in small cottages outside Folsom's walls. Today, the Folsom Prison Museum occupies one of them. During the 1903 break, the *Oakland Tribune* said, "Too well, [the families] know the savage character of the ringleaders of the conspirators and their fears conjured up scenes of torture and death, in which their loves ones were the victims." The wife of Frank Lockhart, lieutenant of the night watch, told one newspaper, "I shall never forget the yelling of those men in the yard. I believe I shall hear it to my dying day. I looked down and saw my husband with his gun, but he did not use it. I could not understand then why he did not shoot, but, of course, I know now. He is out with the posse now in pursuit of the convicts and I pray he will come back unhurt. But you cannot tell about these things."

be read and made a defiant speech from the scaffold"—a speech not printed in the papers.

In the end, Guard Cochrane became captain of the guard, convict James Roberts received a second-degree murder conviction, and fellow escapee Fred Howard, who was finally captured in 1910, pleaded guilty to Cotter's murder. Rumor had it that authorities found Frank Miller's body in Colorado, "shattered with lead," in an unmarked grave.

In 1908, construction of a wall around Folsom began. The three-sided structure met the American River on each end. Completed in 1923, the wall finally secured Folsom Prison, twenty years after the break.

Captured: Harry Eldridge: hanged; Joseph Murphy: hanged; James Roberts: life sentence; Albert Seavis: life sentence; Fred Howard: life sentence; John Woods: sentenced to hang, committed suicide.

Died on the Lam: John Allison, Fred Miller.

Never Captured: Richard "Red Shirt" Gordon, Ray Fahey, Edward Davis, Frank Case, and Joseph Theron.

CRUELTY AT FOLSOM PRISON

The recaptured convicts blamed harsh cruelties as their reason for making the prison break. Prison officials denied any such cruelty at Folsom and responded to public criticism by saying, "We do not believe that there is any prison in the world where prisoners are better fed than in the penitentiaries of California; and certainly there are no prisons where they are fed as well for the same cost. The health and physical condition of the convicts are the most carefully guarded, and it has been frequently a matter of criticism made by those familiar with prison methods in other countries and in other states that our convicts are too well treated." In his own defense, Warden Thomas Wilkinson claimed prisoners became "saucy" and, in turn, the guards "became angry and took it out on their unfortunate victim." Wilkinson pointed to Captain of the Guard R. J. Murphy as responsible for dealing out punishments, an accusation not seriously entertained by the courts.

The following methods of "controlling" inmates were banned in 1903. They continued unofficially until Warden James A. Johnston abolished all corporal punishment at Folsom in 1912.

The straightjacket: Called "the springs" or the "bag" by inmates. The prisoner wore a corset-like coat with his arms pinioned into pockets sewn inside. While lying facedown on the floor, the guard pulled the ropes tight—to the point of near-suffocation. At Folsom, Warden Thomas Wilkinson created a smaller straightjacket to worsen the punishment. Guards inserted a "Spanish windlass" (a two-inch-thick stick) through the laces and turned it to tighten the jacket as much as possible. Those lacing the jacket often weighed over 200 pounds. Denied water, the prisoners lay in a dark cell, sometimes in their own urine and excrement, barely able to breath. They experienced excruciating cramps that shot through the body and numbed their hands and arms, while the jacket's brass rivets dug into the skin. Inmates often suffered permanent crippling in their hands and arms. Some died. Prisoners often wore the jacket for ten to fifty hours at a time. Jake Oppenheimer (story #28) withstood this punishment for a staggering 110 hours.

Epsom salts: Once cinched in the straitjacket, the prisoner was held by one guard, while another poured Epson salts down his throat.

The iron maiden: Standing between two iron doors, the prisoner was in a virtual vise. Unable to move, his ankles swelled and blood clots formed in his legs.

The "Hooks," or Tricing: With his wrists in steel cuffs behind his back, the prisoner was backed up to a wall. A leather chain was threaded through hooks above his head and then fastened to his handcuffs. Thus shackled, the prisoner was pulled upward. The prisoner's arms twisted behind him and his upper body wrenched forward while his feet strained to touch the floor.

"After it was done, the excitement and everything, of course I realized that I had done something, probably made trouble for me . . ."
—George Easton, 1905

21. George Easton, April 6, 1906

Twenty-six-year-old George Easton frequently visited Josephine "Belle" Quick's house of ill-fame in the town of Dixon, in Solano County. In late October of 1904, Easton created a disturbance there. He was thrown out of the house, arrested, and told to leave town. A few nights later, Easton returned to the establishment, where he found Quick, Charles Horigan, and another woman sitting at a table having dinner. Despite the previous disturbance, they permitted Easton to join them. Easton asked Quick if she happened to have a razor, and she handed him one. While Quick was distracted trimming the wick of a lamp, Easton crept up behind Horigan, pulled his head back and, with one motion, used the razor to slit his throat from ear to ear, nearly severing his head. After threatening to do the same to Quick, Easton fled into the night. He turned himself over to authorities the following morning, lest a mob find him.

Initially, Easton claimed jealousy as his motive. He felt jealous over the attentions Quick gave other men. He told the house's barkeep, "She [Quick] seems to think more of them than me. I don't care a damn. I'll get even." At his trial, Easton feigned insanity, saying he'd been "crazy from dope" on the night of the murder. He testified to having used drugs three to four times a day for three years. The jury didn't buy Easton's story, declared him sane, and found him guilty of murder. Upon hearing his death sentence, Easton said, "Bring me a pencil and paper, that I may write to my mother and tell her I am to be hung." He also asked that someone go to Quick's house and bring him his mother's picture. This, he told the officer, was "all I had left." On April 6, 1906, just before the executioner placed the black cap over his head, Easton thanked the guards and prison officials for their kind treatment. Fifteen minutes later, the prison physician declared him dead.

". . .there could be no God, else an innocent man would not be hanged."
—William M. Gray, on the scaffold, 1906

22. William M. Gray, April 13, 1906

In mid-January 1905, someone bludgeoned Wong Kuong to death in a downtown Sacramento alley. The only description of the assailant came from Chin Coy, a friend of the victim, who heard it from Kuong, as he lay dying. "If he catch 'em the nigger," Kuong supposedly said, "I know him." Based on Kuong's description, Coy told police: "He big like me; he got a light hat on, got a sweater." Coy also reported that the suspect wore an overcoat and no vest.

Police officer Martin Pennish arrested William Gray the next day. The following April, Gray went to trial. Prostitute Belle Wilks testified that Gray told her he "killed the Chinaman and I have the money for it." She claimed he also had a "small little black greasy purse" on him—the supposed loot from the robbery. Another witness, William Grubbs, testified that Gray asked him to provide his alibi for the night in question, but Grubbs refused. On behalf of the defense, however, two officers testified that Wilks and Grubbs had bad reputations. One said he wouldn't believe anything Wilks said, even under oath.

Pennish admitted at trial that he had not written down the description Coy gave him, nor was it recorded in the "bug book," the criminal log at the station. A rumor also circulated that Pennish would receive a reward for arresting Kuong's murderer. Gray did not take the stand, nor did the defense offer a closing statement. Despite the lack of physical evidence, the jury convicted Gray of murder in the first degree. The defense appealed on the basis of several issues. Coy's description of the assailant, considered hearsay, should have been inadmissible. Nor was Coy's own credibility ever challenged or questioned. Finally, another black man fitting the same description had been arrested before Gray, but this was never addressed at trial.

Gray lost his appeal. On the day before his execution, he sent an application for pardon to Governor George Pardee, but Pardee was away at the time. On April 13, 1906, "Gray mounted the gallows with courage," reported the *Oakland Tribune*, and he "expressed the belief that there could be no God, else an innocent man would not be hanged."

"I don't fear death, it is only a long sleep, no different from night's unconsciousness, except it is longer."
—Adolph Weber, the night before his execution, 1906

23. Adolph Julius Weber, September 27, 1906

Twenty-year-old Adolph Weber sat under a magnolia tree and watched his family's home become engulfed in flames. Blood snaked down his arm from a cut on his hand. The bodies of his mother Mary, sister Bertha, and younger brother Earl lay smoldering in the grass. His father Julius wouldn't be saved either. Having been shot before the start of the conflagration, Julius's lifeless body burned in a locked bathroom.

The beautiful home of the wealthy Weber family sat just outside the town limits of Auburn, California, too far from a hydrant to quickly extinguish the fire. Neighbors raced to the scene, but found the doors and windows locked. Thinking the family wasn't home, they broke windows to gain entrance in an effort to save furniture. In the dark and smoky interior, rescuers stumbled over the bodies of Mary and Bertha. They passed the bodies through the window to people gathered on the porch, who then respectfully placed the bodies on the lawn.

Mary's lower limbs had been badly charred, while Bertha's upper body, including her face, were barely recognizable. Curiously, their lifeless bodies had been discovered in the parlor, a room not yet touched by flames. George Ruth handed eight-year-old Earl Weber to Undersheriff William May. The boy appeared alive, but struggled to breathe. Earl suffered from an unknown disease which affected his ability to walk or speak. His head had been beaten severely. Moments after being laid next to his mother, Earl died from smoke inhalation.

The suffocating smoke drove the rescuers out, preventing them from searching for Mr. Weber. As both men and women screamed and sobbed over the deaths of members of this prominent and well-respected family, Adolph continued to sit emotionless under the tree. Given his usual peculiar and detached nature, onlookers didn't view his behavior as suspicious or odd.

At the scene, Coroner W. A. Shepard examined the bodies of mother and daughter and discovered their deaths had resulted from .32 caliber bullet wounds. Law officials immediately surmised that the killer had attempted to disguise the true nature of the crime by setting fire to the house. The act was "...either the work of a madman, or a cool, calculated, premeditated crime," wrote the *Oakland Tribune*.

Adrian Wills, a former childhood friend of Adolph's, approached him as he sat under the tree. He brought Adolph to the Wills's house, where a doctor dressed his injured hand. Adolph claimed he received the cut when he broke a window. "I must go home; I think my mother is hurt; I know my little brother is all right, because I brought him out myself," Adolph told Adrian's sister. Adolph then suggested that Adrian and a few others go downtown for sodas and ice cream, then go on to the American Hotel to "see the girls." Adrian, thinking his friend suffered from shock, obliged.

The following morning, Sheriff Charles Keena interviewed Adolph, who insisted he left at 6:30 the night of the fire to go jogging, that he tripped and tore his pants, and he went to a shop to purchase a new pair. He had the clerk wrap his old trousers in paper, then he left the store. At 7:42, Guy Lukens, a town resident, encountered Adolph in the streets and frantically told him his house was on fire.

Adolph said he arrived back at the house and, in an effort to save his family, he kicked in a lower window. He threw his bundled-up pants inside and crawled through, cutting his hand. Once inside, however, he said the smoke drove him out.

Keena then accompanied Adolph to his aunt's house for a change of clothes, even though Adolph and his aunt had not been on speaking terms for some time. Bertha Snowden, one of Mary's sisters, lived on land adjoining the Weber property. She described how Adolph "was hateful to his people," and that Adolph's sister feared him, telling her aunt that Adolph was mean enough to kill anyone. Snowden pointed a finger at her nephew and said, "Dolphy, you know who did that!" Adolph denied any involvement in the murders, but Snowden persisted, telling Adolph that if he couldn't prove his innocence, she'd like to see him hanged.

Keena ended the conversation.

The two men left the house and were joined by Wills and investigator Clarence Geear. Authorities had found fifty-two-year-old Julius Weber's body and discovered a .32 caliber bullet lodged in the patriarch's chest.

On November 12, 1904, two days after the fire, an article in the *Sacramento Bee* appeared, recounting Snowden's conversation with Keena and Adolph. Somehow, a reporter had got wind of Bertha's accusation, which led to the brazen headline, "Adolph Weber Is Suspected of Murdering Entire Family." Adolph confronted his aunt and demanded an explanation, but she denied that she had spoken to the reporter. "Dolphy," she said, "you know who did the deed. You dare not deny it to me."

Adolph shook his fist at Snowden. "Your turn is next," he said and left the house.

That night at the coroner's inquest, District Attorney Robinson called Adolph for questioning. Adolph's tone turned aggressive and surly, and he answered the district attorney with short, snippy answers. He claimed he left his family alive and well at 6:30 the night of the fire. As Adolph left the courtroom with Robinson and Keena, Justice of the Peace O. A. Smith approached the three men. He carried a warrant for Adolph's arrest.

Moments after being locked in a cell, Adolph began complaining about the conditions, demanding different bedding and clothing. Once furnished with these items, Adolph phoned Ben Tabor, his father's attorney, who came immediately.

As the prosecution compiled its case against Adolph, the team also worked to piece together the details of a bank robbery that had occurred six months earlier in Auburn. In May 1904, the Placer County Bank had fallen victim to a robber who was wearing a false beard and blue goggles. He handed the clerk a note identifying the gun-wielding bandit as none other than R. J. "Red Shirt" Gordon, the infamous escaped convict from Folsom prison. The man demanded "all the money in the Placer County Bank." The robber leaped over the counter and fired a shot at the clerk, but missed. Then he shoved money into his canvas bag, scaled the counter, dashed out to his horse and cart, and escaped into the hills with more than six thousand dollars.

"The robbery surpassed all feats of daring recklessness in the annals of crime in this county," wrote the *Sacramento Bee*. "The affair, when told at first, had such a dime-novel flavor that many were loath to believe it. So sudden and unexpected was the robber's invasion, and so calm and deliberate his actions while in the bank, that many declared [it] the act of a man of unsound mind, so unmindful of the dangers of capture and death the robber seemed to be."

Posse members found the small .22 caliber pistol in the hills, along with the bandit's shirt, false beard, and overalls. Sheriff Keena tracked the gun's origin to a pawn shop in Sacramento. The dealer described the buyer as "a young man about twenty-years old, slender, light complexion, and looked like a Swede." With nothing else to go on, the case went unsolved until authorities noted similarities in build and athleticism between young Weber and the bank robber. Before turning reclusive, Adolph was a talented athlete, excelling in several sports. His alleged appetite for "reading sensational dime novels" also figured into the district attorney's theory.

Adolph responded to such suggestions by saying, "When a fellow is down everyone is against him. I wonder what I will be charged with next." Adolph also denied the insinuations that he "was a lover of trashy literature." He told a *San Francisco Call* reporter, "I have not been reading trash of that sort. I have confined my reading entirely to biography and to standard history for the last two years. Reports that I have devoted my time to reading trashy stuff of the dime novel sort are detrimental to me and to my case."

When the inquest continued that evening, Adolph opted to stay in his newly carpeted cell, an upgrade he requested and paid for, as well as the use of three adjoining cells. He did, however, provide a statement to the court: "If a person murdered his father, would he leave his brother alive? Earl was not shot: Would he be left to tell on him? If a person murdered his family, leaving his brother unshot, would he rescue that brother from death to tell on him? If a person in possession of his wits had murdered his family, would he leave their bodies in a room where there was no fire? If he had set the house on fire to cover the crime, would he not leave the bodies in the flames to burn?"

The prosecution had its own theories. Several witnesses contradicted Adolph's claim of carrying Earl from the house. District Attorney Robinson felt the reason Adolph didn't shoot Earl was because he couldn't risk the noise of another gunshot. According to Robinson, Adolph confronted his father in the bathroom at the rear of the house. Witnesses heard Bertha playing the piano at the other end of the house at around 6:30, drowning out the noise when Adolph shot his father. Adolph lit his father's body on fire, locked the bathroom door, and quickly walked to the parlor where Bertha sat at the piano. Blood on the stool indicated Adolph shot his sister in the chest while she played. Mary Weber had been putting Earl to bed when she heard the second shot. Rushing down the stairs, she saw what her son had done. She ran to the phone in the hall and as she picked it up, Adolph shot his mother at close range, the bullet striking under her left arm. She fell, dropping the phone, but still alive. Adolph stood over his mother and fired again, sending a bullet into her chest.

Robinson said Adolph bludgeoned Earl with the butt of the revolver, leaving him for dead. Adolph then dragged Earl and Bertha to the hall, laying Bertha head-to-foot with his mother. He then lit them on fire. This, Robinson said, explained why mother and daughter had burns on the opposite ends of their bodies. Adolph then set fires at two ends of the house, hoping the house would be engulfed in seconds. However, the locking of the doors and windows blocked the flow of oxygen, extinguishing the flames in the hall.

The route Adolph claimed to have taken into town was completely contradicted by several witnesses. The most damaging testimony came from May Clark, a prostitute. She said she saw Adolph walk under a street lamp at about 6:43 P.M., passing her house, which was situated on a different route than Adolph claimed he had taken. Clark testified she again saw Adolph "hanging around" the post office at 7:00.

Somewhat earlier than 7:00, J. A. Powell testified he entered the bathroom of the American Hotel and saw Adolph washing his hands. Startled, Adolph quickly left without turning off the water or drying his hands. Powell also testified he saw the same man enter the hotel's lobby with Adrian Wills later that night and heard Adolph say, "Let's go up and see the girls."

When the coroner's jury pronounced Adolph guilty, it came as no surprise to anyone, including Adolph. However, what the public really wanted to know was, *why*? Some said he murdered for the inheritance, an estimated $80,000. Others conjectured that Julius Weber discovered his son had robbed the Placer County Bank and Adolph believed he had to silence him. Many said the motive included both theories. However, the prosecution had nothing else to go on: no witnesses, no murder weapon.

Throughout the preliminary examination, Adolph frequently read a book while witnesses testified against him. Oftentimes, a cynical smile slithered across his face. When Clarence Geear took the stand, a loud clanging noise startled Adolph as he wrote notes. A revolver, wrapped in cloth, had dropped onto the edge of a table. The barrel of the gun showed bloody fingerprints, and two light-colored hairs stuck to its side. It had been found during the court recess earlier that morning. Inside the Weber's barn, where Adolph spent much of his time, Sheriff Keena's men had discovered a cleverly concealed entrance to a passage that led underneath the barn. One of the men ran his hand along the sill of the low-ceilinged, narrow space, and came upon the .32 Iver-Johnson revolver.

"[Adolph] turned deathly pale; [he] squirmed about in his seat and nervously fingered the pencil with which he was making notes of the evidence being offered," reported the *San Francisco Call*. Robinson passed the revolver to the defense attorneys, who appeared to be just as shocked as their client. Things only deteriorated for Adolph from there. After being charged with the murders of his family, he learned that Geear and others had also discovered the bank loot. Just outside the Weber barn, buried eighteen inches under the ground, they found a lard can containing nearly six thousand dollars in gold, short $825 from the amount reported stolen from the Placer County Bank. Bank officials identified the gold coins as those taken in the May robbery.

When informed of the latest find, Adolph replied, "Oh, I thought you had discovered the motive for the murders. The bank robbery is a trivial matter. It's not bothering me. It's the other case I am thinking about." Then, Adolph finished with what Keena deemed a confession: "If I did take it, it was not because I needed the money, but only to see what I could do."

"Officers say that the accused man's downfall will surely come from his conceit," wrote the *Oakland Tribune*. "The fact that the authorities have been able to uncover most of his carefully laid plans has been more motivating to him and has done much toward weakening the boy."

The days of confinement and the compounding evidence against him began to take its toll. Adolph refused to eat and even appeared in court wearing slippers. He laughed at rumors of an insanity plea and remarked, "I'm not going to let myself go crazy, never fear." While awaiting trial, Adolph read books, wrote notes for a memoir, and enjoyed flowers and candy from women admirers.

By late January, Adolph's trial commenced, but the only charge was the murder of his mother. Much of the witness testimony contradicted Adolph's claims, including the route he took into town, his actions therein, and his involvement in saving Earl. Prosecutors, including Attorney General Ulysses S. Webb, theorized that Adolph did, in fact, re-enter the house, but only to drag the bodies into the parlor where the fire was just beginning to take hold. Afterward, Adolph sat under the magnolia tree, watching the fire rage on and holding his injured hand, which the examining doctor, Robert F. Rooney, determined was self-inflicted.

Unbeknownst to the defense, the prosecution had found a San Francisco pawnbroker who claimed he sold the gun to the defendant. Henry Carr identified the gun—before knowing its involvement in the crime—as one he sold in July 1904, during the same time Adolph and his family had visited San Francisco.

Even though the gun was found on the Weber property, the case against Adolph still hinged on circumstantial evidence. The defense challenged the prosecution's witnesses, particularly May Clark and Henry Carr, accusing them both of having unreliable reputations. When Adolph took the stand, he rebuked the prosecution testimony and during cross-examination he responded to fifty-four of Webb's questions with either "I don't know" or "I don't remember."

After three weeks of testimony, prosecutor George Hamilton addressed the jury in his closing argument. "I thank God his father is dead, that his sister is dead, that his little brother is dead, for they will not be compelled to take the stand and swear this boy is the murderer of Mary Weber. Gentlemen of the jury, give him the same mercy that he gave his mother as she knelt before him begging for her life."

Defense attorney Grove L. Johnson implored the jury not to convict Adolph based merely upon circumstantial evidence; he argued that Julius Weber, known to have a fierce temper, could have done this to his family and dropped the weapon in the cesspool. Expert testimony, however, concluded that the shot that killed Julius couldn't have been self-inflicted.

After the jury returned a guilty verdict, Adolph told the press, "Of course, the verdict was a keen disappointment to me, but I am not at all discouraged. We will take it up to the Supreme Court and if that will grant me a new trial, this will be only the beginning of the fight. It's no use to complain, I cannot change the result . . . I will have to try harder the next time, that's all." Adolph kept up an air of confidence and cheerfulness. "I want to conquer so much that I don't allow any other thought to enter my mind. A man can do nothing if he allows fear to get the best of him. He must maintain his supremacy over fear and discouragement if he wishes to win out. He cannot afford to lose his grip. My poor health is troubling me more than anything else at present. This confinement is telling on me and I was not well when I came here." Then he laughed and said, "It was a queer way of celebrating Washington's birthday for me, wasn't it? I wonder what Mrs. Snowden thought of it."

Adolph then dismissed two of his three attorneys, despite facing charges of robbing the bank. The matter settled out of court after Adolph agreed to turn over the money to the bank and cough up the remainder, amounting to $6,700 with interest. Amazingly, concerning the agreement, Adolph remarked, "I want it understood, however, that my acceptance of the proposition has no connection with my guilt or innocence of the bank robbery charge."

While awaiting the Supreme Court's decision, Adolph refused to speak to the press and appeared in court looking rough. "His hair has grown long, his face is unshaven; he is thin and has a general unhealthy look," reported the *Los Angeles Herald*. The case of his inheritance had come up in court and Adolph wanted his money. A question lingered over the proceedings: Can a person profit by a wrong he committed in order to inherit an estate? In California, the answer at the time was yes. The judge had no choice but to award Adolph the nearly $71,000 in the estate. Because Adolph was tried and found guilty only for the murder of his mother, he could inherit his father's money; also, no specific law prevented him from benefiting as a result of the murder of his family. In 1905, the California state legislature passed the "Patricide Law," prohibiting one from inheriting an estate by way of murder. Although the law has been amended several times, it remains in effect today.

In June, the suspense ended. The Supreme Court upheld the lower court's decision, although one judge dissented, saying the case lacked sufficient evidence beyond a reasonable doubt to convict Weber. Undersheriff May asked Adolph if he would continue his fight and Adolph responded, "No, why should I? My youth is gone, my health is gone, and my honor is gone. . . I abandon the case."

Adolph's last hope resided with Governor George Pardee. Because Adolph had dismissed all of his attorneys except Tuttle, Undersheriff William May, who had recently passed the bar exam, resigned in order to assist Tuttle in preparing the plea. Affidavits from several jury members accompanied Adolph's application, stating that since the trial, after considering the evidence and other sworn affidavits, they now had a reasonable doubt as to Adolph's guilt. Pardee granted Adolph a sixteen-day stay of execution in order to review the affidavits.

The night before his hanging, Adolph spent hours playing chess with prison physician Dr. C. H. Gladding. Guard P. J. Cochrane entered his cell around 8:30 P.M. and informed Adolph, "Weber, it looks pretty black for you. We have had no word from the Governor and it looks like there's no hope for you."

"That's where you and I differ," Adolph replied calmly. He and the doctor continued to play chess until nearly midnight and Adolph awoke early the next morning and enjoyed a hearty breakfast as if it were any other day, but by 9:30, his resolve began to wither. He sent a telegram to Tuttle, asking for word. Tuttle replied that he hadn't heard anything. Adolph tried again, this time begging, "Prevent execution. Insanity plea. Anything." He sent a duplicate message to May, who informed his client "that all hopes are gone."

"That settles it," Adolph said, realizing the inevitable. "I have no statement to make, no writing to leave behind and I have no statement to make regarding the disposition of my body." As the noose swung in front of him on September 27, 1906, he inclined his head, as if to facilitate the process.

Bertha Snowden arranged for undertakers to retrieve her nephew's body and transport it to Sacramento where he'd be displayed for hundreds of curious onlookers. Before cremation, Adolph's doctors at the Cooper Medical College dissected his brain, apparently to determine whether Adolph truly was insane. Their findings revealed nothing of importance.

WAS ADOLPH WEBER INSANE?

In May 1908, Dr. Robert F. Rooney published his findings in the *California State Journal of Medicine*. Having been the Webers's family physician since before Adolph's birth, Rooney observed the marked change in behavior of the Webers's eldest son. He described Adolph as a bright, healthy, and promising young boy who loved and obeyed his parents and devoted himself to the care of his disabled younger brother.

Adolph excelled in sports and was an avid runner. At school, Adolph achieved high marks and had many friends. Then, during his final year of high school, Adolph began to fall back in his studies, had irregular attendance at school, and often complained about his health. He turned "sullen and morose," distancing himself from friends and family, and he barely attended school during the last semester. His only activities seemed to be playing chess, reading "quack literature," and frequenting brothels. He also started conducting cruel and senseless experiments on small animals and wringing the necks of chickens for his own amusement.

At eighteen, he came to Rooney requesting a circumcision, hoping to alleviate his excessive masturbating. For months after the procedure, Adolph regularly complained to the doctor of "vague nervous symptoms," which Rooney dismissed, attributing them to the influence of Adolph's choice in reading material. Adolph consulted other doctors, all of whom concurred with Rooney's opinion. Still, Adolph continued to approach Rooney with many "imaginary troubles."

Adolph grew abusive toward his mother and sister, and he often physically struck his invalid brother. He assumed "lordly airs in his family relations," demonstrated by sleeping late, demanding a special diet, and insisting on eating in a separate room. "He spent his time mostly in brooding reveries," wrote Rooney, "resenting any interference, and could not bear to be crossed in any way, flying into violent rages at trivial causes." During his trial, he remained stoic and indifferent to his predicament. In prison, "he wrote bloodcurdling doggerel and filthy verses; [he] quoted much poetry, in an erroneous manner, and applied it to his own position."

In his report, Rooney discussed the mental disease of paranoia, most prevalent after the age of fifteen, "…occurring in individuals capable of, at times, fine education and brilliant acquirements, yet possessing a decided mental twist." According to Rooney, those with paranoia suffered delusions with hallucinations, often chronically progressive, misguided ambition, contempt toward others, and indifferent to the suffering of those outside their own personality. Rooney blamed Adolph's vanity, egocentrism, and delusions of grandeur on the disease, and he asserted that it wasn't uncommon for the paranoid individual to be "cunning and scheming, capable both of devising a plan and choosing the best moment for its effective execution…" Rooney concluded "that the unfortunate young man was insane when he planned and executed his abhorrent deed."

Rooney's opinion, based on evidence learned after Adolph's death and from the findings of leading psychiatrists, reflected his own regrets about his professional dealings with Adolph: "[I] did not recognize the symptoms of the disease when they lay open to anyone skilled to read them."

PART III: 1907–1912

Folsom Wardens:	Archibald Yell, December 1, 1903–February 14, 1908
	William H. Reilly, February 14, 1908–June 1, 1912
	James A. Johnston, June 1, 1912–November 16, 1913
California Governors:	George Pardee, January 6, 1903–January 9, 1907
	James Gillett, January 9, 1907–January 3, 1911
	Hiram Johnson, January 3, 1911–March 15, 1917

Aside from corrupt government, Californians had much to celebrate. Electric streetcars, established by the Pacific Electric Railway, offered low-cost mass transit across counties in the southern part of the state. A San Jose air show intrigued people with a potential new mode of transportation, and, in March 1910, the first motion picture played in a Los Angeles theater. Miners in Southern California enjoyed prosperity, selling precious gems such as tourmaline, kunzite, topaz, garnet, and more. In fact, the San Diego area provided the Dowager Empress of China with 120 tons of pink tourmaline from 1902 until her death in 1911. The same year, men voted to allow women the right to vote, making California the sixth and largest state to approve women's suffrage.

However, the state remained steadfast in its stance against Asian immigrants. In 1910, Angel Island, an island in the San Francisco Bay, became known as the "Ellis Island of the West," processing approximately one million Asian immigrants. The station detained immigrants for days, months, or even years before allowing them into the country, if at all. Virtually a Chinese prison, Angel Island remained in operation until 1940.

Southern Pacific lobbyists continued to dominate the state legislature, wheeling and dealing to further their own interests. Governor George Pardee, backed by the railroad in his first election, lost in 1906 after he offended his backers with a modest support of reform. Instead, James Gillett, called a "mule" for the Southern Pacific, easily won the governorship. Voters had had enough in 1910 and took a chance by electing San Francisco attorney Hiram Johnson to the governorship. He promised to "kick the Southern Pacific out of politics." Johnston immediately began the "Progressive Era," a period of unprecedented reform. He ended the railroad's corruptive reign, supported workers' compensation, and provided greater rights to women, among other accomplishments.

Mirroring its government, California's prison system stood in dire need of reform. In response to a 20 percent increase in inmates, Folsom's warden, Archibald Yell, lobbied in 1903 for funds to build a new cell building and a wall around Folsom. In 1907, legislators approved $168,000 for both projects. The building wasn't completed until 1916, the wall until 1923.

To combat increased prison populations, the parole system began to allow low-risk offenders to make good on the outside. Continued reports of cruelty at the prison troubled the Board of Prison Directors and citizens alike. Reformers favored abolishing corporal punishment in prison, and they promoted indeterminate sentencing, including segregating first-time offenders from "hardened" criminals. With the lack of rehabilitation, work programs, or prison industry, reformers dubbed the penitentiaries "Schools of Crime." The only thing inmates learned, they said, was how to be better criminals.

When James A. Johnston became warden of Folsom in 1912, he immediately discontinued corporal punishment, started a school for the inmates, and regularly checked food for quality. He also began farming operations on the premises, making Folsom a completely self-sustaining prison until the 1960s. Considered one of the "best known men of penal affairs," Johnston left Folsom after only a year to take a position at San Quentin, where he also made many positive changes.

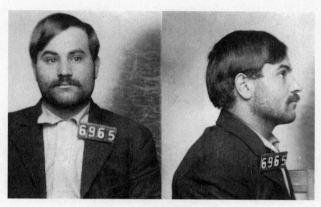

"That's all right, boys."
—Antonio Cipolla's final words from the scaffold, 1909

24. Antonio Cipolla, April 30, 1909

Italian laborers Antonio Cipolla and Joseph Piraino shared a room in a lodging house in Sacramento in 1908. Both were unemployed, and the men often sought work together. On the morning of March 3, at Cipolla's suggestion, the men followed a trail along the Sacramento River to Yolo County to look for ranch work. When they reached a levee, they encountered two other Italians, both of whom were strangers to Piraino. The men held Piraino down while Cipolla slashed him with a knife and stole the gold coins he kept in a money belt. California Supreme Court justice J. Henshaw later wrote, "The wounds across the abdomen were of a frightful character, extending from the spine upon the left around and across to the spine on the right, severing the intestines and nearly cutting the body in two."

Piraino's assailants threw him in the river. Remarkably, Piraino dragged himself onto the shore, where a steamboat crew rescued him. From his hospital bed, Piraino described the attack to police, who later arrested Cipolla at the lodging house. Cipolla had shaved off his mustache, but he was identified and one of his shoes contained $20 gold pieces. Police never found the other two men. Joseph Piraino died on the operating table two days later.

Cipolla pleaded not guilty, but witnesses who had been nearby at the time of the attack testified against him. The jury convicted Cipolla of murder in the first degree and the judge sentenced him to death. Cipolla's defense motioned for a new trial based on venue, claiming the crime occurred in Yolo County, not Sacramento County. However, evidence showed that Piraino was found lying 196 feet inside Sacramento County. The court denied Cipolla's appeal.

On April 30, 1909, Cipolla stood "perfectly cool" on the scaffold and remarked, "That's all right, boys," to witnesses.

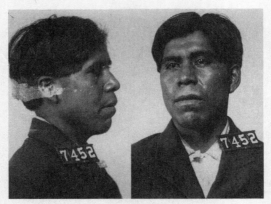

"**Wilbur is my only son, I have lost two by death, but this hurts me worse than the loss of either of them.**"
—William Benjamin, father of Wilbur, 1909

25. Wilbur Benjamin, October 28, 1910

On a lonely mountain trail outside Rumsey, California, William Gilmer searched for his fourteen-year-old daughter, Violet. She hadn't walked the three miles home from school on Monday, October 4, 1909, but Gilmer and his wife didn't worry initially, assuming Violet had stayed with a classmate or teacher because the weather looked ominous. When she failed to return by Tuesday, her parents feared the worst.

The next morning, Gilmer walked Violet's route, searching for any sign of his youngest daughter. Gilmer recalled his ordeal:

> I got almost to the end of the trail and found nothing to show any harm, and I thought I was about through; all at once at my left hand I saw a storm cape, I would call it, a pair of old shoes and some books on the ground, a dinner bucket on the ground upset . . . I stopped, I turned partly around to the right and there was the body of the child and laying right on the other side of the trail; the head up the hill, lying on her back, her face turned some to the right, feet and lower limbs spread wide apart, very wide apart.

As she was found, lying on her back, bloodied and partially clothed, the child had obviously died as a result of a horrific assault. School books and postal mail were strewn about and her hat rested on her chest. It proved too much for the sixty-year-old father. Leaving the body undisturbed, he hastened to Rumsey to seek help. Coroner Kitto and District Attorney W. A. Anderson soon arrived at the desolate part of the foothills. Authorities determined the sweet, dutiful, and affectionate young girl had been raped and choked; her lungs were torn and filled with blood, and from all indications she had put up a very brave struggle. Her head and neck displayed obvious signs of strangulation, and her abdomen was heavily bruised. Her battered legs were partially stripped of her stockings.

Violet, described as bright, pretty, and exceedingly shy, lived with her father and helped care for her invalid mother. The *Woodland Daily Democrat* wrote, "… she was such a lovely character that all who knew her became deeply attached to her." Due to her mother's illness, Violet performed the household chores in the morning, walked the three miles to school, and returned in time to help with the evening duties.

The town was outraged and the newspapers wrote of angry mobs threatening to lynch the killer. Thus, it was no wonder the authorities kept Wilbur Benjamin's arrest that afternoon under wraps. Called a "miscreant half-breed" by some, the Native American had lived and worked in Yolo County on his family's farm for about four years. Other farmers for whom he also worked described him as a man of good character and reputation. Suspicion first fell on the twenty-one-year-old when witnesses described seeing him on his bicycle at the Rumsey post office, a mile from the murder scene, about an hour after school dismissed.

Police asked his father, William Benjamin, to bring articles of clothing and other personal effects belonging to his son, including a pair of shoes, to the station. The muddy shoes produced by William Benjamin fit the tracks found near the body.

Police had discovered Wilbur Benjamin sitting on a pile of tires on Lou Everett's farm, where he worked picking plums. Benjamin protested his innocence, even displaying great surprise that investigators suspected him. In fact, the Everett family and other workers at the farm that night were shocked, noting they had spent the evening with Benjamin, whose demeanor and behavior had appeared normal. Sentiment ran strong on the part of those who lived, worked, or attended school with Benjamin, most declaring him incapable of committing such a heinous crime.

Looks can be deceiving. While being held in the county jail, Wilbur Benjamin confessed to the district attorney and other officers that he had, in fact, encountered and assaulted Violet. However, he insisted Violet was alive when he left her. Benjamin claimed he had come upon Violet on the desolate road where she had stopped to change her shoes, as she often did before the long trek home over hills and mountain trails. She informed Benjamin that she was in a hurry; he told her that there was no rush.

He forced her onto the ground with the intention of raping her, holding his hand over her mouth for two minutes while he unfastened her clothing. But he said she put up such a desperate fight that he left her lying just off the trail—alive. He hopped on his bicycle and went directly to the post office; he arrived at the Everett ranch by six in the evening. Benjamin asserted he didn't know the girl was dead until Wednesday afternoon when the news broke.

A man highly respected in the community, William Benjamin sat devastated as he listened to his son's confession. "Wilbur is my only son, I have lost two by death, but this hurts me worse than the loss of either of them. I have tried to raise my boy to do right. If he has done wrong, I cannot help it and am not to blame." He asked that nothing further be asked of his son until his attorney arrived.

While some supported Wilbur Benjamin, others threatened violence, prompting rumors of a change of venue for the trial. District Attorney Anderson insisted he hadn't witnessed any such ill-sentiment or threats. He believed the people of the area to be law-abiding citizens, interested only in due process of the law. He further stated, "As to the case against the defendant, we are satisfied that it is in good shape. All of the officers connected with the case have worked untiringly and have been favored with extremely good luck. When we think how rapidly one discovery followed upon another, we naturally think of the old saying, 'Murder will out.'"

At the preliminary hearing, Benjamin's attorney, T. A. Ragain, accused Anderson and other officers of inducing a confession by asking leading questions and confusing his client. Officers testified that Anderson had told the prisoner that he needn't talk if he chose not to. This closed the examination and Ragain announced the defense would not present any evidence at that time. The trial was set for November 16, 1909.

It took two days to secure a jury of twelve men to hear the state's case, which was based mainly on circumstantial evidence. Benjamin claimed that after his arrest, District Attorney Anderson told him that Violet wasn't dead and advised him to "Tell the truth; it won't cost you much." Moreover, Benjamin said Anderson told him, "It would be better for you and easier for us if you make a complete confession." Anderson denied the conversation took place. A witness testified that around 5:30 on the evening of the crime, he saw Benjamin riding his bike "as fast as he could . . . and did not speak and barely raised his head" when he passed him. The witness also testified to seeing Violet Gilmer an hour earlier, walking toward her home.

Constable Parker and other investigators told the court they found bike tire tracks where a bicycle had been thrown down against a clump of chemise near the crime scene. Benjamin never denied meeting Violet on the trail, but he continued to insist the young girl wasn't dead when he left the scene.

In closing, Anderson stated that it "would be an insult to the intelligence of the jurors to assume that they could believe under such circumstances some other man had gone to the scene, after Benjamin left, and murdered and ravished the body of a little, weak, and defenseless girl." Mr. Ragain, who earlier proposed to submit the case without argument, replied briefly and dispassionately. He insisted that the circumstantial evidence did not prove his client's guilt and that Benjamin's "intellectuality is not of a high order." He also accused officers of taking advantage of his client's simple mind during his interrogation.

The jury returned to a quiet courtroom an hour later, bringing a guilty verdict. Ragain offered no motions and Benjamin appeared ignorant of his fate. At Benjamin's sentencing a few days later, Ragain motioned for a new trial. Judge Hawkins handed down his decision:

> The evidence shows that, forgetting your good old father, and unmindful of the lessons that your elders would strive to have you learn, you sought out this little girl with the fixed purpose of raping her. Whether or not you intended to kill her is immaterial. In the silent woods, unseen save by the all-seeing eye of God, you laid your heavy hand upon her slight and tender form with evil intent. She fought, fought desperately against tremendous odds, and, fighting, died to save her honor while you completed your hellish task. For such a crime that law decrees that you shall suffer death. Let those who would tamper with little girls beware of your awful fate.

Attempting to appeal the February 4 execution, Ragain stated the jury did not take any other elements into consideration "except stern justice itself," and it had pulled the "race card." Ragain closed his appeal by saying, "From the fact that this is an Indian and that the Indians have been dealt with so harshly by the white people that the race is so nearly extinguished, and that this is the first crime of its nature which has ever been committed by an Indian, I can't see that it is going to further the ends of justice to inflict the death penalty."

Following the appeal, Ragain became ill and his doctor advised him to cease work immediately. Benjamin faced the judge alone. In July, the higher court affirmed the earlier decision and Benjamin made no reaction when he was re-sentenced to hang on October 28.

On October 28, 1910, Benjamin stood on the scaffold, a cigarette protruding from his mouth as the warden read the death warrant aloud. The prisoner remained stoic and said nothing before falling through the trap. William paid a visit to his son on the day before the execution, but he did not claim the body afterward.

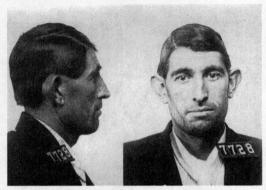

"If I am hung, I'll come back after I'm dead and get even with some of these people who have been prosecuting me."
—Michael Leahy, 1910

26. Michael Leahy, February 8, 1911

Michael Leahy had become infatuated with Mary Chateau, a woman with whom he'd been having an affair. When John M. Chateau learned of his wife's infidelity, he made her choose. She opted to stay with her husband. On May 9, 1910, Mrs. Chateau told Leahy of her decision, and he threatened to kill her if she didn't elope with him. Frightened, Mary informed her husband. He swore out a warrant charging Leahy, his fellow Southern Pacific railroad worker, with disturbing the peace.

The next morning, when John Chateau went to retrieve firewood from his shed, Leahy sprang from the outbuilding, wielding a revolver, and shot him. Leahy picked up an ax to finish Chateau off when a neighbor, who witnessed the crime, tackled Leahy to the ground. The forty-one-year-old Chateau died ten days later. He left behind two children.

"I blame the woman for this trouble," Leahy said of Mary Chateau. "I asked her to elope with me, and when she refused I found it necessary to kill her husband. I would have killed any other man just the same." While awaiting trial, Leahy feigned insanity by refusing to talk, eat, or even sleep. When he became emaciated and too weak, he pleaded guilty, hoping for a life sentence. In desperation, he claimed Chateau pulled a gun on him first. Even though Chateau carried a gun, witnesses insisted only Leahy fired a shot. The entire trial lasted six hours and the jury deliberated merely thirty minutes. They found Leahy guilty of murder.

Days later, just before Judge Prewett announced his sentence, Leahy declared, "If I am hung, I'll come back after I'm dead and get even with some of these people who have been prosecuting me." Prewett sentenced Leahy to hang at Folsom on February 8, 1911.

According to the *San Francisco Call*, Leahy spent his last evening telling stories to the evening watchmen about his time as a brakeman for the railroad. In the morning, he woke in good spirits and joked with Warden Reilly. Reportedly displaying "...a cool indifference that marked his actions since his arrest," Leahy died nine minutes after the trap sprung, making it the quickest execution during Reilly's term of office.

"This is going to be my execution and the only one I've ever had and there ain't going be no wailing and gnashing of teeth."
—Edward Delehante, the night before his execution, 1912

27. Edward Delehante, December 6, 1912

While serving time at San Quentin for criminal assault in Fresno County, Edward Delehante stabbed two fellow convicts in the prison yard. In the breakfast line, Delehante, without warning, stepped out of line and plunged a knife into the side of William Peterson. Next, he stabbed William "St. Louis Fat" Kaufman in the chest. When Kaufman ran, Delehante pursued him and stabbed him in the back until he fell to the ground. Peterson survived his attack, but Kaufman did not.

Guard W. J. Duffy found Delehante against the yard wall, still clutching the sharpened file. "You better give me that thing, Ed. You're apt to get into trouble." Delehante obliged and Duffy escorted him to his cell. The press reported that Delehante and his victims had been friends until, for some unknown reason, a bitter feud began. The three men had all participated in the annual minstrel and vaudeville performances presented by the San Quentin inmates less than a month earlier. On January 1, 1912, the *San Francisco Call* reported that "Edward Delehante and his Tar Baby Troubadours" sang "Way Down Mississippi" and performed "characteristic plantation sketches." The paper also listed Delehante as the director and manager of the show.

Guards believed the feud may have stemmed from jealousy over singing parts in the show, although Delehante stated, "Kaufman goaded me until I was insane." Called the "Black Demon of San Quentin" by the press, a heavily shackled Delehante gave an "ornate and finished address to the judge." Delehante's defense team insisted their client had sustained a head injury during a race riot in Joplin, Missouri, causing mental illness. Delehante also claimed his parents and sister died in the 1903 riot. He pleaded insanity.

Delehante received a guilty verdict and was sentenced to hang at Folsom prison. He asked the judge to change the execution date to December's Friday the 13th, in order to be consistent with his back luck in life. The judge denied his request.

J. Henderson, editor of the *Oakland Tribune*, described Delehante's last evening: "The table in his death cell was piled high with pies, cakes, chickens, candies, and other delicacies, which Ed had asked [for] when Warden Johnston had told him he could have anything he wanted." Delehante also asked for a phonograph and records of ragtime and instrumental songs. Appearing jovial, Delehante said, "Bring me four niggers to play the banjo! Fetch on your chicken and chocolate cake and bring me a watermelon so big I can hide my head in it."

Delehante asked Johnston if he could dance a jig on the gallows, saying, "This is going to be my execution and the only one I've ever had and there ain't going be no wailing and gnashing of teeth." The warden, who would see his first execution in the morning, told Delehante to "get a good sleep tonight" and let him know in the morning if he still wanted to dance the jig.

By morning, Delehante had changed his mind and told the warden, "No, warden, that wouldn't be no ways fitting for me to dance at my own funeral." Instead, according to Henderson, "the big negro placed his feet firmly on the trap and then looked down on [the witnesses] with a smile. He actually laughed and then said: 'I guess you all is guessing why I laugh. Well, I'm going find out something that you'd give anything to know. I'm goin' learn what's in the beyond.'" With that, Delehante went to his death on the Folsom gallows on December 6, 1912.

WARDEN JAMES A. JOHNSTON

As Chairman of California's State Board of Control, James A. Johnston implemented systems within state departments, commissions, and institutions. He shared his opinions about the state's responsibility in caring for inmates with then-Governor Hiram Johnston, who was impressed with Johnston's ideas and insight. James Johnston took over as warden of Folsom Prison in June 1912. He quickly gained a reputation as the most highly regarded warden of both Folsom and San Quentin, credited with not only reforming prisoners, but also those in charge of them as well. The governor had tired of reports of cruelty, overcrowded conditions, and ill prisoners, remarking, "There were hard faces showing hatred, resentment, and despair, ready for revolt if incited." Johnston's philosophy was simple: "The effort to redeem the man should begin from the moment he reaches the prison gates." Johnston worked with the state university at Davis to begin offering correspondence classes at the prisons. At the initial registration, hundreds of inmates filled the chapel and library, eager to learn to read, write, and do arithmetic. Others studied agriculture, economics, commercial law, history, and foreign languages.

Despite having no prior experience, Johnston immediately began work on building a farm—with the help of the university. Inmates planted orchards of peaches and plums and started vegetable gardens. Cattle and hogs were raised, and a modern dairy soon followed. This foresight helped the prison become completely self-sufficient until the 1960s.

Appalled by the squalid conditions, Johnston added ventilation to each cell and built a bathhouse equipped with showers and tubs, replacing the single shower and four tubs that had previously serviced 1100 inmates. Johnston also inspected prison food, testing it himself to ensure quality.

When Johnston realized that 95 percent of incoming inmates required the attention of a dentist, surgeon, or eye doctor, he brought in a resident dentist. Every prisoner received a thorough exam and treatment. Many inmates suffered from various diseases, such as tuberculosis and syphilis, or needed glasses or a root canal. Johnston made an effort to meet with every prisoner, listen to his story or request, and come up with a solution.

But of all the changes Johnston made, abolishing corporal punishment was arguably the most important. Upon becoming warden, he immediately did away with the straitjacket, hooks, and other forms of physical punishment. "It is not wise or advisable to coddle or baby men who have committed crime," he said. "Nevertheless, there should be kindness, mercy, charity, humane treatment, and encouragement on the road uphill, for it is uphill work for a man going out of prison to put the past behind him and go forward." Many guards were dismissed and some resigned, unable to fathom controlling the inmates by any other than brutal methods. "I saw no sense in suggestions that would continue the barbarity of breaking men's bodies instead of trying to open their minds," Johnston said.

Johnston had made more changes at Folsom in one year than any warden in its history. The Board of Prison Directors asked Johnston to take over administration of San Quentin. That same year, 1913, Governor Johnson sponsored and signed the law prohibiting corporal punishment. Nicknamed the "Golden Rule Warden," Johnston spent twelve years at San Quentin. In 1934, he was appointed Alcatraz's first warden, a position he held until he retired in 1948.

"I was anxious to see men leave the prison better than they entered."—James A. Johnston.

PART IV: 1913–1918

Folsom Wardens: James A. Johnston, June 1, 1912–November 16, 1913

J. J. Smith, November 16, 1913–February 2, 1927

California Governors: Hiram Johnson, January 3, 1911–March 15, 1917

William Stephens, March 15, 1917–January 9, 1923

In the mid-1910s, California's 2.5 million residents found success in agriculture, industry, entertainment, and mining. The state became one of the principal producers of grapes, citrus, and deciduous fruits, which kept California's canning factories prosperous. Paramount distributed thirty feature films in 1915, showing them in new "movie houses" or converted opera houses. Miners continued to discover gold, particularly near Barstow, yielding $1,400–$3,000 per ton. However, by 1917, the number of miners sharply declined as the country called on soldiers to fight in World War I.

Industries boomed and unions kept busy. The I.W.W. organized and led strikes, demanding living wages for its 100,000 members, many of whom were migrant field workers. The Union Labor Party practically had electoral control of San Francisco, creating a militancy of the city workers.

Further limiting the rights of immigrants, California passed the Alien Land Act in 1913, depriving Asians of the right to own land (the United States Supreme Court deemed this act unconstitutional in 1952). In 1915, roughly 20,000 Chinese lived in San Francisco, about ten thousand fewer than before the 1906 earthquake that destroyed all of Chinatown.

Segregation took place inside prisons as well. In the continued effort to reform California penitentiaries, lawmakers passed the Indeterminate Sentence Law in 1917. It sent all "hardened" and habitual offenders to Folsom prison, while first-time offenders and petty criminals served their terms at San Quentin. Prison officials hoped that classifying and separating its prisoners would give young offenders a chance to rehabilitate before being paroled. Officials called the move a success after a few years, but overcrowding at both prisons in the early 1920s made adhering to the law impossible.

According to a later study, some of the prison population increase in 1915 was "due chiefly to a large influx of criminals visiting the Panama-Pacific Exposition being held in San Francisco." The two-year expo attracted more than 3.7 million visitors who paid a quarter to celebrate the opening of the Panama Canal and also to tout San Diego as a port of call for ships traveling north.

Fortunately for the expanding prison population, Folsom's new cell building—said to "embody the most advanced ideas in prison construction," with heating, ventilation, and plumbing—was completed in 1916. Warden Johnston also oversaw completion of a school, which enrolled 500 inmates in fifty-eight different classes per week. The prison farm continued to produce livestock, chickens, fruits, and vegetables. Most inmates preferred the farm work over backbreaking jobs in the quarry. Low-risk prisoners were allowed outside the prison walls to assist in the building of state highways. These prisoners enjoyed leaving the confines of prison, while the state benefited from cheap labor.

Johnston also brought dental care to the prison in 1913. The first resident dentist took home $1,200 per year for his work. Other medical professionals came to the prison to diagnose mental and physical illnesses, provide medications, and supply inmates with eyeglasses. After years in solitary, Jacob Oppenheimer (story #28) likely appreciated the improved conditions and care during his last year of life at the prison. No one imagined the "Human Tiger" and the prison warden would strike up a friendship, but Johnston's kind and humane treatment softened the heart of even the most hardened criminal.

"So, the sooner I cash in my chips, the better, as it will save me a lot of trouble and unhappiness."
—Jacob Oppenheimer, 1913

28. Jacob Oppenheimer, July 12, 1913

Called the "worst criminal in California history" and dubbed the "Human Tiger" by sensationalizing reporters, Jacob Oppenheimer spent eighteen years in solitary confinement. Despite his reputation, many considered him a great thinker, reader, and writer. He possessed a vast vocabulary, high intelligence, and incredible insight into both the outside world and the human psyche, as evidenced by his many letters and essays, and by his autobiography, *Thoughts of a Condemned Man*.

Feared by guards and fellow inmates, Oppenheimer "defied and mystified the officials of California's two prisons," said James Johnston. "He made many murderous attacks on prison officers and fellow convicts. His killings and assaults terrorized. His keepers were puzzled because he had demonstrated uncanny ability to improvise weapons and get at his victims despite confinement, surveillance, and restraint."

Oppenheimer's murderous career eventually caught up to him. In 1901, a law written especially to apply to him passed the legislature: Any prisoner serving life imprisonment who assaults or murders a guard or fellow inmate must face the death penalty. Oppenheimer became the first prisoner to be affected by this law. Of Folsom's ninety-three, Oppenheimer was the only one executed for assault.

In 1890, seventeen-year-old Oppenheimer worked as a messenger for the American District Messenger Company in San Francisco. The company often sent him to prostitution and dope houses, delivering cash and telegrams.

In 1892, a fellow messenger made a crude remark about the company's cashier. She thought it came from Oppenheimer and told her brother and supervisor, Frank Wehe. Denying the accusation, Oppenheimer refused to apologize and Wehe discharged him. Oppenheimer later noticed sums missing from his final check and he confronted Wehe with a revolver. Oppenheimer fired three shots at the supervisor, who escaped with minor injuries.

During his trial, Oppenheimer said he couldn't recall anything about the shooting due to "intense excitement." The defense presented over twenty witnesses who testified to Oppenheimer's character of "peace and quietness," but evidence from eyewitnesses contradicted the positive defense witnesses. The judge sentenced Oppenheimer to eighteen months in the House of Corrections.

Oppenheimer blamed exposure to these disreputable places for launching his criminal career. He philosophized on the situation he had encountered, saying, "Is it any wonder that the messenger boys, beholding these sights and coming in daily contact with all sorts of people and vices, grow demoralized?" Oppenheimer later wrote to the state legislature, outlining several proposed restrictions and bans to prevent exposing young men to San Francisco's underworld scene.

By 1895, Oppenheimer had a few minor robberies under his belt, most of which he committed with brothers John and Berry Holland, as well as Charles and Walter Ross. Although considered the usual suspects in various crimes, the group repeatedly eluded arrest. When the four other men decided to rob the Garrett and Taggart Drugstore, Oppenheimer bowed out, preferring to go solo. He had grown tired of constant police surveillance.

During the robbery, the Holland brothers and Charles Ross tied and gagged the drugstore's clerk. An officer approached the door and spoke with Ross, who convinced the cop he was a friend of the clerk's. The officer left and the three men made off with three hundred dollars. Within a week, the pair of brothers robbed a saloon owner, John MacIntosh, of cash and diamonds. Police soon arrested all four men for the two robberies. The officers struck a deal.

Charles Ross would turn over Oppenheimer and admit to the drugstore robbery with the Holland brothers. Ross would also admit to the MacIntosh robbery and finger his brother Walter for participating. In return, all would receive lesser sentences.

The officer who identified Charles Ross as the man he spoke to at the drug-store later testified at trial that it was actually Oppenheimer. The drug-store clerk, however, couldn't positively identify Oppenheimer as the third man. Regardless of the inconsistent testimony, the jury found Oppenheimer guilty. Judge Abraham Lincoln Frick took the opportunity to make an example of the defendants and to send a message to young criminals.

"Your whole demeanor during the course of the trial," Frick told Oppenheimer, "was such as not to commend you to the mercy of the court. You have previously been in trouble of a serious character. The nature of the crime of which you have just been accused of convinces me that reformation in your case is out of the question." He sentenced Oppenheimer to fifty years in Folsom prison.

"Much obliged," Oppenheimer replied to Frick and took his seat. John Holland received thirty-five years, while his brother, Berry, got life. In exchange for handing over Oppenheimer, Charles Ross earned fifteen years for the saloon robbery, and his brother went free. Unfortunately for Charles, he would have to serve his time at Folsom alongside the man he had framed. For three years, the two men avoided contact, but it was apparent that one sought protection, while the other sought revenge.

On September 29, 1898, Ross approached Oppenheimer in the yard, a prison-made knife at the ready. Tired of watching over his shoulder, Ross planned to eliminate his enemy. Oppenheimer, always prepared, wielded his own knife, catching Ross off guard. Oppenheimer stabbed Ross several times. While Ross lay dying, guards hauled Oppenheimer to the dungeon cell block, throwing him into solitary. His fifty-year term already felt like a life sentence and he barely flinched when the judge sentenced him to life at San Quentin.

In May 1899, while working in the jute mill, Oppenheimer stabbed Guard James McDonald several times. For this, a newspaper reporter dubbed him the "Human Tiger," a name that Oppenheimer loathed. Warden Charles Aull of Folsom blamed leniency at Oppenheimer's previous trial, saying, "I consider that this tragedy is due to no other cause than the miscarriage of justice in the trial of Oppenheimer at Sacramento for the murder of convict Ross. In that case, the jurors held out for life imprisonment. In order to prevent a total disagreement, the other jurors consented to a verdict of life imprisonment. The result is seen in today's assassination at San Quentin."

Surprisingly, McDonald survived, but lawmakers wanted Oppenheimer to pay with his life. They knew it was only a matter of time before Jake would strike again. In 1901, legislators passed the law, especially written for Oppenheimer, that would seal his fate.

For now, Oppenheimer escaped with his life, but it was one of solitary confinement where he endured hours in the straitjacket, being hung from his wrists, and exposed to chloride-lime fumes that burned his eyes. George Wilburn, an Oppenheimer biographer, described the prisoner's new living arrangements in the "incorrigible ward": "The convicts were given clothes every three weeks. Each prisoner was allowed to exercise thirty minutes a week in the hallway in front of his cell. Jake was given two meals a day and was permitted to bathe, under guard, once every two weeks. His cell was kept between fifty and sixty degrees."

Oppenheimer grew restless, but refused to request anything of the guards. Like the caged tiger they said he was, he could only pace his dark cell. His four-by-six-foot home provided just enough room for him and his thoughts of escape. Guards did supply him with three weekly copies of the *Christian Advance and Volunteers' Gazette*. Oppenheimer found them useful. He removed an inside page from each and, after five weeks, he had acquired fifteen sheets of paper. With these, he fashioned a periscope eleven-feet long. While Guard Jones stood at the end of the hall, Oppenheimer guided his paper tube through the wicket in his cell door, igniting it from the gas light hanging ten feet away. Jones spotted it just as Oppenheimer withdrew it and lit his mattress on fire. Guards yanked Oppenheimer from his cell and extinguished the flames. Warden Charles Aguirre ordered another bout in the straitjacket. "Jake Oppenheimer's spirit was broken sufficiently," reported the *Mountain Democrat*, with tongue in cheek, "that he sent for Aguirre and declared his craving for a smoke was more than he could endure and he had taken that means of securing it."

EXCERPT FROM OPPENHEIMER'S ACCOUNT OF HIS 110 HOURS IN A STRAITJACKET

I had not been in it 15 minutes when sharp, needle-like pains began shooting through my fingers, hands, and arms, which gradually extended to my shoulders. Within half an hour, these pains shot back and forth like lightning. Cramping pains clutched my bowels; my breath pained with a hot, dry sensation; the brass rivets on one side ate into my flesh, and the cord ground into my back until the slightest movement, even breathing, was an added agony.

My head grew hot and feverish, and a burning thirst seized me which compelled me every few minutes to call the guard for water, whereupon I was slightly raised and the fluid poured down my throat.

As the hours and days passed, the anguish became more and more unbearable. I slept neither night or day, and how slowly, especially at night when all was silent in the prison, the hours dragged as though weighted with lead!

The bodily excretions, over which I had no control in the canvas vice, ate into my bruised limbs, adding pain to pain. My fingers, hands, and arms finally became numb, and paralyzing shocks stunned my brain.

Had I been offered a dose of poison, I would have drunk it with gratitude.

Thus I suffered for four days and 14 hours incessantly.

In prison [the straitjacket] is an instrument of hellish torture, and its very innocence of appearance serves to divert attention from it. Prisoners have been killed and crippled for life in the jacket. I know of four prisoners in San Quentin who in one year attempted suicide rather than be subjected to its tortures.

There are ways enough to punish a prisoner without resorting to such savage methods, and, in my opinion, kindly treatment can more easily soften the heart of the most hardened criminal than all the straitjackets that any man's devilish ingenuity ever manufactured.

Oppenheimer told Aguirre of his scheme. "My intention, according to the plan, was to set fire to my mattress and pass the burning tube along to a few other of the prisoners, and when the blaze grew fierce we were to huddle against the doors of our cells and yell fire to get Jones to come and unlock the cells in order to save us from being cooked alive . . . Then we would have waited till three or four of the boys were released and fallen upon him and killed him, or rendered him insensible at least."

Those housed in the solitary ward were forbidden from speaking to one another, but Oppenheimer devised a communication system. During his dark and lonely days, he developed and perfected a method similar to the Morse Code. On the rare occasion Oppenheimer could speak to a fellow convict, either during their exercise or through the walls of the cell, he disclosed his method. He created a diagram of the alphabet, with five letters across and five letters down. The last row contained six letters. Each letter represented a certain number of taps. For example, "E" required one tap (first row) and then five taps (fifth letter). Over several months, Oppenheimer and the other inmates perfected this system and taught it to incoming convicts. This was how they formulated their escape attempt using fire.

Nearly four years passed before The Tiger tried to flee his cage again. Using a long file, Oppenheimer unscrewed twenty-six bolts that fastened the steel roofing of his cell. Suspicious, guards kept a close watch over the convict. Sure enough, as Oppenheimer lifted one end of the roof, guards stood waiting for him to emerge.

The following year, in 1904, after saving the black pepper from his meals, Oppenheimer threw it into the face of a guard, hoping to escape. Another time, he choked a guard, but was hit on the head by another officer before he could do further damage. Over the next few years, he endured numerous punishments. Guards removed his mattress, blankets, books, and magazines, and, at times, they chained Oppenheimer to the wall in his dark cell.

Guards and convicts questioned Oppenheimer's sanity when he babbled and insisted that snakes were in his cell. Then something came along that quieted Oppenheimer's demons and softened his heart. A tiny black kitten, belonging to one of the guards, had wandered into his cell and developed a fondness for the hardened criminal. "He was allowed to keep the pet," said Wilburn, "and would spend hours playing with it. When his little friend would crawl through the grating of the door and go to the other convicts, Oppenheimer would be sullen and morose until it returned."

With nothing but time and patience on his hands, it didn't take long for Oppenheimer to formulate a new escape plot. Somehow, he secured several sack needles used in the jute mill. He would use them on the four bars running crisscross in the small area at the bottom of the door. For months, Oppenheimer tirelessly chipped away at the bars. A fellow incorrigible, Jack O'Neill, heard Oppenheimer tampering with his cell door, but didn't know what the convict was doing. He reported it to the guards. They didn't discover Oppenheimer's plot, but nevertheless, moved him to another cell.

Oppenheimer spent the next couple of years plotting revenge against O'Neill. In the meantime, guards continually moved Oppenheimer from cell to cell, always anticipating his next scheme. In April of 1907, Oppenheimer found himself in his original cell—the one with the partially sawed bars. The work had gone undetected during his moves over the previous two years. But this time he didn't have any needles.

San Quentin's new warden, John Hoyle, allowed Oppenheimer to have writing materials. Oppenheimer wrote day and night and began studying languages, history, and law. He asked for a needle to bind his work together. He compiled his pages during the day, and by night he crouched by his cell door and continued his work on the bars. He used grease saved from his meals to lubricate the needle. Nine months later, Oppenheimer completed the task. He later wrote a letter to guard Miller, thanking him for "allowing" him the time to chisel away at the bars.

Oppenheimer waited until the guard moved to the end of the hallway before he slithered his small, lean body through the tiny opening. The dark, empty hallway obscured The Tiger as he hunted his prey. His determination to find O'Neill propelled him quietly down the hall and into the dining room and kitchen. He spotted a bread knife on the counter. Trustee John Wilson, working in the area, immediately saw what Oppenheimer wanted. The two men went for it and Wilson snatched it up a split second before the escaped inmate. Wilson tried to conceal the knife under his arm as the men scuffled. However, Oppenheimer grabbed the knife and drew it out violently, cutting the inside of Wilson's arm. The commotion drew other inmates and guards who overpowered Oppenheimer.

Oppenheimer insisted he never intended to hurt the trustee: "I realize my predicament is a most serious one, but there was nothing premeditated in my

A LETTER OF GRATITUDE

To Guard Miller: Noble Swede, allow me to express my thanks to you for the opportunity you have given me to work upon the door every afternoon. You did me a great favor every afternoon in taking a siesta from a trifle after four till the other guard woke you up by rapping on the door. Your sleep was long enough each day to allow me to exercise on the door of my cell with this needle. The work was slow, but as long as you slept, sure. Allow me, as a slight testimonial of my gratitude, to offer you the remains of the needle that enabled me to get out of my cell. It is the only favor I have ever known you to do anyone, but as you have done it unintentionally I don't hold you to blame. So remember, majestic Swede, that it is never too late to mend—the door. So now I will bid you au revoir. J. Oppenheimer P.S. Also remember—that he who laughs last usually laughs best. Savey [sic], J. O.

attack on Wilson, and as far as he is concerned, I am only sorry that he was injured, as I had nothing against him personally...I would have got to O'Neill and sooner or later I will get him yet."

The state of California had no intention of letting that happen. The 1901 law was clear about Oppenheimer's punishment, but he wouldn't go down without a fight. He pleaded insanity at the preliminary hearing and acted as his own attorney. Mentally unstable or not, Oppenheimer conducted his defense with the knowledge and sharpness of a skilled attorney. "He displayed far more courtroom etiquette than the ordinary San Francisco police court lawyer and was cool and collected," reported the *San Francisco Call*. Time and time again, Oppenheimer befuddled the prosecution's witnesses. By the time he finished with Wilson, the trustee couldn't say for sure whether Oppenheimer even grabbed the knife from him. Similarly, Warden Hoyle had to admit he had no clear notion of what took place in the kitchen.

At his arraignment, Oppenheimer told the judge that the years in solitary confinement made him desperate and forsaken. Oppenheimer made an impassioned statement:

> So far as my being desperate is concerned, what attitude would any man have were he confined as I have been in solitary imprisonment for eight years and only allowed thirty minutes' exercise once a week? Imprisoned, as I have been, men are practically forgotten, not alone outside of prison walls, but inside as well, and officials only remember that you are a criminal and an outcast. They say I spend all my time in exercising in my cell in order to have the necessary strength to throttle some guard . . . As a matter of fact, I have for a long time practiced certain movements. If I did not do something to pass away the time, I would have been dead long before this. My eyes are so weakened from absence of light as to cause me constant pain, and I don't look like a pugilist, do I? A four-by-six cell doesn't provide exceptionally good training quarters.

Guards scoffed at Oppenheimer's claims of insanity. "Oppenheimer is not insane," said Captain of the Guard S. L. Randolph. "He is no more insane than I am, but he has a lust for killing. He wants to murder someone always. Yet he has a shrewdness and mentality that is remarkable in the type he represents. He is a degenerate who delights in murderous and fiendish ideas."

Others disagreed, including Rabbi Levy of San Francisco, with whom Oppenheimer often consulted. Levy asked new law graduate Gus Ringolsky to take Oppenheimer's case. Ringolsky refused, saying, "I don't want to take the case. It's too important, [as] the man's life is at stake. I haven't opened my mouth in a courtroom. I don't know how to try a case." Levy persisted and Ringolsky reluctantly accepted the Human Tiger's case.

The young attorney arrived in San Rafael to meet with his first client—the most hated criminal in the California prison system. After discussing the case, the two parted. Jake immediately penned "Comrades," a somewhat autobiographical short story about an unfortunate prisoner and his loyal and trustworthy dog.

> ## THOUGHTS OF A CONDEMNED MAN
>
> Many people do not discover their talent until they are ready for the grave.
>
> The high road of truth is always open.
>
> When enlightenment flourishes her torch, ignorance flees.
>
> A man should till his mind like a farmer tills the soil, tearing up weeds, exterminating all poisonous matter, and fertilizing it with watchful care.
>
> One who has a beautiful mind has a picture gallery beyond price.
>
> The reason birds are so happy is because they don't know the value of money.
>
> A thief is always on the lookout for stars but he doesn't look up to the heavens.
>
> A feather pillow is as hard as a stone to a guilty conscience.
>
> Conscience is the umpire who distinguishes right from wrong.
>
> He who conquers a weakness is a warrior.
>
> He who surrenders himself to disappointment proclaims himself a prisoner of failure.
>
> The pendulum of time is the hammer-stroke of impending death.
>
> The wisest man that ever existed knows no more about future life than the greatest fool that was ever born.
>
> There are more men in cages than animals.
>
> — Jacob Oppenheimer

Working strictly pro bono, Ringolsky immersed himself into the case, examining every detail. On October 9, 1907, he faced his first courtroom. He told the court that the long solitary confinement caused Oppenheimer's mind to become unhinged, as, he said, ". . . the defendant was born with a predisposition to insanity and that he needed only, gentlemen of the jury, the eight years in one of these coffinlike [sic] cells to produce in flower and to make bloom those seeds that were implanted in his mind by an inscrutable providence."

On that first day of trial, Oppenheimer wrote the beginning of *Thoughts of a Condemned Man*, a compilation of reflections from a man forced to face his inevitable death upon the gallows.

Oppenheimer must have predicted the outcome of his trial early on. Despite testimony from a doctor declaring Oppenheimer insane, the prosecution convinced the jury the defendant was mentally sound, using several of Oppenheimer's own writings as proof. Oppenheimer was sentenced to die at Folsom Prison. Ringolsky reassured his client: "I'm not through yet. In fact I haven't started." Within a week, Ringolsky filed an appeal with the California Supreme Court.

During the long wait after his transfer back to Folsom, Oppenheimer and his attorney became close friends, frequently exchanging letters with one another. On Christmas Eve, 1907, Oppenheimer expressed his gratitude toward Ringolsky and assured his friend of his well-being, saying:

I have been notified of your visit up here last Saturday and was told that the lateness of the hour prevented your seeing me. I was somewhat disappointed at not beholding your pleasant countenance, but as this is a world of disappointments, like Socrates, I have accepted it philosophically. I am feeling in better health than I have in the past five years. In other words, Jacob is himself again. True, I can only manage to sleep ten hours of the twenty-four, but I hope to do better presently. My appetite, whilst not so voracious as a wolf's, is slightly better than a hummingbird's. The solitude which surrounds me is delightful to a poet for in soothing meditation I soar to heights among the fleecy clouds and into the blue atmosphere. . .

The following year, Ringolsky received requests from astrologers, needing Oppenheimer's birth date in an effort to study the Human Tiger. "Born September 19, 1872," Oppenheimer wrote to his attorney. "Refer you to almanac for day, hour unknown, as I never noticed the clock at the time. Excuse the joke. Never was inquisitive as to ask the hour. Am convinced that whatever hour it was, it couldn't have been unluckier."

Prompted by Ringolsky and a sympathetic doctor, Oppenheimer began work on his autobiography, hoping it would be cathartic. He began his autobiography by writing about his time as a messenger, recalling a San Francisco rampant with drugs, gambling, and prostitution. He implored legislation to pass laws prohibiting

---

PREFACE TO OPPENHEIMER'S AUTOBIOGRAPHY

Some readers may object to this true history being written in a humorous style. Possibly they would enjoy it better were it written in a dry and scholarly manner. But the reader must forgive us if we decline to do so for two reasons. First, we have always thrown down with disgust, not unmingled with thirst, those histories which seem to have been written in the dryest [sic] spot of the Sahara desert. Second, we have never darkened the doorstep of a college and consequently Greek, Latin, Hebrew and the balance of the ghosts are dead to us. By the gods of mythology! If anything makes us want to put on the boxing gloves for a combat to the death, it is with that ancient scholarly historian author who understands one gross of Greek words and twenty of Latin and is always, when writing a book in English, placing them in nosegays between honest English words without translating them. Some of our modern writers are equally as bad with their bouquets of German, French, and Italian, when writing an English book.

Therefore, be prepared reader, not one iota, nay not an atom of Greek, Latin, Hebrew, German, French or Italian shall darken these pages. If they do it was while we were in a trance and therefore legally not responsible for the crime. In conclusion we will state, all names for various reasons are fictitious with the one exception of the main personage of this history.

—Jacob Oppenheimer, Cell 1, Condemned chamber, July 4, 1908

anyone under the age of twenty-one be a messenger; that no one sell "dime novels" to a boy under twenty-one; that no one under twenty-one be allowed in disreputable establishments, or be sent to fetch or deliver any type of drug or liquor.

In January of 1909, Oppenheimer received news that the State Supreme Court had denied his appeal. Ringolsky began preparing documents for a rehearing. He contended that the 1901 law, which he dubbed the "Oppenheimer Law," constituted cruel and unusual punishment, and he argued that the trial court wrongfully admitted improper testimony prejudicial to his client. After a meeting with Ringolsky, reviewing the prospects for further legal maneuvers, Oppenheimer returned to his cell and added further entries to his *Thoughts of a Condemned Man*.

In the meantime, Oppenheimer formed an alliance with two other death row inmates, teaching them the tap code used to communicate. The three concocted an escape plot. Securing a saw, which they passed back and forth, each prisoner labored at the bars on his cell door. In January 1910, their work paid off and the three men escaped for a time, but only to be subdued eventually by guards.

Days later, Judge Thomas Lennon re-sentenced Oppenheimer, after denying his request for a rehearing. Ringolsky had already met with Chief Justice Warren H. Beatty of the U.S. Supreme Court regarding a petition for Writ of Error. The justice allowed him to submit the document to the highest court, thus staying Oppenheimer's February execution date.

Celebration of the good news was short-lived. A feud between Oppenheimer and Francisco Quijada, one of the other attempted escapees, began to unfold. During their exercise time, the one-armed Indian blamed Oppenheimer for their failure and struck Oppenheimer in the face. For the next year, Oppenheimer's hatred for Quijada festered and the men often exchanged threatening messages. In September of 1911, a guard opened the cell doors of the condemned row for ventilation. "Come out and fight, Jake!" Quijada yelled. Released from his cage, The Tiger darted at his enemy and drove a long iron wire into the man's chest, which pierced his heart. Quijada died within minutes.

With the gallows edging closer, Oppenheimer saw his opportunity to finish telling his story slowly dwindle. Thus, he jumped at the chance to speak with reporter Gilbert Parker, who had requested an interview. "The newspapers have gone out of their way to abuse me," he told Parker. "I have been called 'The Man Tiger of the Prison,' fiend incarnate, hyena, human monster, parasite, and every epithet that is vile and debasing. Is it any wonder that people all over the country have come to regard me, a human being, as something to shun and tremble at? My very name inspires fear. I haven't deserved all of this, not by a long shot."

When Parker asked him why he killed so many, Oppenheimer claimed self-defense: "I hope someday people will begin to regard me as a human being instead of an animal." Warden William Reilly sat in on the interview and later told the reporter that should the Supreme Court allow Jake to live, he would let him work in the yard among the other convicts. "He was sincere when he said he wanted to live on the square," Reilly said. "Jake is not wholly bad. He is a victim of circumstances. The newspaper accounts of his viciousness are overdrawn."

When James Johnston took over as Warden in June 1912, he visited Oppenheimer in his cell. Johnston described standing nearly nose-to-nose with Oppenheimer, who insisted the warden see for himself what it was like to be confined in the small space. "I've been in this rat hole for five years," snarled Oppenheimer. "Five years, day and night. Here's where I live. Here's where I eat. Here's where I sleep. Here's where I exercise. Whadda yuh think of it?"

Johnston was appalled at the prison's squalid conditions and immediately implemented changes. He abolished corporal punishment, checked food for quality, and provided adequate medical treatment to the inmates. He allowed Oppenheimer to have light to read and write, as well as pencils and books. Johnston met regularly with Oppenheimer and they had many intellectual discussions. "I got to know him well," said Johnston. "He was sharp, shrewd, suspicious. He asked no favors. He didn't expect law officers to help him. He redressed his own wrongs. His code was simple, certain, decisive. If any person did him an injury—he killed him."

Given plenty of writing materials, Oppenheimer composed some of his most poignant and thought-provoking works, and he continued to work on his life story.

CHILDREN (AN EXCERPT)

Children are the most precious gems that come from nature's treasury. They are the virgin gems which sparkle and dazzle one by the purity of their light. They are the flower beside which the rose and violet fade into insignificance. They are the perfume which purifies the atmosphere.

They are the fragrant flowers which make hearts beat with joy, make the eyes beam with pride and tenderness, make the mother brave death, make the savage and cruel minded pause and inhale the sweetness of their essence.

There doubtless are many who love gold, have no eyes except for ambition, no care but for the cry of glory. And, if their selfish aims are gratified, they imagine themselves rich, blessed, and famous beyond the average of mankind. But these self deluders are poor, very poor, compared to the parents who possess those priceless treasures of nature, children. They who have children are far wealthier than the multi-millionaire or the most powerful king who has none . . . Let us then take more notice of these lovely flowers of nature and cultivate their love with greater assiduity than gold, ambition, and glory, for they are the joybringers [sic] of the human race. Anyone who passes them by, preferring such empty baubles as gold, glory, or ambition is simply closing his eyes and missing the happiest hours of his life.

—Jacob Oppenheimer, Folsom Prison, 1912

Warden Johnston's kind treatment was not lost on Oppenheimer, who immersed himself into books and writing. Again, Parker came to talk with Oppenheimer, who expressed abhorrence at the lack of prison reform, remarking, "The fault with our prisons today is that they do not reform. The men in prison should be taught trades so that when they come out they could go to work instead of walking the streets to get into further trouble. Then there should be a school where men could be taught to read and write." Oppenheimer said that given the chance at parole, he'd make a living writing articles, lecturing, and traveling with a "moving picture machine."

However, Oppenheimer would never receive that opportunity. The U.S. Supreme Court denied his appeal. Oppenheimer picked up his pencil once again.

In June, 1913, as Johnston sent invitations to Oppenheimer's execution, Governor Hiram Johnson received a petition signed by four thousand citizens, hoping to save the condemned inmate. Oppenheimer continued to write down his thoughts and urged lawmakers to reform what had become his home for the last eighteen years. "The guards now employed at both prisons should be ousted and men of education, intelligence, broadmindedness, liberal heartedness, and judgment installed in their places," he wrote. "Guards of this kind should endeavor to cultivate a good feeling toward prisoners by making study of them, so that they may be able to arrive at a conclusion what sort of character each particular prisoner is and treat him accordingly . . . Kindness should be the watchword, not nagging, brutality, and falsifying."

His final appeals to the governor yielded a denial. Resigned to his fate, Oppenheimer wrote to his lawyer and only friend: "I am unluckiness personified, for everything I have ever done or attempted to do has always met with one result—FAILURE. So, the sooner I cash in my chips, the better, as it will save me a lot of trouble and unhappiness."

Oppenheimer spent his final night listening to music from a phonograph and indulging candies and baked goods sent by well-wishers. On the morning of his execution, Oppenheimer called capital punishment a "relic of barbarism." He would be a "martyr to the cause." Ringolsky spoke about his friend and only client. "There's a lot that's fine in Jake," he said. "He has a lot of character, gentleness, and ability."

When the two men met in the death house, Oppenheimer reassured his friend, saying, "You know, this is no punishment for me. This is nothin'. I have suffered a thousand deaths in the prisons. To walk these steps is just nothin'."

On July 12, 1913, without a tremor, Oppenheimer mounted the thirteen steps. As the noose encircled Jake's neck, Ringolsky turned away. A guard handed him a flask of whiskey and he took a long swig. After twelve minutes, doctors pronounced Jacob Oppenheimer dead. Authorities buried him in the prison cemetery between two trees.

Ringolsky was forced to put to rest a case he fought so vehemently, free of charge, for six years. He went on to a successful career as an attorney, passing away at the age of seventy-nine in December 1962.

FINAL THOUGHTS OF A CONDEMNED MAN

Remorse is the disagreeable phantom of an evil action.

Some people think more than they talk—others talk more than they think.

Attempting the impossible is what produces many failures.

Good is the mind which is never worked out, for much as you can take out of it so much more remains.

A man's shadow is the silent historian of his actions.

There are some men so utterly devoid of fortitude that when misfortune overtakes them they lay [sic] down and die.

A year is a short time to some people, but to some prisoners it is a lifetime.

Better to have joy, knowledge, and love late in life than never.

When magpies chatter—wisdom is mute.

Women are generous in everything—even with their tears.

There are two sides to human nature, and in order for a person to comprehend both sides, the good and the bad must be freely exposed.

There is a tender melancholy about a drooping flower that touches a kind heart.

The tender vine as it entwines itself about a hardy tree is like a child who clasps its arms about its mother's neck for protection. Thus, does the strong protect the weak.

The violet's invitation is—enjoy my company whilst you may and inhale the perfume of my breath for I cannot stay with you long.

He who destroys the illusions of a child is heartless.

The chain of life is linked promiscuously with success and failures, hopes and despairs, sorrows and joy, doubt and confidence, tears and smiles, memories discordant and memories pleasant, sight and laughter, love and hate.

Nature is a broad minded and progressive dame who believes in giving everything and everybody a chance.

If all the laws of the state were condensed into one volume and all the laws applied to all the states alike, there would be less juggling and more justice.

—Jacob Oppenheimer

"I am not afraid to go to my finish. It is not courage, but fate."
—Samuel Raber, 1915

29. Samuel Raber, January 15, 1915

Cherry de St. Maurice owned the Cherry Club, a luxurious and profitable brothel in Sacramento. The *Des Moines Daily News* called it "the most widely known resort in the West—a place of sybaritic splendor." The papers often called Cherry a "notorious character," though most knew her as "Queen of the Tenderloin," referring to her role as Madam to the *demimonde* in the Red Light district.

Said to be in her mid-thirties, Cherry hailed from Chicago, and now traveled under a different name. She was widely read, keen in argument, and resourceful. She frequently discussed the social and economic impacts of the *demimonde*, the Tenderloin's celebrated prostitutes, with clergymen, priests, and reformers. Cherry declared it useless to fight the Tenderloin so long as money ruled and "gave everything a price."

Cherry candidly upheld prostitution as a social expedient and openly opposed the Red Light Abatement Act. In 1913, she appeared before Governor Hiram Johnson to protest the passage of the act. "Our business has its place," she insisted, believing the *demimonde* different and more respectable than women who flaunted vice on the streets.

Cherry enjoyed the irony of giving wine suppers during sessions of the legislature and on other occasions for politicians who publicly scorned her occupation yet privately employed her services. Rumored to be worth nearly one hundred thousand dollars, she once said with a laugh, "Money! Why everything I touch turns to gold! And yet, what does it buy?"

THE RED LIGHT ABATEMENT ACT

With the Panama-Pacific Exposition set to take place in 1915, Californians launched a "moral purity" campaign to rid its cities of prostitution houses they called "public nuisances." The act passed in 1914 and was signed by Governor Johnson, shutting down brothels across the state. It gave the city power to fine brothel owners and to allow property owners to keep single women from renting an apartment on the first floor, or any apartment at all. Without housing, prostitution moved to the streets, exactly what Cherry de St. Maurice had lobbied against. The Barbary Coast, San Francisco's infamous "Red Light District," was one of the last districts to shut down after the state supreme court ruled the act constitutional.

On July 9, 1913, Cleo Sterling, one of the prostitutes, or "inmates," of the club, found Cherry's nude body in her bedroom. Cleo claimed she last saw her mistress with two men in Cherry's bedroom. No obvious signs pointed to cause of death, but police noted a drop of blood under her nose. They then discovered a crumpled piece of tape, the kind boxers use to bind their hands, beneath her body. Further examination showed that the hyoid bone in her throat had been crushed by strangulation—"the work of a master garrotter who knew to a terrible nicety how to snuff out a life without leaving a mark in the flesh," reported the *Des Moines Daily News*.

Police began searching for two men seen leaving the club in the early morning hours, men whom they soon identified as being Samuel Raber, a café singer, and Jack Drumgoole, a successful prizefighter. Officials blanketed the state with telegrammed descriptions of the two men. Meanwhile, Ms. Sterling was arrested on suspicion and sat quietly in a jail cell. Soon she admitted to her relationship with one of the accused. "I love Sam," she said. "I know nothing about the murder."

After discovering several thousands of dollars in jewelry missing from Cherry's suite, police contended the murder occurred during a robbery gone wrong. From the little information Sterling gave, authorities discovered Samuel Raber and Jack Drumgoole had been in her company that night. According to the *Nevada State Journal*, Drumgoole and Raber were well-known in Reno. Drumgoole, a quiet, law-abiding man, began a successful career there as a prizefighter. Raber entertained in local cafés. Police described him as a "hop-head" and "more or less a worthless fellow." Authorities searched the apartment the two men had shared in Sacramento and found tape matching that found under Cherry's body. They also learned that Raber and Cleo Sterling began living together less than six weeks after Raber's wife succumbed to an illness.

On July 27, a San Diego pawnbroker phoned authorities saying he had just done business with a man who "did not look right to him." It was subsequently revealed that Drumgoole had pawned a hundred-dollar bracelet for thirteen dollars, while Raber waited on a nearby street corner with six-thousand dollars worth of Cherry's jewels sewn into his coat lining. When confronted by police, Raber claimed he bought the gems from a man in Los Angeles for fifty dollars. After a search, a pendant inscribed with "Cherry" prompted an admission from both men.

Raber revealed an elaborate plan to divert the jewels by shipping some to Salt Lake City, and picking them up later at the Wells Fargo Express Company. He later decided on shipping the jewels to San Diego. The jewels arrived days before their arrest. Raber, who gave his real name as Sam Beasley, admitted being "in on the deal," but said he did not kill the woman. He blamed Drumgoole and said he didn't know Cherry was dead until reading it in the papers the next day. Drumgoole claimed Cherry fought back and he choked her to stifle her screams. He tried unsuccessfully to revive her. Both men said they sought out Cleo, and gave her twenty-five dollars to buy her silence.

Raber refused to elaborate for authorities and said he would tell his full story in court: "I just want to tell you enough to convince you that I am not guilty of murder. I don't believe there was ever a man convicted of murder who was not guilty and I know that I will never be convicted of the murder of Cherry de St. Maurice." Raber also concealed a seven-hundred dollar diamond under his tongue during the four-hundred-and-fifty-mile trip to Sacramento. When one of the detectives eventually realized it and demanded the gem, Raber spit it into the detective's palm. "I've had that thing under my tongue for three days," he said.

Next, both men claimed Cleo Sterling planned the entire crime. They said she blackened their faces in her room, moments before Raber posed as a messenger with a telegram at Cherry's door. During the robbery, Raber thought he heard Cherry say, "Don't do that, Sam!" Drumgoole heard her say, "Take all I've got boys, but don't kill me. God bless you!"

Stories circulated about the size of Cherry's supposed estate, her previous life in Chicago, and her apparent obsession with a beautiful doll, the size of a two-year-old child. Police found the doll lying on her bed dressed in a fine nightgown. A complete outfit for the doll lay on a chair next to the bedside table. Housekeepers said Cherry often rocked the doll, as though it were alive. Some said that Cherry had borne a daughter nearly fifteen years earlier in Chicago, shortly before her husband left her. What became of the girl is unknown, but many suspected she had died.

Afterward, many women came forward claiming to be the daughter of the murder victim, but when Anna Held got involved, people took notice. A Polish-born actress, Held was married by common law to Florenz Ziegfeld. She suggested the format for the famous Ziegfeld Follies in 1907, helping Ziegfeld establish the most lucrative phase of his career. Held said that when she played in Sacramento in 1911, she met Cherry in her private car, where she told Anna, "You are my only heir. If you outlive me, I shall leave you everything I have. My mother was a sister of your father." Cherry didn't leave a will. In an interview, Held could not remember the full name of her benefactress, except that "she was French," and she stated, "It is very sad that the poor woman was murdered. She visited me when I played in Sacramento. I saw her many times. Of course, money is money but the woman was sweet to me. I have received word that the estate belongs to me and I will take the case into the courts if necessary." Upon further appraisal, Cherry's debts exceeded her assets and Held withdrew her claim.

Raber, Drumgoole, and Sterling were all granted separate trials. In mid-October, Raber faced the jury. Raber offered to plead guilty in return for a lighter sentence, but the district attorney refused him this "luxury." His attorney attempted to prove that while Raber grabbed valuables, Drumgoole intentionally strangled Cherry to death. On October 18, 1913, after thirty-five minutes of deliberation, a jury found Samuel Raber guilty of murder in the first degree. At sentencing a few days later, Raber collapsed when he learned he was to hang on January 2, 1914.

Jack Drumgoole's trial took place just days after Raber's sentencing. Drumgoole arrived in court in a nervous state, dressed shabbily and scarcely able to articulate. His only discernible words came when he denounced Raber. Drumgoole insisted that Raber held him at gun point in order to gain entrance to Cherry's apartment and kill her.

While Drumgoole awaited to learn his fate, Raber entertained occupants of the Sacramento county jail and several residents of Woodland, California, with the cheerful and warbled ditties that made him famous as a café entertainer. People gathered around the jail and listened to Raber sing through the night. Jailers forced him to stop singing after sleepless prisoners complained. Women and girls stood outside the jail calling out to trustees and asking them to allow more songs.

On October 24, the jury found Drumgoole guilty, but couldn't agree on his punishment. Eventually, he was sentenced to life at San Quentin.

The trial of Ms. Cleo Sterling proved more fascinating and entertaining than those of her co-conspirators. The *Nevada State Journal* wrote, "Attired in a stylishly tailored blue suit, white shirtwaist, velvet pumps, and wearing a large black hat, Cleo appeared little worried when she went into court." She had good reason. It took more than two days to obtain a jury since most potential jurymen opposed the death penalty for women. The court disqualified 158 men before seating a jury composed completely of married men. The court also ruled that confessions from Raber and Drumgoole could not be used, and attorneys for both men managed to keep them from having to take the stand at her trial.

After an hour of deliberation, the jury acquitted Cleo of all charges. The crowd that jammed the courtroom rushed to her with congratulations. Women threw their arms around her and kissed her, while the men shook her hand. "I'm going back home to my parents in Europe," she said, but by December Cleo had received a floater[1] in Reno, Nevada, for "consorting with the Chinese" in Chinatown.

Raber filed an appeal and even Cleo herself appeared before Governor Johnson to prevent her lover's execution. In July 1914, Cleo sent Samuel twenty dollars to help him in his plea for a new trial. He was now scheduled to hang December 18. The California Supreme Court justices agreed that it did not matter who actually killed Cherry, ruling, "Each of the parties to the criminal enterprise was responsible for all acts done by the other in the prosecution of that enterprise. Nor is it of the slightest consequence that the conspirators may not have intended to bring about their victim's death. The killing, having occurred in the perpetration of robbery, was murder of the first degree."

Luckily for Raber, Governor Johnson granted a reprieve to allow time for further investigation. Raber's attorney's said he could prove Drumgoole intentionally killed Cherry. Meanwhile, residents of Joliet, Illinois, Raber's hometown, rallied around him, stating they remembered him as a little boy with good character. Religious women from Sacramento also corroborated Raber's claim that he had converted to religion in Folsom. Petitions circulated in hopes of saving him. They weren't enough.

On the eve of Raber's execution, Drumgoole had something to say. Declaring no friendly feeling toward Raber and prompted only by remorse, he said that Raber should not be condemned to die. Drumgoole insisted Raber hadn't laid a hand on Cherry and called Cleo the instigator of the crime. He said the three of them planned the operation. Drumgoole was to overpower and hold Cherry, while Raber ransacked the apartment.

Governor Johnson refused to grant another reprieve. Raber wrote two messages, one warning others to avoid following in his footsteps and another expressing his religious faith. He also received and answered several letters from friends in Aurora and Joliet, Illinois. On January 15, 1915, Raber stood, unflinching, on the platform of the gallows, where the *Oakland Tribune* reported he declared, "I am not afraid to meet the finish. It is not courage, but fate." He thanked the church for the comfort given to him and died twelve minutes after the trap sprung.

---

1. A conditional pass. Offender must leave town within a specified number of hours to avoid arrest.

30. Frank Creeks, August 27, 1915

On October 16, 1914, exemplary convicts Frank Creeks and his cell mate George Phelps engineered a prison break that the *Oakland Tribune* described as "unrivaled in daring and ingenuity." At 8:30 in the evening, the two crouched behind a door to the main corridor, opening into the yard. They knew guards customarily brought firearms into the cell block for the night guards at about this time.

Unaware of the convicts behind the door, night captain J. Drewery and guard Joe Kerr approached from the outside with four firearms. Phelps gripped the handle of a prison-made knife, while Creeks carried a dumbbell. They had also fashioned a makeshift key for access. "As I opened the door to let [Drewery] pass through," said Kerr, "Creeks stepped through the door with his hand upraised. I was struck in the head, the blow sending me to the floor." Phelps then attacked Drewery with the knife, leaving the forty-six-year-old captain with six stab wounds, including three to the head. Drewery died within minutes. A guard at Folsom since 1908 and captain for only thirteen months, he left behind a wife and two children.

Kerr, dazed and unsteady, got to his feet and made a break for the open door, hoping to prevent the men from escaping, but Kerr needed the key in his fallen partner's pocket. Creeks shoved the barrel of a revolver into Kerr's stomach and the two men scuffled until a tower guard fired a shot. Kerr watched Creeks and Phelps flee. Kerr was not inactive, however; he recalled the situation, saying, "I still had my revolver in my belt and drew it, firing the five shells in it at the two fleeing convicts. Phelps fell." Phelps died from a bullet wound to the back of his head. Escaping into the yard with two revolvers and ammunition, Creeks engaged guard Frank Maher in a gun battle, wounding Maher in the hip. Miraculously, Creeks cleared the yard and escaped into the night. Maher died eleven days later from the gunshot.

The next day, with the aid of bloodhounds, authorities discovered Creeks asleep in a rooming house in Loomis, thirteen miles north of the prison. Asked by the prison directors about the circumstances surrounding the break, Creeks said, "I don't remember." He blamed Phelps for plotting the escape and for the death of Drewery. Creeks said Phelps threatened him until he agreed to the plot. Warden Smith considered Creeks's story to be flimsy, at best.

After visiting his son in jail, John Creeks told prison officials that Phelps forced his son at knifepoint to join in the escape plot. In an effort to save his son, he then vowed to begin a statewide movement to abolish capital punishment. At his trial, Frank Creeks continued to insist Phelps coerced him into taking part in the escape. Prosecution witness Guard F. L. Platt testified that Phelps didn't have a weapon, but the defense argued that Pratt didn't inspect the body until the following day, by which time a weapon could have been removed. Frank Creeks was found guilty of murder.

In April 1915, while awaiting his appeal's outcome, Creeks and fellow inmates Earl Loomis and Zollie Clements attempted another daring escape. They made keys to unlock their cell doors and intended to allay suspicion by relocking them. Guards discovered the three men in the gallows room, attempting to climb down a ladder they fashioned using the rope that hung #28, Jacob Oppenheimer. The men surrendered and guards escorted them back to their cells.

The California Supreme Court acknowledged that even though Creeks did not kill Drewery himself, he participated in the event that led to the captain's death. The court denied Creeks's appeal. On August 27, 1915, Creeks had to be supported by guards as he was led to the scaffold. The *Modesto Evening News* reported, "[Creeks] was in a fainting condition when the trap was sprung." Called "one of the worst prisoners ever confined," Creeks took nine-and-a-half minutes to die in front of seventy-five witnesses.

"I'm glad it's almost over. Will they hang an insane man? Would a jury hang me?"
—David Fountain, 1914

31. David Fountain, September 10, 1915

On December 5, 1914, ten-year-old Margaret Milling walked to the German Lutheran Church, two blocks from the state capitol grounds in Sacramento. Margaret, the eldest of seven children, went to meet with her sewing circle. The club members had been making doll dresses and decorations for the upcoming Christmas celebration.

The Sunday school room sat empty. Margaret had made a mistake. The sewing circle didn't meet that day. She went to the piano for a little practice before returning home. Margaret didn't realize she had an audience. The music had attracted the attention of the janitor, who stood in the doorway and listened for a while before joining her at the piano.

Police found Margaret's bruised and mangled body later that afternoon in the basement, stuffed into a large crevice in the wall. The janitor, David Fountain, had reported the crime to the police, claiming he had discovered the body while cleaning. Charles Oehler, the church's pastor, recognized the young choir member and took upon himself the unfortunate duty of informing John Milling and his wife. The news was devastating and the parents collapsed in grief. John swore vengeance on the still unnamed killer.

Margaret had been severely beaten, raped, and strangled. A three-quarter-inch binding rope—the kind used to tie bundles of the church's leaflets—was wound tightly around her neck like a noose. Coroner Gormley, in his twelve years of work for the county, had never seen such a savage murder: "It is inconceivable that there are such brutes in the world as [the] man who killed this innocent child."

Suspicion immediately fell on fifty-four-year-old Fountain, who stoutly maintained his innocence. However, he did admit to being a "five-time loser" and a resident of an Iowa insane asylum in 1889. Dr. Oehler told police he had rebuked Fountain more than once for "getting familiar with little girls of the church." Police led Fountain to the belfry where they discovered traces of blood. They also pointed out blood spots on Fountain's pants. He claimed he had killed a turkey on Thanksgiving, a fact which Oehler corroborated.

When Fountain's questioning resumed in District Attorney Worchorst's office the next day, the suspect confessed. Fountain said that after playing the piano with Margaret, he suddenly lost control. He admitted, "I seemed to go mad, passions got the best of me. I forgot everything except my desires." Fountain continued to recount the events of the crime. He threw her to the floor and struck her repeatedly. Fountain stated, "Blood spurted from her cuts on her face and maddened me." He chased her into the kitchen where he grabbed the cord, strangled her, and then sexually assaulted her.

Fountain told Worchorst that he couldn't recollect what happened next, only that he found the girl's body in the belfry after he returned from a brief trip downtown. He took her to the basement: "I thought she should have a proper burial. I did not want her body to decompose."

Later, Fountain produced a slightly different version. "I cannot remember having killed her. I do not know how the little girl's body got up in the belfry. I can't remember tying the rope around her neck. She was such a cute little girl, but I was crazy, crazy. Everything went wrong with me and I can't remember." Fountain wondered if confessing would save him from the gallows, saying, "I'm glad it's over. Will they hang an insane man? Would a jury hang me? I've confessed and I feel better." Despite "clearing his conscience," Fountain worried about the uncertainty of his future. It ate at him. The following day, he spoke to a reporter and repudiated his confession, declaring he only confessed to avoid further "grilling" by the authorities. He said he would plead not guilty and wanted an attorney.

Fountain's retraction didn't concern Worchorst, but it infuriated John Milling, who said, "If that beast—that murderer—is sent to prison [for life] or an asylum, I'll kill him." Fountain feared not only Millings' wrath, but also those of Sacramento residents. He begged Worchorst to move him to a stronger cell in the county jail, fearing his current cell wouldn't withstand an angry mob. Authorities denied his request.

The court appointed Fred Harris to defend Fountain and trial was set for February. In the meantime, Fountain underwent mental and physical examinations where doctors determined the prisoner to be "insane along certain lines"—at least when it came to perverted and violent tendencies. However, this conclusion wasn't enough to support an insanity plea.

When Fountain entered the courtroom to begin trial, John Milling, enraged and grief-stricken, lunged at Fountain. "Let me get my hands on him!" he shouted. Three officers restrained Milling, who continued to scream and kick chairs, attempting to reach the confessed killer. Fountain sat nearby, showing little concern. One spectator even observed a faint smile on the defendant's face. Officers led Milling out of the courtroom before the trial resumed.

The defense asked for more time to secure affidavits to outline the insanity plea, but presiding judge Herbert White denied the motion. In fact, the defense lacked any available testimony regarding Fountain's alleged insanity, as well as his supposed term in an insane asylum some twenty-eight years earlier.

The jury returned with a guilty verdict. At the sentencing, the judge fixed the day of execution for the first Friday after the expiration of the legal grace of 60 days. "I do not care to waste my time on a man of your caliber," stated the judge. The defense immediately filed an appeal and in July the California Supreme Court upheld the lower court's judgment. The court contended that none of the submitted affidavits were sufficient to prove Fountain's insanity at the time of the murder. The court referred to Fountain's early confession and said it "showed that the killing of the child was committed by him in connection with a lecherous and brutal attack which he had made upon her for the purpose of arousing and gratifying an unnatural passion."

Scores of individuals applied to Warden J. J. Smith for invitations to witness the execution of Fountain in September. For the first time in the prison's history, invitations on white cards outlined in black were sent out. Police and others involved in the case attended the "neck-tie party." John Milling, however, was not allowed to witness the death of his daughter's killer. (The following month, the State Board of Prison Directors ended the invitation practice, beginning with the execution of Burr Harris (see story #32). "The death chamber will no longer be used as a curiosity shop," said Warden Smith.)

Fountain maintained that his mind was blank at the time he killed Margaret Milling. Regardless, on September 10, 1915, spectators claimed Fountain "trotted" or "walked briskly" to his place on the gallows, seemingly as anxious as the witnesses for his death.

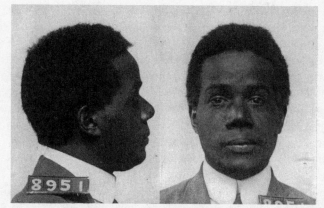

"Never knew Mrs. Gay . . . I just wanted to kill some woman."
—Burr Harris, 1913

32. Burr Harris, October 8, 1915

The crime scene made even seasoned investigators queasy. One reporter remarked, "With the force she was killed, [one was] led to the supposition that the murderer killed with hysterical violence." Blood-splatters coated the walls and floor; the victim's brain oozed from its skull. Religious cards and papers covered the corpse. One read, "The Lord is my Shepard [sic]; I shall not want." A bloody gas pipe lay on the floor near the victim.

The bludgeoned body belonged to Rebecca Gay, a prominent Christian Scientist of Los Angeles and leader of the Pacific Coast branch of the church. She kept an office on the fifth floor of the H. W. Hellman building. There, on a Friday afternoon in 1913, Gay's killer methodically washed his hands of blood at the sink, wiped them on a towel, and laid the stained rag on the body. He then hung the sign on her office door that read: "Mrs. Gay will not return until Monday." A janitor discovered the body the following morning.

Investigators found Gay's purse empty, although her jewelry remained untouched. After snooping around the scene, a newspaper reporter spotted a man's bloody detachable collar on the roof directly beneath the window of Gay's office, but it didn't appear to provide any critical leads.

A couple of women who saw Gay in her office the afternoon of her murder provided the only viable clues investigators had to go on. They described a black man sitting in the building lobby, holding what appeared to be a rolled up piece of paper. He approached Gay and she asked him, "Are you the man who telephoned?" He entered her office and the door closed.

Not far from Gay's office, police approached a black man banging his head on a pole. He gave his name as Robert Askew and told investigators he once worked as a chauffeur for John Gay, Rebecca Gay's former husband. According to newspapers, at the time of his ex-wife's murder, John Gay was worth an estimated four to five million dollars, making him the fifth wealthiest man in San Diego. For the previous twenty years, the former Mrs. John Gay reportedly had received $1,500 per year in alimony.

Askew claimed he had been drinking and couldn't recall his recent actions. The two women in the office building couldn't positively identify Askew as the killer, only that he strongly resembled the man they'd seen in the lobby and later seen enter Gay's office.

Based on a reliable alibi and the uncertain identification, police released Askew after he served a term for drunkenness. Police directed their efforts to San Diego, where they arrested Burr Harris, a local character under surveillance in connection for previous murders. He also fit the description of the suspect. Investigators found a gas pipe, similar to the one that killed Gay, in the backyard of Harris's mother's home. They arrested the twenty-seven-year-old Harris.

On October 6, ten days after the murder, Harris confessed. Wearing a smile, he said, "Yes, I killed her. I must have been crazy. I have spells when I am queer in the head." Harris alleged that voices in his head told him a Mrs. Wallace—in the Hellman building—intended to kill him and that he needed to kill her before she had the chance to do him in.

"Never knew Mrs. Gay," Harris said. "I didn't go to the Hellman building to find her. I just wanted to kill some woman. I took a gas pipe from the backyard, went to the building and up to the fifth floor. I saw her name on the door." He sat in the reception room for about thirty minutes when he heard the voices again, informing him Mrs. Gay was the mysterious Mrs. Wallace. "I knocked and when it opened I asked if Mrs. Wallace was there."

The telephone in Gay's office rang and when she turned to answer it Harris closed the door, pulled out the gas pipe that he had wrapped in a sheet of music, and then "beat the life out of her." Harris struck Gay several times on the head with the pipe and, as investigators had earlier theorized, Harris tried to throw her body out of the window. Her weight proved too great, so he left her on the floor and covered her with religious papers. He then took a train to San Diego where he buried his bloody clothing in a field near his mother's home.

The next evening, guided by Harris and the faint light of a lantern, investigators unearthed the clothes. Harris confirmed the blood-splattered coat, trousers, and shirt belonged to him, along with a pair of white gloves he wore to prevent leaving fingerprints. After further questioning, Harris told police a wild story that a man paid him to kill Gay, and that another black man acting as an agent delivered $500 to Harris. Harris said he buried the money near Tijuana. The confessed killer then recanted this story, insisting that "recurrent murder mania drove him to the act."

Based on a plea of not guilty by reason of insanity, Harris's trial began on November 10. He testified that he had no remembrance of killing Gay until after the officers arrested him and described the circumstances of the crime. He told jurors that for three years he suffered from "spells"—lasting anywhere from days to weeks—where he'd experience sickness, loss of consciousness, and memory loss. During these times, voices in his head told him that other people threatened to kill him and he must protect himself by finding and killing these people first. Harris insisted he suffered from epileptic insanity, and even defense medical experts testified they felt the defendant did indeed suffer from "a spell of this insanity" when he killed Gay. However, the court instructed the jury that "irresistible impulse" was not a defense.

The *Los Angeles Examiner* called Harris an "ebony statue" as he calmly described killing Gay, as well as his other crimes, reporting, "It was a story which caused women to weep and men to grip their chairs for control." Harris told of killing Melvina Haskins, a murder for which a jury had acquitted him years earlier. He claimed that he had also sent poisoned candy and a homemade bomb to another person, and he had set fire to the Coronado Hotel in Los Angeles. All of these crimes, he said, were the result of an uncontrollable desire to kill—voices in his head urging him to commit murder.

Ignoring Harris' plea of insanity, the jury returned a guilty verdict after eighteen minutes of deliberation. Exhibiting his usual stoic demeanor, Harris smiled, shook hands with his attorney, and left the courtroom, escorted by the bailiff.

While awaiting the outcome of an appeal, Harris confessed to the murder of Charles Pendell, a diamond broker, a year earlier. Some of the details Harris provided didn't match up with the evidence, while he did relay other particulars only investigators knew about. Nevertheless, in keeping with his usual modus operandi, Harris retracted his confession, stating he only wanted the chance to see his mother again. Police did investigate Harris' possible role in the murder, and they never ruled him out as a suspect.

The higher court handed down its decision in the fall of 1915 and Harris's execution took place on October 8, 1915.

"I will have nothing to fear in death, for the good Lord will take care of me."
—Earl Loomis, days before his execution, 1915

33. Earl Martin Loomis, November 5, 1915

On the evening of August 17, 1914, Marie and Clifford Hollcroft sat at the counter of their shop, Purity Ice Cream Parlor, on 17th Avenue in Sacramento. Harold Peterson, a thirteen-year-old employee, sat with them. At 9:30, nineteen-year-old Earl Loomis rushed in, brandishing a revolver and yelling, "Hands up!" Everyone obeyed except Marie, who raised one hand while the other grasped a revolver under the counter.

After pressing the dollar key on the register, Loomis reached for the money, but hesitated. At that moment, both Marie and Loomis fired a shot at one another. Loomis's shot struck Marie in the chest. As Loomis ran out the door, Marie leaned over the counter and fired three more shots at him, one hitting the bandit's left eye, blinding him. Marie died moments later.

Police found Loomis collapsed four blocks from the ice cream parlor. He initially told officers that bandits had shot him and he had taken their gun. Later, at the hospital, he admitted to killing Marie Hollcroft. Loomis pleaded not guilty due to moral insanity. He claimed the evening's drinking, combined with a family history of mental illness, physical abuse, and lack of schooling, kept him from knowing right from wrong when he shot his victim.

After ten minutes of deliberation, the jury found him guilty of murder. Soon after, many women's groups fought to save Loomis from execution, citing his age and poor upbringing. "Wouldn't it have been better for [the state] to have spent a little money some twenty years ago to have helped that mother raise her children better?" read one editorial. Others sharply criticized the "Sob Sisters," calling Loomis a cold-blooded killer with "no use to society," and a person who had cursed his own mother when she came to visit him in jail. "Oh hell, get away, can't you," he reportedly told her. "I took a chance, and I'll take my medicine." Interestingly, Loomis's brother, Boyd, was serving a three-year term for burglary at Folsom and prison officials "did not favor the idea of keeping him in Folsom, where his brother Earl is to be hanged." They therefore transferred him to San Quentin.

While awaiting the results of his appeal, Loomis, Frank Creeks, and Zollie Clements attempted to escape from condemned row. Guards found them descending a ladder they devised from the noose that hanged Jacob Oppenheimer. In October, the higher court denied Loomis's appeal. The day before his execution, he spent his time reading the Bible. "I am taking up religion," he told Warden Smith. "I guess it's pretty late to take up religion, but I hope it will do me some good." On November 5, 1915, Loomis greeted the witnesses to his execution with a "Hello, boys," before he dropped through the trap.

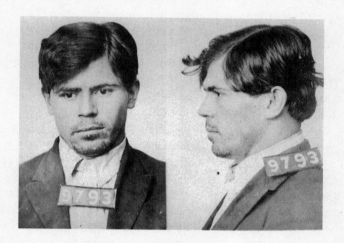

34. Rito Bargas, January 21, 1916

On July 4, 1915, Jesus Chavez, his wife Rufujio, and their six children rode home in a large buggy from Goose Lake near Wasco in Kern County. Francisco Amador, a family friend, accompanied them. They encountered Rito Bargas and Trinidad Gonzalez on the road and exchanged pleasantries. The two men, traveling in a horse cart, continued on toward Goose Lake.

Later, Jesus Chavez left the party on a horse to visit a nearby ranch and Amador took over the buggy reigns. Eleven-year-old (some newspapers reported his age as six) Domin Chavez rode in his lap. A short time later, Rufujio saw Bargas and Gonzalez behind them. Bargas yelled, "Stop, Chavez!" The men rode up alongside

PUTTING PRISONERS TO WORK

In 1914, San Quentin warden James Johnston proposed that low-risk prisoners work as road workers on California's state roadways. The following year, state legislators approved the measure and hundreds of convicts began building remote highways across the state. Most notably, they built the Redwood Empire Highway, Walker Pass Highway east of Bakersfield, as well as roads leading to Yosemite Valley and Lake Tahoe. In return, for every two days of work, the convict laborers received a one-day reduction of their sentence. The arrangement, entirely based on the honor system, proved successful and, in 1923, legislation amended the act to provide convicts up to $2.50 a day in wages. By the mid-1930s, 10,113 men had worked on the state's highways. During the entire time, only 102 escaped and were never recaptured. Today, the California Department of Corrections employs convicts in Conservation Camps with the Department of Forestry and Fire Protection, working on various projects, including restoring historical structures, park maintenance, and clearing fallen trees.

the buggy and fired at the driver, killing both Amador and Domin. Presuming they had killed Chavez, Bargas yelled, "Where is Amador?" They fired again into the buggy, wounding Rufujio. The shooters then fled the scene, leaving two dead and Rufujio with two bullet wounds to her arm.

The men arrived at the ranch of Juan Rivera, who was boarding Gonzales's two young daughters. When Rivera demanded payment, Gonzales refused and fired shots at Rivera, inflicting only superficial wounds. Making yet another escape, the men spent a week on the lam. Driven by hunger and lack of ammunition, they settled approximately thirty miles away in Bakersfield. They came to a small cabin owned by Juan Cervantes, an elderly Mexican. Up against a six-shooter, the man allowed the daring duo to take refuge in the house. After befriending the pair and earning their trust, Cervantes was permitted to leave to gather supplies. He used the opportunity to inform police of his house guests.

Bakersfield police descended on the cabin and kicked in the front door. Gonzales, "crouching like a tiger" in the center of the room, slowly raised his hands and succumbed to the authorities. He wouldn't divulge his companion's whereabouts, but police knew he couldn't be far. Searching the surrounding tall brush, officers came upon Bargas, surprising him as he acted as a lookout. Police did not find a gun on Bargas, assuming he had disposed of it in the nearby irrigation ditch or hid it among the surrounding brush. The "rough-looking, typical desperados" refused to talk as they were taken in custody. In classic, dramatic fashion, typical of early newspaper reports, the *Bakersfield Californian* described the two fugitives: "Gonzales is a tigerish-looking fellow with eyes like those of a rattler and a jaw set and determined. His hair, grown long, fell about his face, giving him the appearance of an aboriginal savage. Bargas is a more civilized man in appearance and several years younger than his companion. He is of the cool, calculating type, possessing a stronger mentality and greater cunning." The newspaper went on to report, "[Bargas] is believed to have planned the murder of Amador, inciting Gonzales, who has a wild and passionate nature, to take the initiative." This description prompted the press to further refer to the pair as "tiger men." As far as the Chavez family, reporters described them as ". . . above the ordinary Mexicans in intelligence and culture." Bargas had left a wife in Mexico to drive teams for U.S. businesses.

In October, Bargas and Gonzales were tried separately and each man blamed the other for the deaths. Gonzales's attorney urged Bargas to confess, intimating he'd receive a life sentence while at the same time save Gonzales, who also implored his friend: "Don't keep quiet and let me suffer all my life." Bargas refused to incriminate himself and maintained his innocence, bringing attention to the fact that the caliber of bullets that caused the deaths of Amador and the boy were not of the same caliber of his revolver, a .38. He offered to go with police and look for his weapon. The officers searched the area and discovered a fully-loaded .38-caliber Colt. They were skeptical, however, as to whether or not someone attempting to throw doubt on the case against Bargas planted the gun.

Gonzales received a life sentence. Upon hearing his partner's fate, Bargas pleaded guilty, hoping to avoid the extreme penalty. The judge endeavored to uncover the motive for the shooting, but Bargas declined to shed light on the subject. When questioned by the judge, Mr. Chavez offered very little, only saying that he employed Bargas at one time, but discharged him because of unsatisfactory work. Chavez stated he was away from the home quite often and reportedly said with a smile "there may have been some relations between his wife and Amador," but did he not know. Unable to ascertain a motive, the judge called Bargas "the more intelligent of the two defendants," and sentenced him to hang.

The night before his execution, Bargas retracted his earlier accusations of Gonzales and asked for his partner's forgiveness. Bargas then slept seven hours, which the *Woodland Daily Democrat* called "unusual for a condemned man." Bargas died on the gallows on January 21, 1916.

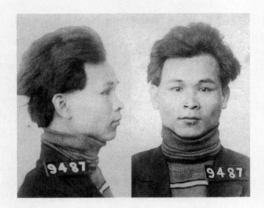

35. Sing Ung, February 18, 1916

Just after midnight on November 3, 1914, Y. Iwanaga was walking down a street in Stockton, California. As Iwanaga, a barber, approached his place of business, two men came from behind and shot him three times in the back. He died instantly.

Police found a .38 caliber Smith and Wesson near where Iwanaga fell. A bullet from the gun was lodged in the body, the other two bullets came from a .25 caliber weapon. Within minutes, police apprehended Sing Ung in a lumberyard, where he admitted fleeing the scene but denied taking part in the murder. He claimed two men pursued him and he fired his gun at them. Searching Ung, police found a recently fired .25 caliber revolver.

Police arrested another Asian, Uee Quey, and the two suspects were tried separately. Several witnesses who were voting in the general election at a polling place across the street from where Iwanaga was killed identified Ung as one of the shooters. Throughout his trial and subsequent imprisonment, Ung stoutly maintained his innocence. Uee Quey pleaded guilty and earned a life sentence. A judge sentenced Ung to death.

On February 18, 1916, twenty-four-year-old Ung, born and raised in Sacramento, went to the gallows, still claiming his innocence. Weighing only a hundred and ten pounds, Ung was the lightest man ever hanged at Folsom.

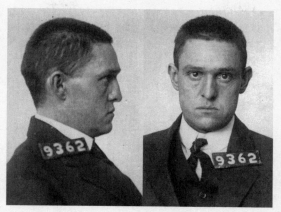

"Gentlemen, I am innocent and being railroaded from life."
—Glenn Witt, on the scaffold, 1916

36. Glenn Witt, March 3, 1916

At two in the morning, Charles Oxnam and Glenn Witt stood on the spacious lawn and surveyed the large mansion. All of the lights were extinguished in the home. The men removed their hats and shoes and dropped them onto the cold, wet grass.

Inside, wealthy attorney William Montrose Alexander, Sr. was asleep beside his wife, Cora. Their teenage children slept in their separate rooms. Alexander had moved his family from Texas to the fashionable Wilshire District of Los Angeles just a week earlier, in December 1914.

Seventeen-year-old Oxnam and twenty-two-year-old Witt quietly entered through a ground floor window. Their bare feet silenced their footfalls as they crept upstairs to the master bedroom.

Awakened by a noise, Cora turned on a light and roused her husband. Their son, whose room adjoined theirs, also awoke and burst into the room. He carried a pistol, loaded with one cartridge, and he immediately exchanged shots with Oxnam, who had entered the room from the hallway. William, Jr. had a finger blown off and sustained a nonfatal wound in the chest. Oxnam was shot in the leg. Mrs. Alexander had begun removing her rings, willing to give the intruders anything as long as they ceased fire. William, Sr. jumped at Oxnam, but the youth was too quick and he shot the fifty-seven-year-old Alexander in the chest. Oxnam then fled from the house.

Cora tended to her dying husband while William, Jr. struggled with Witt, who by now had entered the master bedroom. The teenaged Alexander daughters, Penelope and Louise, burst into the room and beat on Witt's face and head with silver-back hairbrushes. Witt later remarked, "Those girls fought like tiger cats." Finally, Witt extricated himself and escaped, leaving a trail of blood. William Alexander, Sr. died in his wife's arms.

In their haste, the burglars left their shoes and hats in the yard. Police found the two men later that day at a rooming house where they had sought medical attention for their wounds.

On Christmas Eve, a coroner's jury charged Witt and Oxnam with murder. A distraught Mrs. Alexander exclaimed, "May God have mercy on you and help you." Oxnam moved to have his case tried in juvenile court since he was only seventeen, but a 1914 U. S. Navy recruiting affidavit, co-signed by his mother, showed his age to be twenty. He pleaded not guilty by reason of insanity. Witt appeared indifferent to his predicament. When asked how he would plead, he briefly replied, "Not guilty, of course."

The district attorney decided to try the men separately. Oxnam's court-appointed attorney intended to show that his client's childhood fever stunted his mental development and that he was "never able to learn anything in school and that he [was] not responsible to the same degree as a grown man." Oxnam's stepmother described his behavior as "wild and wayward," following the apparent incident of "brain fever."

The Witt family hired attorney Clyde Cate, who aimed to show that Witt, unarmed, never came near Alexander and, in fact, tried to persuade Oxnam to leave without shooting. "They can't soak me," Witt stated. "I didn't kill Alexander. The burglary was over and I had left the room. I had no revolver and there would have been no murder if Oxnam had not lost his head."

Witt called Oxnam a "hair-trigger," saying, "I never would have had anything to do with him. It wasn't necessary to kill Alexander." Witt claimed that moments before William, Jr. came rushing into the room, he touched Oxnam's shoulder and said, "[We] better get out quick." When Witt turned to leave the room, the shooting began.

Oxnam admitted he shot the "retired capitalist," but refused to harbor all the blame, asserting, "Witt got me into that business. I never thought of being a burglar until he told me how easy it was to rob houses." However, the most damaging evidence against both men came from their own confessions upon arrest. The two admitted feeling desperate, and both claimed the killing of William Alexander did not occur until the family members had them surrounded.

Oxnam's trial began January 11, 1915. As predicted, he pleaded insanity. Twenty-three witnesses testified for Oxnam, depicting him as a morose, violent, and backward child, once nicknamed "Crazy Oxnam." Even Dr. Charles Locke, a staunch supporter of capital punishment, declared, "I do not believe the state of California will take the life of this boy . . . I do not think this is a case for such punishment. I believe this boy was stunted mentally and therefore his case is different."

The jury disagreed. They found Charles Oxnam guilty of murder in the first degree and they made no recommendation for leniency. Oxnam would hang.

Witt's trial followed. He testified he couldn't sustain employment and entered the Alexander house at Oxnam's suggestion, unaware that his partner-in-crime had a gun. Attorney Cate hoped his client's lack of a criminal record would sway the jury, but Witt received an identical verdict. "This is worse than Mexico," Witt shouted, "there is no such thing as justice here, but mark me, there will be before long!" Newspapers characterized Witt, a member of the Industrial Workers of the World, as a "typical IWW thug" and "the mastermind of the crime."

The judge delayed sentencing when Witt's friends protested outside the courtroom, declaring officials were "railroading him to the gallows." Eventually, Witt and Oxnam were sentenced to hang on April 16, 1915, Witt at Folsom and Oxnam at San Quentin.

Both teams of attorneys filed appeals, earning the men a reprieve, but, again, the courts disagreed with counsel. The California Supreme Court acknowledged that even though Witt did not fire the fatal shot, he participated with Oxnam to

THE INDUSTRIAL WORKERS OF THE WORLD (I.W.W)

At a Chicago convention in 1905, socialists, anarchists, and radical trade unionists formed the Industrial Workers of the World, an organization which fought to abolish the existing wage system for workers and replace it with a uniform wage. The I.W.W. constitution read, "The working class and the employing class have nothing in common. There can be no peace so long as hunger and want are found among millions of the working people and the few, who make up the employing class, have all the good things of life." Besides the Knights of Labor, the I.W.W. was the only American union that welcomed all races and both genders. Much of its membership consisted of immigrants. In fact, in the mid-teens, the organization vastly improved conditions for migratory farm workers.

Politicians and the press, however, disagreed with the I.W.W. philosophy, believing the union threatened labor markets by trying to monopolize them. This feeling, coupled with the I.W.W. condemnation of World War I, caused the eruption of vigilantism. Both local government and groups and organizations of citizens waged war against the union. Members were lynched, tortured, and imprisoned. They were charged with hindering the draft and encouraging desertion. The press repeatedly referred to members as thugs and criminals, making public enemies out of members of the organization.

Over the years, the I.W.W. has declined in membership and experienced structural changes, but it still organizes unions across the world for companies such as Starbucks and other food companies. Today, there are roughly 5,000 members, a far cry from the 100,000 at its peak in 1923.

perpetrate the crime and, therefore, was equally guilty in the eyes of the law. The Court also declared that Oxnam had sufficient mental capacity to understand that such an act was criminal and liable to be punished. Sentenced for the second time, Witt and Oxnam now faced a September 24, 1915 hanging.

In an effort to stay Oxnam's execution, Dr. Herbert Goddard, a well-known authority on insanity, pronounced him a "low moron," unaccountable for his acts. Witt also had his own advocates. Prompted by petitions, the Advisory Board of Pardons issued the results of its investigation. Governor Hiram Johnson issued another reprieve.

On October 30, good news finally came for Witt and Oxnam. The Advisory Board recommended their sentences be commuted to life imprisonment. Given the report from the board, Governor Johnson gave the men another reprieve until January 21, but he made no final decision on the matter.

In the meantime, four "lunacy" experts examined Oxnam. They called him "defective" and backed up the claims made by his stepmother and others. Witt was still counting on the board's recommendation to grant him a permanent reprieve from the gallows.

The Governor had other plans. Although acknowledging Oxnam as "somewhat sub-normal," Johnson didn't feel the mental deficiency was sufficient enough to interfere with the execution. He refused to grant clemency. The two were now scheduled to die on March 3.

The *Oakland Tribune* said Oxnam went to his death sobbing, while Witt remained calm. Though pale, he showed no fear. "I stand here innocent," Witt said. "I am being railroaded from life." Witt spent his final hours with his mother and two of his five sisters, who had taken up residence near the prison while awaiting the outcome of his appeals. The warden refused to allow anyone to report on the conversations, holding that the last meeting between mother and son was sacred. Until his last breath, on March 3, 1916, Glenn Witt proclaimed his innocence.

After living to see her husband's killers executed, Mrs. Cora Alexander died in Texas the following year at the age of forty-six.

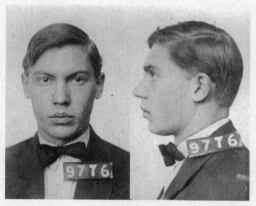

"Write my mother. I haven't the heart to do it."
—Kosta Kromphold's last request, 1916

37. Kosta Kromphold, September 1, 1916

Native Russian Kosta Kromphold, a twenty-one-year-old machinist from New York City, robbed a Chinese restaurant and escaped with an undisclosed amount of cash. Marysville police officers and brothers-in-law Chester Smith and John Sperbeck responded on bicycles to a call from witnesses who saw the suspect flee to a lumberyard. The men cautiously cased the area. Smith spotted a man crouching behind a pile of lumber, with a handkerchief spread out in front of him.

"I was under the impression that he was just finishing his lunch," said Smith, who didn't feel Kromphold fit the suspect's description. Smith called to the young man to come out so he could have a look at him. Smith reported ". . . and at that, the gun flew in my face and the handkerchief fell off it and I jumped back . . ." Smith warned Sperbeck. "Look out, John, he has a gun."

Two teenage boys who were playing nearby at the time of Smith and Sperbeck's contact with Kromphold later testified that Kromphold hid behind a woodpile, "threw his gun around the corner," and fired. The bullet entered Sperbeck's mouth and exited behind his left ear. Kromphold fled the yard. Smith pursued but lost him. He returned to find his brother-in-law's dead body.

An hour later, a posse of officers and citizens discovered Kromphold hiding in the brush beside the Yuba River, just outside of town. He exchanged shots with members of the posse, including the arresting officer, Francis Heenan (who was later killed by subject #51, John Connelly, in 1922).

Kromphold insisted he shot in self-defense, saying he never saw Sperbeck and only intended to scare Smith. Citing witness testimony, the defense argued Sperbeck stood roughly thirty-seven feet from Kromphold, making it impossible to aim. The two young boys could not opine whether Kromphold shot Sperbeck intentionally.

In the end, the jury found that Kromphold deliberately aimed at, shot, and killed the officer, and he was condemned to death. Sperbeck, a fourteen-year veteran of the police force, left behind a wife and young child. A Mrs. A. Meyers of New York City wrote to Governor Hiram Johnson on behalf of her housekeeper, Johanna Kromphold, the condemned man's mother, saying that Mrs. Kromphold had already lost two of her three children. Mrs. Meyers's message continued, "By taking this young boy's life, you not only take one but two, as I am positive she will never live through this terrible ordeal."

Johnson refused to interfere, making way for Kromphold to mount the gallows. On September 1, 1916, Kromphold gave his last request to the prison chaplain: "Write my mother. I haven't the heart to do it."

38. Joseph Schoon, July 12, 1918

In December 1916, Dutch sailor Joseph Schoon made parole after serving time at San Quentin for grand larceny. The terms, however, required Schoon's deportation. While being escorted to New York, the twenty-seven-year-old Schoon successfully escaped from federal officers in North Dakota.

On the evening of February 4, 1917, Schoon and a companion visited several Stockton saloons and restaurants. When their money ran out at one in the morning, the two "kind of hard-looking characters" resorted to begging. One bar owner said of Schoon, "I didn't like his talk because it was professional talk, like a hobo. Like a man that just beats the trains." When the panhandling became aggressive, a bartender called the police.

Thirty-six-year-old police officer John Louis Briscoe arrested the two men and proceeded to walk them to the police station, located a block away on Weber and El Dorado streets. Attorney C. L. Neumiller, who later became a prominent member of the Board of Prison Directors, was staying at the Hotel Stockton when he heard four gunshots. Looking out his window, he saw a body lying outside an alley on El Dorado Street. Officer F. H. Ingalls also heard the shots and saw two men running from the scene, but he lost sight of them. Briscoe, a husband and father of four boys, attempted pursuit of the fleeing men and fired three shots. He then collapsed in the alley and died of a single bullet wound to the chest.

An hour later, not far from the shooting, police spotted someone crawling under a bridge and soon pulled Schoon from his hiding place. Schoon was sweaty and breathing heavily, and he had a bruise over one of his eyes. Officer Ingalls arrived on the scene and said Schoon fit the description of one of the men he had seen running earlier. Schoon carried a loaded .38 caliber pistol in his vest pocket. The gun had been recently fired and when police asked about it, Schoon remained silent. Schoon confirmed that he was now alone, and he insisted his earlier drinking companion had nothing to do with the shooting. Police never located this man.

Schoon stood for trial in April and maintained his innocence, yet he didn't testify on his own behalf. Found guilty and sentenced to death, Schoon appealed, citing his membership in the unpopular Industrial Workers of the World (I.W.W.) as a reason for jury bias. Schoon also pointed out that no one had witnessed the shooting. Further, he said he and his companion were frightened and ran after hearing the shots. His appeal was denied, and Schoon stood on the Folsom gallows on July 12, 1918. He reportedly spent his final night singing German hymns and songs, and he had become so belligerent by morning that four jailers had to forcibly dress him for his execution and subsequent funeral.

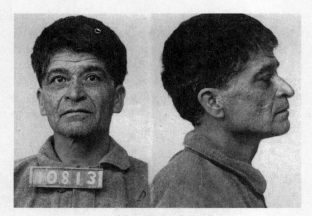

"I'm glad I did it."
—Jose Negrete, referring to murdering his victim, 1918

39. Jose Negrete, November 29, 1918

While serving a twenty-five year sentence at Folsom Prison for second-degree murder, Jose Negrete finally had had enough of fellow convict M. Castellano's insults. The two men worked in the prison's flower garden and, according to Negrete, Castellano called him a "chingara," or son of a bitch, saying also, "I'm going to get you." Two days later, on January 19, 1918, while prisoners gathered at the gate after breakfast, Negrete and Castellano exchanged more hostile words. Negrete then stabbed Castellano and "twisted the file in his victim's heart," reported one newspaper.

"I'm glad I did it," Negrete told Warden J. J. Smith, giving no other explanation. The *Oakland Tribune* reported, "It is almost an unwritten law among the convicts, it is said today, never to explain such attacks." The prosecution later theorized that Castellano had received his own private plot of ground in the flower garden, which infuriated Negrete. Castellano, said to have had a good record during his short imprisonment, was serving a four-year sentence for robbery.

Despite a self-defense plea, Negrete received the death penalty after a guilty verdict. On the morning of November 29, 1918, Negrete stood on the scaffold, muttering in Spanish—words not translated by the press—before falling through the trap.

PART V: 1919–1924

Folsom Wardens: J. J. Smith, November 16, 1913–February 2, 1927

California Governors: William Stephens, March 15, 1917–January 9, 1923

Friend Richardson, January 9, 1923–January 4, 1927

The Roaring Twenties began with the passage of Prohibition in 1919. The ban on alcohol paved the way for speakeasies and bootlegged liquor, both adding to the increasing prison population. In its annual report to the governor, the Board of Prison Directors stated, "Prohibition had not decreased crime, as it was hoped it would, and that violations of the Drug Act had shown an alarming increase." The unpopular ban brought with it a new breed of criminal. Organized crime rapidly spread across the country and it not only consisted of iconic criminals like Al Capone, but corrupt politicians and police officials, as well.

The era also marked the first time women's voices were heard politically. In 1920, the Nineteenth Amendment gave women the right to vote and a newfound independence flourished among American women. They looked up to the likes of Zelda Sayre Fitzgerald, the famous flapper wife of F. Scott Fitzgerald; "The Empress of Blues," Bessie Smith, who dominated the airwaves; and Georgia O'Keefe, who didn't adhere to the rules of the art world. Women could finally excel in the arts and sports, as well as the working world, where they took secretarial jobs from their male counterparts.

The early part of the decade experienced a rebound from the Great War, saw its first transcontinental flight, and welcomed the emergence of jazz. California's population skyrocketed to 5.7 million people, a stunning 66 percent increase—the highest rate of increase since the Gold Rush of 1849. When the Los Angeles population surpassed that of San Francisco, making it the largest city in the West, Bay Area residents were livid. It sparked a rivalry between the two cities, each one trying to outdo the other with events and attractions. L. Frank Baum (author of *The Wizard of Oz*), who lived on Hollywood Boulevard, said of L.A., "Here the

American people were erupting like a volcano; here was the place for me—a ring-side seat at the circus."

Unfortunately, this "Lawless Decade" was also considered the golden age of the Ku Klux Klan and saw a sharp increase in violence against blacks. The group boasted a staggering four to five million members by 1925. They preached "One Hundred Percent Americanism" and introduced cross burning to their reper-toire. Minorities became public enemies to hate groups. Lynchings increased dramatically, prompting an anti-lynching bill to be passed by the U.S. House of Representatives in 1922, only to be defeated in the Senate then and again in 1923 and 1924.

Racial discrimination spilled into the courtroom, where some judge's own biases often determined a minority person's fate. Newspapers offered little support, using racial slurs, including calling Native Americans "half-breeds."

Folsom Prison saw a large influx of prisoners in the early Twenties, particularly among minorities. Overcrowding at San Quentin in 1923 resulted in 137 new wards at Folsom. Construction on a new Folsom dining hall began that year, and additional farmland was purchased to feed the growing prison population.

After seven years, legislators approved compensation in 1923 for the prisoners involved in the road camps, a work program considered a huge success. Warden J. J. Smith told the Board of Prison Directors, "A man leaving prison with a comfort-able amount of money earned by road work is certainly not apt to drift back into crime."

Finally, after fifteen years, the wall surrounding Folsom was completed in 1923. Although it thwarted many escapes, the wall never stopped desperate men from trying.

40. William Shortridge, May 2, 1919

On May 7, 1918, at around two-thirty in the morning, Officer James Wesley Mock attempted to arrest William Shortridge for robbing the Dawson House Hotel in Marysville. Shortridge had escaped to the railroad tracks in a brushy area when Mock found him. Mock whistled for assistance from other officers, but received no response. Shortridge resisted Mock's efforts to handcuff him. The two men wrestled and Shortridge grabbed for Mock's gun, prompting Mock to strike the suspect in the forehead several times with his club. Without being restrained by handcuffs, Shortridge was able to wrestle Mock's gun away and fire.

A bullet struck Mock, who fell to the ground, while, once again, Shortridge made a getaway. A posse of citizens and officers later found him in a grain field, where they arrested him. A week later, Mock died from the gunshot wound. Shortridge pleaded not guilty, claiming he shot Mock in self-defense. He testified that he promised Mock he'd go peacefully, but only if Mock didn't cuff him. Of course, Mock wouldn't agree to that. When the men struggled, Shortridge claimed Mock threatened to kill him.

After receiving a guilty verdict and death sentence, Shortridge appealed, citing several court errors, including allowing Mock's dying statement to be read in court. The defense deemed it invalid, questioning whether Mock believed he'd die. The California Supreme Court ruled otherwise, stating, "While the evidence is meager, nevertheless, it sufficiently appears from the statement of the district attorney, which deceased adopted as his own, that [Mock] later made the declaration and answers to the questions put by the district attorney, believing that his wound would prove fatal, and under a sense of impending death."

As a last request, Shortridge asked that someone write to his mother in Louisiana, informing her of his death. Reportedly "stolid until the end," Shortridge died on the gallows on May 2, 1919.

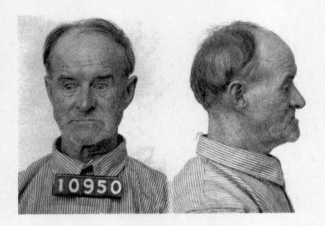

41. James Tyren, May 22, 1919

On May 6, 1918, Ida Mae Tyren, who was separated from her husband, threatened him with a divorce, citing Tyren's verbal and physical abuse toward their adopted son, twelve-year-old Holland. James Tyren allegedly responded, "Yes, you start it, and I will do the finish." The following day, Holland and his seven-year-old sister Alice left for school from their mother's house, then walked to their father's home for lunch. When the children didn't return home after school, Ida Mae called Tyren, demanding he bring their children to her. He refused. When she arrived, he answered the door and said, "I have killed them."

Investigators came upon a gruesome scene at Tyren's home. In the second story bathroom, they found the tub filled with bloody water, and the bodies of Holland and Alice were found lying on a bed in the adjoining room. Holland had been strangled and submerged in water. Alice's throat had been slashed. Tyren was discovered sitting on the floor of the room with a self-inflicted, but superficial, slash across his throat.

Arraigned for Holland's death, Tyren pleaded insanity, claiming he had no recollection of the crime. Tyren insisted he had been struck over the head numerous times in his life, suffering serious head injuries, including a kick from a mule. The defense also cited several head injuries he had sustained while working for the city of Sacramento streets department. Calling their client "shell shocked," defense attorneys pointed out several scars on his head. The defense called attention to other injuries Tyren suffered, including a missing toe and a "badly misshapen back," which caused Tyren constant pain.

To prove premeditation, the prosecution relied upon a disjointed, rambling handwritten note Tyren had scribbled on the back of the divorce summons:

Now that I have worked so hard for what we have got and you want to take the children and everything in it is too much for me and I never was in court and I hope I never will be only before my God and you will suffer just as much as I by the time you see this I hope me and my boy and my little sunshine will be no more trouble to from yours James Tyren.

Tyren had nicknamed his daughter "Sunshine." The jury convicted Tyren of murder in the first degree. Sentenced to death, Tyren appealed, but the higher court affirmed the judgment. On May 22, 1919, just over a year after the heinous crime, Tyren swung from the noose at Folsom Prison.

42. David Clifton, October 21, 1921

During April 1920, David Clifton shared a house with Harry Smith and two women, Cora Fisher and a Miss Watson. Trouble between Clifton and his friend Smith began when the former sprinkled red pepper throughout the building in an apparent effort to dispel the "hoo-doo" and evil spirits he felt inhabited the house. According to Watson, Clifton drew a knife and Fisher threw him out of the house.

Watson testified in court that the day before the crime, Clifton and Smith had argued over money and Smith told Clifton to leave the house. The following day, Watson reportedly witnessed Clifton sharpening a large knife, saying, "It would do the work." On April 9, Smith and Clifton were drinking heavily with another man named Pat when a fight over who would go out to get more liquor broke out between Smith and Clifton. Watson and a witness named Miller saw Clifton repeatedly stabbing Smith with a knife, while Smith pleaded with him to stop.

Clifton fled the house but police found him shortly thereafter, leaning on a fence, the bloody knife still in his pocket. Clifton claimed he killed Smith in self-defense, despite having told investigators that Smith didn't have a weapon on his person. The court relied on Watson's testimony, even though no one could corroborate her statements. California Supreme Court Chief Justice Frank Angelotti called Watson's testimony "somewhat rambling and unconvincing."

In fact, Angelotti wrote to Governor William Stephens urging him to commute Clifton's sentence to life, calling Clifton and the others "ignorant and superstitious."

Stephens refused clemency. Clifton was hanged on October 21, 1921.

43. Felipe Bisquere, January 26, 1923

Twenty-year-old Felipe Bisquere worked in the box factory for the M. J. Scanlon Lumber Company in Plumas County. He had previously been employed in the company cookhouse. On October 31, 1922, Superintendent C. N. Cox ate breakfast in the company dining room with his wife. Bisquere sat at a nearby table.

When Cox and his wife got up to leave, Bisquere turned his stool, making a noise that prompted Cox to ask what was the matter. Bisquere jumped to his feet and shot Cox twice, once in the neck and once in the chest, killing him instantly. Police arrived and immediately arrested Bisquere.

On the advice of his attorney, Bisquere pleaded guilty, although he provided no clear motive for the shooting. During his testimony Bisquere made an obscure statement: "I was working in the kitchen and putting food on the table and the people say they going to kill me for the electric." Bisquere said that he then purchased a gun. Over the next three months, he became convinced that Cox was plotting to murder him. The jury had difficulty deciphering Bisquere's responses, calling them incoherent and confusing, and returned with a guilty verdict. The judge sentenced Bisquere to death. Less than three months after the killing, on January 26, 1923, Bisquere was executed.

**"Dope started me in my way. I've seen the time I'd give my life for the stuff.
Now I'm giving it any way."**
—George Donnelly, on the scaffold, 1923

44. George Donnelly, February 23, 1923

In 1874, at the age of five, George Donnelly and his family emigrated from Scotland to San Francisco. At fifteen, Donnelly landed himself in Preston School of Industry, a reform school in Ione, California. For the next thirty-seven years, Donnelly bounced between California's two state prisons for burglary convictions. In November 1921, in the midst of serving his sixth prison term for burglary, fifty-three-year-old Donnelly stabbed fellow Folsom convict Earl Morse to death.

The murder that signaled the end to Donnelly's sad story happened as about eighty convicts lined up for breakfast. Morse and another inmate began arguing. Donnelly stepped in and stabbed Morse in the jugular, severing his spinal cord. Morse stayed conscious long enough to tell prison officials that the "cell tender" did it (at the time, Donnelly held that particular post). Another convict found the bloody prison-made knife in a bathroom trash can. Donnelly admitted killing Morse and said, as reported by the *Modesto Evening News*, "I'd kill the same man over again for what he did to me." Donnelly never elaborated on his motive, but only said that a sudden quarrel arose between him and Morse. Later, he implied in his appeal that because Morse's strength was superior to his own, Donnelly feared bodily harm from Morse.

Found guilty and sentenced to death, Donnelly appealed to the higher court, but to no avail. As he stood on the scaffold, he told the gathered witnesses, "Dope started me in my way. I've seen the time I'd give my life for the stuff. Now I'm giving it any way." He also said, "Goodbye, Eddie," presumably to a newspaperman he knew. Donnelly dropped through the trap on February 23, 1923.

"I've taken a life and I'll give one, but don't ever tell my wife."
—Alex A. Kels, 1923

45. Alex A. Kels, January 4, 1924

In September 1923, wandering laborer Edward Meservey found himself at an employment agency in Lodi, California. Jobs were scarce and he knew that, being in his sixties, he'd encounter tough competition from younger, stronger workers.

Into the employment agency walked Alex Kels, a wealthy butcher who kept a ranch outside of town. Kels eyed Meservey. As one newspaper put it, "He picked [Meservey] out from a group as carefully as he would a cow for butchering." Kels told Meservey he needed work done on a windmill located on his property, and, in return, he promised $2.50 a day, plus board. The pay exceeded Meservey's expectations and he agreed to go to work as soon as possible. The men shook hands and left together in Kels's car.

That night, September 12, ranchers found the car burning in a haystack in a farmer's field near Lodi, the finishing touches to a gruesome crime. The intense heat prevented neighbors from approaching the vehicle. When the burning mass had cooled, residents recognized the car as the one owned by the thirty-eight-year-old prominent butcher. They discovered a charred body in the back seat, on which they found Kels's keys and other personal belongings. Kels's wife Annie made a positive identification of the body. Investigators also found the butt of a revolver in the remnants of the car. Authorities declared robbery as the only plausible motive, noting that Kels had set out that day on a collection tour and had expected to deposit a large sum of money at the end of the day.

An autopsy revealed the victim had been shot twice and struck under the right eye with a blunt instrument, crushing his skull. After a couple of days, authorities abandoned the theory of robbery as the motive and started to investigate the victim himself, or the person whom both the public and the authorities presumed was the victim. Investigators learned Kels had recently taken out a few life insurance policies, equaling nearly a hundred thousand dollars, payable to his wife. At the same time, he organized a new meat company, incorporated for seventy-five-thousand dollars.

Amid the quiet investigation, Mrs. Kels planned her husband's funeral, sparing no expense for the interment of the highly respected businessman. Hundreds of mourners attended the funeral and did their best to console the pregnant Mrs. Kels and her nine-year-old daughter, Laverne. Soon after the services, Mrs. Kels, overcome with grief, became bedridden. Newspapers described her as "making no effort to live" and suggested that her death and the death of her unborn child was expected any day.

Mrs. Kels had heard, but refused to entertain, rumors that her husband had possibly staged his death to collect the life insurance. She fully believed she buried her beloved Alex and even offered a $1000 reward to the first person to prove they had seen her husband alive after September 12. "I do not understand where all the terrible rumors have sprung [from] insinuating that Alex is alive. They found his money and keys in his burned automobile. Isn't that proof enough that he perished in the flames?"

She remained under the around-the-clock care of physicians, nurses, and priests. Newspapers, incoming mail, and magazines were kept from her; she was told that in her frail condition they were "bad for her eyes." Laverne, who enjoyed reading the newspaper, would be given the papers only after her aunt cut out any articles pertaining to her father, and she was told the missing sections were recipes and coupons.

The insurance companies formed their own suspicions and demanded another autopsy. The results proved startling. The victim's spine measured shorter than Kels's and an exam by dentists indicated the remains were those of someone else. Furthermore, pieces of clothing recovered from the fire did not correspond with articles worn by Kels. The absence of sardines, however, clinched it. Kels had purchased two cans of sardines that day, but the stomach of the charred body revealed no such trace of the canned fish.

Investigators had already concluded that the body in the car could not be Alex Kels when Thomas Bawden, a resident of Nevada, reported seeing Kels, his long-time friend, in a hotel lobby in Reno.

On October 1, San Joaquin County sheriff William Reicks and district attorney Marion Woodward, both old friends of Kels, made their way to the railroad yards of Eureka, California, where a man fitting Kels's description was reportedly walking around with a rifle. Inside an empty boxcar, the investigators found Alex Kels, sitting with a rifle barrel held in his mouth. Kels attempted to pull the trigger with his toes. After the gun failed to discharge, Kels gave himself up to his two friends. Kels carried three letters, one addressed to Reicks, another to his sister, and a final one to W. H. Lorenz, his friend and the president of the First National Bank. The letter to Lorenz asked him to do the best he could for Mrs. Kels and his children. "Please see that my sweethearts—my wife, daughter, and unborn child— are properly cared for."

Kels told different versions of the crime. Initially, he stated that he and his companion, "Mac," were held up and his companion killed. Then he claimed business rivals killed Mac, mistaking the laborer for Kels.

Eventually, Kels confessed: "I have always paid my bills and come clean, and I will come clean now." Kels told Reicks of going to the employment agency to hire a ranch hand who he insisted he knew only as "Mac." They left in Kels's car for his ranch outside Lodi and, once there, Kels ordered Meservey out of the car. He shot the laborer twice in the back with a .32 caliber revolver. Meservey groaned, but did not fall. Unsure his victim was dead, Kels hit him over the head with a heavy iron bar, crushing Meservey's skull. He wrapped the body in a blanket, laid him in the backseat of the car, and drove around for several hours, contemplating how to dispose of the body. He stopped at a service station to fill up and purchase the sardines.

At around nine o'clock in the evening, Kels pulled into a field fifteen miles from his ranch. He backed into a haystack, placed his keys into one of the dead man's pockets, and ignited the haystack with a lighted candle. He walked to Sacramento and bought a round-about ticket for Los Angeles, his subsequent wanderings taking him through Texas, Colorado, Arizona, Mexico, Nevada, and then back to California.

"You fellows have got it all figured out pretty well. I was heavily insured and I thought that was the best way to clean up," he told Reicks. He claimed his business affairs had become so tangled, he wanted to drop from sight and stage his own death to ensure that his wife had enough insurance money to pay his creditors. Kels intended to desert his family and flee to Mexico. Despite the danger of returning to California, Kels said he couldn't help but return because, "My friends are here and I had to come back." Kels had only one request during the trip home: He did not want his wife to know he was alive, and he expressed his concern, saying, "My God, it will kill her. I am sparing her the embarrassment of a long trial and putting this matter through just as quickly as possible. I hope that it is all over before she knows a thing about it."

On October 3, his birthday, the "Haystack Murderer" arrived in San Joaquin County to face a grand jury—many members of which were his old friends. A majority of the eight thousand residents of the prosperous little Sacramento Valley city knew Kels. Many expressed their sorrow for what had happened, making apologies, such as, "Something snapped inside of Alex's head." Several wild theories about what made Kels commit murder circulated, including the bizarre idea that he had drunk beef blood for nearly two weeks, causing him to go mad. According to Reicks and Woodward, Kels didn't act differently than the friend they had known for years. He was such a model prisoner from Eureka to Stockton that the sheriff found it unnecessary to cuff him.

No one knew how Kels planned to plea at his arraignment, since he had refused legal counsel. "If an attorney would defend me before a jury for twenty-five dollars, I wouldn't spend the money," he said. Reicks explained that Kels had expressed no regrets, denying that guilt or his conscience had prompted his suicide attempt in the railroad yard, but rather the constant fear of being a wanted fugitive. He said that everywhere he had gone while on the lam, he encountered someone he knew.

At his arraignment the next day, Kels pleaded guilty. George F. McNoble, Kels's longtime business attorney, who Kels refused to see, spoke to reporters: "It's all over. You newspapermen may as well go home. It's all settled that Kels will not hang. He will get life."

Kels puzzled officers, interviewers, and townspeople who thought they knew him. Reportedly, he enjoyed being the "life of the party" on the train from Eureka and acted joyful, playing entertainer to his guards. He had also suddenly become a heavy smoker, consuming cigarette after cigarette. However, reports from one jailer described Kels differently. "He is a broken man," he said, claiming Kels had cried on several occasions since arriving, especially when recalling old friends of his, men whom he called by their first names and who had been on the jury which indicted him. Some friends remained, declaring Kels to have been "railroaded," with "undue influence exerted over his mind, which had become unbalanced."

Mrs. Kels, meanwhile, didn't know her husband was alive, let alone sitting in the county jail, having just pleaded guilty to murder. By all accounts, she continued to believe she had buried him a month earlier. Her nurse, Mary Nolan, told reporters the child which Mrs. Kels carried was undoubtedly dead and Mrs. Kels would soon die, as well. The entire town of Lodi, obviously taking pity, conspired to keep the truth from Mrs. Kels and Laverne. Laverne's schoolmates, teachers, and neighbors participated in keeping the secret. Caretakers permitted her to only leave the house for school a few blocks away and to return home immediately afterward. They also "subtly persuaded" her not to venture downtown so that she wouldn't hear the newsboys crying out every published development in her father's case.

On October 8, Kels testified as a preliminary condition to passing sentence. Kels's statement varied in two respects from his original confession to Sheriff Reicks. He denied planning the murder in advance, whereas he had first confessed to taking three weeks to organize it. Second, he now identified the victim as Ed Meservey. Kels continued to refuse legal counsel, telling the judge, "I don't want to change my plea. I want to get it over with. If my wife found this out, she would try to save me." Young warned he would order the strongest penalty for the confessed murderer, saying, "Man, don't you know that I will have a mighty hard time showing you mercy the way you have figured in this case?" Kels nodded, but he wouldn't change his stance.

Judge Young then sentenced Kels to hang on January 4, 1924.

On October 27, to everyone's surprise, Mrs. Kels gave birth to a boy she named John Alex Kels. When Kels heard the news, he broke down in his cell and told the jailer, "I certainly made a horrible mess of things, didn't I?" He took a picture of his wife and daughter out of his pocket. "That's why I came back; otherwise, I wouldn't be here."

In mid-November, Mrs. Kels finally heard the truth about her husband, her friends having determined she had recovered well enough from her shock, grief, and recent childbirth to hear the news. According to Mrs. Nolan, Mrs. Kels "faced it heroically" and "never wavered." Annie Kels sent her husband a telegram: "Dear Alex: They have told me all. Pray God to give me strength to get to you. Your faithful and loving wife."

The following day, Mr. and Mrs. Kels reunited in the office of Warden J. J. Smith at Folsom Prison. With no outward scene, they sat side by side holding one another and talking quietly, tears streaming from their eyes. She came unaccompanied by children. Kels asked about his newborn son, who was still too young to bring in a car from Lodi to the prison. No one mentioned the crime and the meeting lasted an hour, the limit for prison visits. After the reunion, Mrs. Kels collapsed—one of many collapses she'd have—and had to be carried to a car. Through her sister-in-law, Mrs. H. A. Staples, Mrs. Kels released a statement declaring her husband insane: "An examination will prove it."

That statement by Mrs. Kels marked the beginning of what would become a bitter fight of wills between the California Governor, Friend William Richardson, and members of the Board of Prison Directors, pinning Warden Smith in the middle. It became a battle where insults abounded, threats of lawsuits were made, and resignations tendered.

Mrs. Kels told Woodward that her husband had not been himself for three to four months previous to the crime, often displaying "those moody, morose spells." Moreover, she'd repeatedly find him in the rocking chair, head in hands, distracted, and impatient with their young daughter. She said her husband told her a gang was after him and he took to carrying a revolver with him at all times. She asserted, "Mr. Kels always was most of the time very kind and generous hearted toward his family, never cross or mean and in the last three or four months he would be just as hateful and mean as can be."

Mrs. Kels could not understand her husband's claims of financial difficulties, as she worked as the bookkeeper for his business. "None of the banks were pressing him for money and he was successful and making good money," she said.

Mrs. Kels and Dr. Fred Clark, superintendent of the Stockton asylum, requested approval from Albert Boynton of the Board of Prison Directors for a particular test. Kels had informed doctors of the possibility he had been inflicted with syphilis and feared the disease affected his brain, therefore causing insanity. A spinal fluid test could prove the presence of the disease and, as a result, warrant further insanity examinations. Boynton granted the request despite the fact that the prison physician, Dr. Rogers, had already performed the test when Kels transferred to Folsom.

As warden, Smith had authority to determine if a prisoner was insane or had become insane since incarceration. Smith opposed the second test. "Kels is perfectly sane," he said. "Since he arrived at Folsom, he had been observed both by the prison physician and myself. We have no doubt of his sanity." Only a court order or a request from the governor would persuade him to allow the additional test. But the prison board wanted a "non-biased" test to be performed and suggested that three vials of fluid be extracted, each sent to different medical laboratories.

Ordinarily quiet, Kels said, "I am ready for my punishment. I do not care to have another sanity test made, but will submit to one if my wife and the warden wish it."

After Smith, who was still awaiting a court order, refused to permit the test, the president of the board, Charles McLaughlin, threatened to remove Smith and replace him with a man who would permit the test. Governor Richardson, a vocal, opinionated, and staunch supporter of the death penalty, stepped in. He had harsh words for the board. "The prison board has strangely and illegally ordered the warden to have Kels tested for syphilis . . . the action of the prison board may be of help to the insurance companies. The people, I believe, will be able to detect the Ethiopian in the woodpile."

Richardson had contended from the beginning of the case, he believed Kels to be sane. "If the murderer is sane enough to plan the crime, he was sane enough to foresee the consequences if caught," he said. In response to the governor's statement, Mrs. Kels tearfully declared she would appeal to the governor until the last moment. "The governor will understand and be lenient when he knows my story. My God, why should he try to make an example out of Alex?"

That's exactly what Richardson intended to do. He asserted firmly, "His execution will be a warning to criminals all over California and will thus prove a protection to every citizen in the state."

Feeling pressured, Smith permitted the spinal fluid test and, on December 19, three vials of fluid were extracted from the condemned man's spine. Doctors sent each vial to a different laboratory in the state, one being the Stanford Medical School. The entire attention of the state focused on the gray walls of Folsom Prison to see what political spectacle would happen if the test came back positive. Two days before Christmas, all three tests result were reported, showing no signs of syphilis.

A heartbroken Mrs. Kels collapsed when she heard the news. She had pinned all hope on the outcome of the test. Still, her determination to save her husband from the gallows never waned: "I am going to the governor on Christmas Eve when Peace and Good will are supposed to prevail among all men. Surely, he will commute the sentence of hanging to life imprisonment." Richardson agreed to hear her out, but admitted little could be done to prevent the execution.

Then, on January 2, 1924, Richardson announced he could not grant Mrs. Kels's request. "This law was enacted by the people," he stated, "and Kels must pay the penalty for violation of it. The wife and young children of the murderer deserve sympathy but it should be remembered that Kels deliberately brought this sorrow and disgrace upon them. There is not a single fact in which to base any action for commutation of sentence."

The day before the hanging, Kels visited with his wife and sister, Mrs. Staples. It was the last time Mrs. Kels saw her husband alive. After their hour-and-a-half meeting, Mrs. Kels screamed with agony as guards took her husband to his lonely cell to await his death. The *Nevada State Journal* claimed Mrs. Kels collapsed once more and had to be carried to the warden's office. According to the guards who led him away after his visit, Kels didn't give way to grief, but instead lit a cigarette and picked up his Bible.

Many predicted Mrs. Kels, the "Iron Woman of Lodi," would surely go insane as the result of the mental strain she'd been under for the past couple of months. The *Oakland Tribune* said her screams had disturbed the entire neighborhood. "The condition of Mrs. Kels is serious," said tending physician, E. S. Grisby, "and it is impossible to state at this time whether she will go insane, die of a broken heart or recover. She is a complete mental and total wreck, suffering nervous prostration in the extreme. I hope and believe she will eventually recover, but it will be months. She will not be able to leave her bed for many weeks. Laverne, the daughter, is suffering a complete breakdown."

Jailers claimed that on the night before his death, Kels laughed and joked with his night watchman, narrating amusing adventures concerning his life during the previous September. The newspapers reported that at 10:05 the next morning, Alex Kels went to his death smiling. He had no last words on the gallows, but had earlier thanked the warden and prison officers for showing him every consideration. According to the *Lodi Sentinel*, Mrs. Kels slept "under the effects of drugs" given to her by Grisby, so that she could be "spared the torture of knowing that her husband was being yanked into eternity."

Kels took with him any secrets regarding what citizens considered one of the strangest cases of murder and attempted fraud the state of California had ever seen. His story held not only the attention of Californians, but that of much of the country, which witnessed the series of disputes that rocked the civil structure of the state. The *Modesto Evening News* surmised, "Kels did not die hard, the guards said, who had seen men die thus. To the novices in the death chamber, it seemed that he did die hard—terribly hard. The slightly twitching shoulders, the swaying legs that writhe at first—it must be some such horrible picture that Alex Kels carried in his mind of the death of Ed Meservey, his victim."[1]

Another funeral occurred for "the man who died twice," but unlike the elaborate service held before, the second one paled in comparison, attended only by family. Kels's body rests in a plot less than a hundred yards from his victim, who, thanks to Henry Clay Boniface, caretaker of the St. Joachim's Catholic cemetery, finally received a proper monument. On a slab of concrete, he painted, "Ed Meservey, Died September 12, 1923 A Poor Unfortunate, Famous in Death." "Every man is entitled to a tombstone; just because he had no friends is no sign he should have an unmarked grave," said Boniface.

The *Reno Evening Gazette* wrote that a shrieking Mrs. Kels, overcome with grief, nearly leapt into the grave of her now dead husband, but was caught by her brother-in-law, William. She did, evidently, collapse twice during the service.

Then another development related to the increasingly bizarre case occurred. Kels first wife, Mrs. Ruby Kels—or "Princess Whitecloud," her vaudeville stage name—came forward. She sought partial payment of the insurance money for her and Kels's sixteen-year-old son, Armande Andrew Kels. No doubt, Mrs. Annie Kels had another fainting spell. Everyone knew Kels had married previously, but the news of a child from that union proved shocking.

"Draped in costly furs and wearing expensive jewelry, Princess Whitecloud—as she prefers to be called—told of her marriage at the age of fifteen to Kels, who was then nineteen," reported the *Modesto Evening News*. The pair divorced shortly after she gave birth. "I am asking nothing for myself," she said. "But my boy is not to be cheated." Her attempt to receive money proved unsuccessful.

The political aftermath of the Kels case continued. Still fuming over the dispute with the governor, Boynton and B. B. Meek, another member of the prison board, resigned from their posts, and Richardson did not reappoint McLaughlin after his term expired shortly following the hanging. On March 22, 1924, Mrs. Kels, issued what she called her "final statement to the world." In it, she asserted that her husband, during his last few days, confided in her the truth of the crime:

---

1. According to the *Lodi Sentinel*, as Alex Kels's body left the prison, another car carrying "two negroes from Los Angeles County, both condemned to die," entered the prison. The men were #47 Robert Mathews and #48 Joe Sinuel. Guards apparently remarked,"It was well for the peace of mind of the occupants of the second machine that they were unaware of the contents of the first."

Alex did not commit murder to cheat an insurance company. I wondered why his conscience did not seem to bother him and during the last visit I paid to him at Folsom Prison, I implored him to tell me the truth. He said that he was not alone in what he did, but that he wouldn't reveal the names of those who aided him. "Their consciences will cause them to come out and tell the truth."

She concluded with, "And now, for the sake of my two children, I want the world to know that Alex Kels is not as black as he was painted."

No one came forward offering to shed light on the case, or to come clean with a confession. After threats of a lawsuit, Mrs. Kels eventually received twenty-nine thousand dollars in insurance money and another thirteen thousand for property owned by her husband.

Mrs. Annie Kels never remarried, remaining in the Lodi area until her death in 1977. Her daughter Laverne became a best-selling novelist and her son, John, a first lieutenant in the Air Force, receiving the distinguished Flying Cross in 1944 at twenty-years of age. As of 2012, Laverne's daughter, Janis, served on the board for Murder Victims' Families for Reconciliation and was also the organization's liaison for California Crime Victims for an Alternative to the Death Penalty.

CHANGING OF THE GUARD

On June 23, 1924, Captain of Guard Patrick J. Cochrane was inspecting the rock quarry when a cable snapped and the masthead, or boom, of a derrick broke free. The fifty-one-year-old Irishman and father of four was killed when the masthead struck him. Cochrane began working at the prison in December of 1891. Clarence Larkin, future Folsom warden, took over as captain.

"She was a nice young woman, and looking mighty fine, too."
—Martin Sliscovich, speaking of his victim, 1923

46. Martin Sliscovich, August 22, 1924

On November 22, 1922, Martin Sliscovich stood in the doorway to Jennie Radman's kitchen carrying a loaded .32 Colt revolver. Radman, her friend Domina Lebedina, and John Sliscovich, Martin's cousin, sat in chairs around the small stove. Radman's three young children and Lebedina's child played on the floor nearby. Two of Martin's friends, a man known as "Big George" and another, Matt Klapis, were also present.

Everyone had been drinking "jackass brandy," a bootlegged specialty of Radman's, whose house on Sacramento's O Street doubled as a speakeasy. She had cut Martin off, serving him his last drink moments before he went upstairs for his gun. Martin later said he had no intention of using the gun, but said he merely planned to "Go to say 'Good night.' That is what I do all the time—regular gentleman. I am no bum. I am no—I don't look like a bum, either."

Instead, when he saw Radman and his cousin sitting close, and heard them say his name, everything "turned black." He shot Radman three times and then shot John. Both died almost instantly. Martin went upstairs to a bedroom, placed the gun on the bed, and fled the house. Police didn't locate him until the following May in San Diego.

At his trial, Martin testified that he and Radman had an intimate relationship that turned south when she took up with John Sliscovich and another man, Joe Babich. Martin moved out of the house. A cook by trade, Martin began working on plans to open a restaurant. However, he continued to visit Radman and drink the bootlegged brandy. He claimed that he had become ill on the night in question and that Radman cared for him, even serving him more alcohol. Then "Big

George" and Klapis told Martin that a "colored plasterer" who had worked on the house had been poisoned by drinking Radman's brandy, and that another man lost $80 after drinking the same concoction.

Martin became convinced Radman had attempted to poison him that night. This, according to the defense, coupled with the alleged whispering between Radman and John Sliscovich, led Martin to shoot the pair. Much of Martin's testimony centered on his drinking. Said to have a "keen sense of humor," the Slavic native often entertained the courtroom with his musings. For instance, Martin commented about his drinking habit: "I find out now water better than anything else is; coffee make me nervous, wine makes me feel funny, and jackass brandy make me crazy; beer make me big and fat, you can't work, do nothing, so all that stuff—water make you nice clear mind; you know what you are doing."

The jury rejected the defense's insanity claim and sided with the prosecution, who called the murder a "cold-blooded and atrocious one, [which] seem[ed] to have been committed by a man with utter disregard for human life."

After an unsuccessful appeal, Martin Sliscovich mounted the gallows on August 22, 1924, and parted with his final words, "Goodbye, boys." According to the *Oakland Tribune*, Martin's death took the longest on record at Folsom Prison—fifteen minutes, thirty-five seconds.

Robert Matthews

"Ah jes' wanta thank you all
for the way you've treated
me here."
—Joe Sinuel, on the gallows, 1924

47. Robert Matthews, December 12, 1924, 48. Joe Sinuel, December 19, 1924

On the evening of October 30, 1923, Robert Matthews and Joe Sinuel entered a grocery store owned and operated by sixty-two-year-old Coleman Stone in Los Angeles County. Murphy Williams, Colonel Pope, and James Warmley sat outside in a car owned by Pope's employer, with the engine running.

Stone and his wife were in a back room counting the receipts from the day. Stone saw the men and met them at the counter. Sinuel laid down a dollar to purchase a pack of cigarettes, while Matthews went around the counter to where Stone stood. After a brief scuffle, Matthews struck the grocer over the head with a club. Witnessing the scene, Stone's son-in-law turned to retrieve a gun, but the next instant, Sinuel drew a gun and shot Stone. According to Stone's daughter, who watched the horrifying event, Sinuel leaned over Stone, kicked him in the head, then proceeded to search the body for valuables. The two men then ran out of the store.

Stone died the following day, but not before giving a statement. He declared, "one of the darkies had a slug in one hand and a revolver in the other," while the other demanded money. Stone replied, "I will give you all I got," which amounted to less than two dollars.

When Matthews and Sinuel raced from the store, they discovered their getaway car had left without them. When the men waiting in the car outside of the grocery store heard the shot, they panicked and immediately fled the scene. Sinuel and Matthews escaped on foot. They were driven to La Jolla by Pope a couple of days later, and captured soon after arriving.

Police also apprehended Williams and Pope, but Warmley was never found. Based on testimony from Stone's son-in-law, as well as the four defendants, a jury found them all guilty. Williams and Pope received life sentences, while Sinuel and Matthews received the death penalty.

Both men appealed their verdicts, but the appeals were unsuccessful. In an attempt to at least save his companion, Sinuel wrote to Governor Richardson, taking full responsibility for the murder. The governor determined Matthews to be equally responsible for the murder. Matthews went to his death first on December 12, 1924. One week later, on December 19, Sinuel met the same fate.

PART VI: 1925–1930

Folsom Wardens: J. J. Smith, November 16, 1913–February 2, 1927

Court Smith, March 1927–April 18, 1936

California Governors: Friend Richardson, January 9, 1923–January 4, 1927

Clement C. Young, January 4, 1927–January 6, 1931

The second half of the Roaring Twenties proved just as tumultuous as the first, if not more so. With Prohibition still in effect, Americans continued bootlegging and patronizing speakeasies. Organized crime had also found its niche. Gangsters like Al Capone made millions selling alcohol. Instilling fear through the use of pervasive violence, organized crime quickly monopolized the sale of bootlegged liquor, taking control of nearly the entire black market. Because illegally manufactured alcohol was of such poor quality, deaths by alcohol poisoning rose 400 percent and the unemployment rate soared, most from the loss of formerly legal alcohol-related industries, particularly in agriculture. Police were overtaxed and stretched thin, and the crime rate rose. Those convicted of drug or alcohol charges rapidly filled the prisons. California's legislature responded in 1927 by passing the Habitual Criminal Law, similar to today's Three-Strikes Law, which made a criminal's third felony punishable by life imprisonment.

Gambling helped the decade roar even louder. Notorious bootlegger and gambling kingpin Anthony Cornero operated several gambling ships in the international waters off the coast of California, most notably out of Santa Monica. Patrons lined the piers waiting for their chance to board the *S. S. Rex*, the most luxurious of Cornero's ships, which took in an estimated $20,000 per day.

Fortunately, the decade wasn't completely consumed by vice and crime. Californians enjoyed newfound freedom thanks to Henry Ford. Thriving mass production made one in five Americans a car owner, often for the astonishingly low price of $290. When San Francisco's Great Highway was completed in 1929, motorists lined up to experience the scenic 3.5-mile stretch along Ocean Beach. And in San Francisco, countless riders paid a nickel to transverse the city via the Market Street Railway Company's popular mass transit system.

Millions of Californians filled movie theaters each week, watching Charlie Chaplin, Buster Keaton, and Greta Garbo come to life on the silver screen. The Columbia Broadcasting System began entertaining listeners in 1927 with jazz, as well as sports and live events. The surrealism and art deco movements were showcased across the state, from the Paramount Theater in Oakland to the Los Angeles Public Library. Frank Lloyd Wright left his mark by designing a number of homes and businesses throughout California.

Everything came to a screeching halt in October 1929. The country, already suffering from the early onset of an economic downturn, plummeted into a depression after the New York Stock Exchange collapsed. It would take the United State's involvement in World War II before the country rebounded from "The Crash." With the desperation spurred by the economy came more crime, and Folsom saw another rise in population. Construction began on a new cell building consisting of 310 new cells, a new hospital, and an administration building. Thanks to the foresight of Warden Johnston during the mid-1910s, the established farm at Folsom sustained the prison during the economic crisis.

"I don't think much of that jury, and they have something on their conscience, believe me."
—John Geregac, after a guilty verdict, 1924

49. John Geregac, January 16, 1925

On November 27, 1923, instead of being home with his wife, Charles Chapman sat in his parked car on a secluded "Lovers' Lane" with another woman. Unfortunately for him, John "Smokey" Geregac and his two crime companions, Jack Ferdinand and John Sears, were out that night targeting adulterous couples. Knowing their victims preferred financial loss over publicity, the bandits felt confident they'd elude capture.

The men had already robbed two couples in a car and forced the driver by gunpoint to take them to another location, while the three robbers rode on the running boards of the vehicle. They spotted their next victims and ordered the driver to stop. Ferdinand and Sears approached Chapman's car, while Geregac stayed behind, his gun trained on the four others. Ferdinand forced the couple from the car and rifled through Chapman's pockets. Sears aimed his gun at Chapman's female companion, Catherine Boehmer, after he had ripped open her dress looking for cash.

Chapman remained with his hands up, while Ferdinand stood behind him. Without warning or provocation, Ferdinand shot Chapman in the back. As Chapman lay dying, Ferdinand continued to rummage through the man's pockets. They finally jumped back onto the running board of the hijacked car and left the scene, leaving Catherine Boehmer to find help for Chapman. When she returned several minutes later, she found that Chapman had managed to drag himself several feet toward the car. However, he died before help could arrive.

Meanwhile, the wanton trio robbed yet another couple before ordering their driver to take them to an area near their own car. There, they threw away the driver's car key, leaving the four hijacked victims stranded.

139

Ferdinand and Sears returned their car, a "rent for hire," to the garage, where they were apprehended and arrested by police officers. One of them carried Chapman's wallet. The police chief of Los Angeles boasted of their capture. "Tell the criminals, the highway men, burglars and gunmen just to stay in the city and we'll get them." Ferdinand and Sears implicated Geregac in their confession.

Thirty-year-old Ferdinand, a "hardboiled" criminal, had already spent time in Folsom Prison, yet Sears and Geregac, both in their early twenties, had no prior convictions. All three were tried together, each pleading not guilty. Based on eyewitness testimony, the jury easily found Ferdinand and Sears guilty of first-degree murder, but wavered on Geregac's guilt. It took another day for the jury to finally agree that Geregac was equally responsible for Chapman's death. It marked the first time in Los Angeles County that murder accomplices received the death penalty.

"We're just the goats in a drive on crime," Sears said, referring to himself and Geregac. "We never killed anybody, but just because we don't amount to anything socially, we're to die for a crime we never committed. Everybody knows the rich man or the good-looking woman never gets the death verdict."

Police officers and other officials praised the verdict, calling it a warning to other criminals. It also sparked an interesting observation among citizens and newspaper editors regarding women jury members. One Illinois newspaper applauded the "weaker sex" for remaining obdurate in their decision. It was clear the public had expected the three women jurors to be lenient on the young men because of their "pleasing appearance."

"It's not fair," Geregac said. "We didn't shoot anybody. I wasn't in any way connected with the holdup of the man who was shot. And even if Jack Sears and I could be convicted legally of being accomplices, this was a hard-hearted verdict. Jack here and I are just being made examples of."

That is exactly what the courts intended. Governor Friend Richardson agreed, saying, "This is a matter where society must be protected, where the law must be upheld, and where an example may be made which will help sustain the very foundations of society." Richardson rejected Geregac's plea for clemency, contending that he "made no protest and no effort to disassociate himself from his companions but went ahead and participated in the third robbery."

Even Jack Ferdinand lamented his companions' fate, remarking, "I wish I could pay the penalty alone. There's no need for those other men to die. I'm ready to go. I'm getting what's coming to me." While Ferdinand and Sears mounted the San Quentin gallows, Geregac faced the spectators crowded into Folsom's death house. All three met their deaths simultaneously on January 16, 1925.

That same day, state senator Roy Fellom submitted a bill to the legislature to abolish capital punishment. Fellom commented, "I wish I could have introduced this measure sooner in order to save the lives of those three men. Let's hope that this horrible spectacle of three men being executed in cold blood by the state of California will be the last of its kind and that the state will never again be subjected to witnessing anything so barbaric."

50. Ed Montijo, July 10, 1925

On February 20, 1924, Ed Montijo, Tom Bailey, and brothers Lewis and Oscar Perry arrived at the Merchants National Bank in Los Angeles, intending to rob it. Oscar Perry remained in the car. Montijo positioned himself in the front of the bank, near the entrance. Lewis Perry and Tom Bailey entered at the rear of the bank and pointed their guns at customers and bank employees, including bank security officers Glenn E. Bond and F. W. Forbes.

Witnesses couldn't determine who fired first, Perry or Bond, but a gunfight ensued. Bond received two bullets in the chest, which proved fatal, and Perry sustained one in his chest. Forbes suffered a minor head wound from a shot likely fired by Bailey. The three robbers were able to escape from the bank, but without any bank money. Lewis Perry needed urgent medical attention, so his brother Oscar took him to Dr. Gordon Bayliss, telling the doctor his brother had accidentally shot himself. After treatment, Oscar took Lewis to his home to recover.

After being informed by Dr. Bayliss of his wounded patient, police arrested the Perry brothers at their home. A few days later, Montijo and Bailey were also arrested. Lewis Perry, Bailey and Montijo were tried together, each pleading not guilty. (Oscar Perry was tried separately, found guilty, and sentenced to five years to life. He earned parole after nine and a half years). Because the homicide occurred during the course of a felony, each defendant received a charge of first-degree murder, punishable by death. The trial lasted two weeks. After deliberating for eighteen hours, the jury returned a guilty verdict.

The *Modesto Evening News* reported, "Bailey sat in his cell today shaking, voice husky. 'I must have been crazy,' he mumbled. 'If I had only thought—it hardly seems fair to hang for someone you didn't kill but I should have thought.'" The paper went on to describe Montijo, saying he remained quiet and appeared to have the mental capacity of a ten-year-old. "His eyes were red, showing signs of weeping. He was not nervous, only sad and hopeless."

Lewis Perry, called "agreeable and polite," only smiled, as he made a statement: "It's all in the business. We took a chance and here we are. It's fair enough, I guess, for me, for I'm the one who shot. The bull shot at me, too, though. Wasn't Montijo white about it though? He had a chance to plead guilty and take life, but he wouldn't do it because it would hang Bailey and me."

Lewis Perry attempted to prove he hadn't been eighteen on the date of the crime, the death penalty being prohibited for minors. However, a record from Preston School of Industry had him at nineteen on the date the crime was committed. Perry insisted he had lied to the school about his age, but without further proof, Perry's argument failed. Bailey tried to convince an appellate court that police obtained his confession fraudulently. Bailey contended the police informed him that Lewis Perry had died, but not before confessing and implicating himself. After seeing Perry in the hospital with his eyes closed, Bailey believed the authorities and confessed. Police denied telling Bailey that Perry had died.

Montijo's parents, Mary and George, fought vainly to save their nineteen-year-old son from the death sentence. They presented testimony from five different psychologists who all deemed Montijo mentally deficient, saying his IQ was that of an eleven-year-old. On the morning of July 10, 1925, the day of execution, Dr. B. F. Howard told Judge Charles Busick in a last minute habeas corpus session that Montijo was not mentally competent. Folsom Prison physician C. G. Reynolds, however, told Busick that Montijo had not displayed any signs of insanity since incarceration.

When Judge Busick ruled against the defense, Montijo's mother rushed to her son's side. He had fainted at hearing the judgment. Hysterical, Mary Montijo screamed, "You can't take my boy away from me!" She had to be carried from the courtroom by friends. Within a couple of hours, late in the day of July 10, 1925, Edward Montijo stood with a noose around his neck on the Folsom gallows. Lewis Perry and Tom Bailey met their fate on the San Quentin gallows the same day.

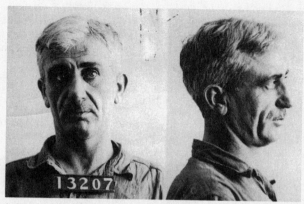

"You can't blame a man in the same condition I am if a chance comes up to make a get-away."
—John Connelly when arrested, 1924

51. John Connelly, July 24, 1925

On February 6, 1922, Officer Francis Heenan of Marysville in Yuba County responded to a gunshot that came from the Canteen Saloon on the corner of Second and C Streets. Inside the saloon, John Connelly, a.k.a. "Silver" Joe Kelly, shot at barkeep George Ladas, while attempting to rob the saloon. Ladas ducked and avoided the bullet. Connelly snagged a hundred dollars from the register, but when he turned to flee, he ran directly into Officer Heenan. Without hesitation, he fired at Heenan's chest and killed him instantly. Connelly stepped over the body and escaped.

Forty-five-year-old Francis Heenan, the oldest officer on the Marysville police force, who had participated in the arrests of two previous Folsom-executed men, had died at the hands of another soon-to-be-condemned man of Folsom. The city of Marysville responded with outrage at the killing of one of the city's finest, forming a campaign to "clean Marysville of bootleggers and criminals."

Police searched for Connelly, but it took two-and-a-half years to locate him. Recognized in part by his streak of gray hair, "Silver" Joe Kelly was captured in Douglas, Wyoming, in June 1924. "You can't blame a man in the same condition I am if a chance comes up to make a get-away," Connelly reportedly remarked after his capture. Both Ladas and Frank Somchano, another officer who had accompanied Heenan to the saloon, identified Connelly as the killer.

At the trial, witnesses placed Connelly at the scene. Pat Malloy, now himself a convict, testified he saw Connelly with the gun that killed Heenan an hour before the crime. Convicted and sentenced to death, Connelly appealed, insisting upon his innocence. In July 1925, Connelly lost his appeal, but it turned out he'd have an unlikely ally in his appeal attempt.

From a prison in Deer Lodge, Montana, inmate Malloy telegrammed Governor Friend Richardson, claiming he perjured himself, "If I did say anything against or for the state at [Connelly's] trial I lied, and what is more, I was so full of drugs I do not recall what I did say." Malloy's admission failed to persuade Richardson to issue a reprieve or commute Connelly's sentence. On July 24, 1925, Connelly "faced the end without fear" and "went to his death bravely, protesting his innocence to the very last."

"The older a man gets, the worse he is, you know."
—Mrs. Eva Bollinger, speaking of her husband's victim, 1924

52. Alfred Bollinger, October 9, 1925

For four weeks, the decaying, mangled body of Alex Summers lay concealed by overhanging boughs, submerged in the shallow, murky water of Simmerly Slough in Yolo County, a mere hundred yards from a well-traveled highway. On May 27, 1924, camper Dan McVey discovered Summers's body, along with a bloody axe, which presumably had crushed the victim's skull. For the next month, investigators attempted to identify the body, but no one had reported a missing person. Their only clues were that the victim wore a light blue work shirt, overalls, and heavy-ribbed underclothes. His feet were bare.

Stymied by lack of evidence, police nearly chalked this one up as the unsolved murder of an itinerant laborer, a common occurrence in automobile camps at the time. Had it not been for the "delirious mutterings" of a Mrs. Eva Bollinger, the crime might have gone unsolved. Her rapidly declining mental state brought Mrs. Bollinger to Dr. Dunlap at the Sacramento County hospital. Bollinger spouted "delirious ravings" that her husband Alfred had killed a man with an axe two months earlier. Her husband had threatened to kill her if she told, but fear preyed so heavily on her mind she could no longer stand it.

The doctor phoned Deputy Sheriff Harry Bryant, a call which immediately led to the arrest of Alfred Bollinger at the Sacramento home of Mrs. J. T. Tulley, his mother-in-law. Initially, Bollinger denied the crime, but after severe questioning, he confessed to bludgeoning Alex Summers to death with an axe. At the time of his arrest, Bollinger wore some of the dead man's clothing and had even shaved with his razor that morning.

Married only a few months, Alfred and Eva Bollinger frequently lived in automobile camps. She often worked in canneries, while he looked for other work. They met Summers at a camp near Sacramento when he sought aid for an arm injury. They became acquainted and decided to seek employment together on the road.

In the early hours of April 27, 1924, at Simmerly Slough near Marysville, Alfred Bollinger quietly crept into Summers's tent, picked up his axe, and raised it high above his head. His victim awoke, but not in time. Bollinger, the father of six from a previous marriage, struck Summers several times. He then gathered the hacked up body, along with the bloody clothing and linens, wrapped it all in a blanket, and hid it in the dense underbrush of the nearby slough.

Bollinger woke his wife and told her they needed to leave. Bollinger later related to officers that Summers had threatened his life more than once, the last time being the night before the murder. Another motive was suggested by Mrs. Bollinger. She stated Alfred was "singularly fond of animals and lavished most of his affection upon his dog." Summers apparently had mistreated the animal.

Eva described Summers as fifty years old. "He used to hang around me all the time," she reported, adding, "The older a man gets, the worse he is, you know. Alex

THE POPULARITY OF AUTOMOBILE CAMPS

During the early 1900s, as the number of cars increased, so did the number of automobile enthusiasts. Having the ability to transport goods, or merely explore, drivers looked to the open roads for work and adventure. Hotels along popular driving routes were still rare, so these auto "gypsies" likened themselves to pioneers by camping alongside the road or in designated areas. In 1924, the number of cars in America reached 19 million, with an estimated 5 million cars and 15 million people occupying campgrounds across the country. As their popularity grew, many municipal campgrounds added cabins with amenities for the weary traveler. These served as ideal stops for those who ventured from town to town, taking odd jobs along way.

objected [to] my supporting my husband and often told me so, right in front of Al." She also stated her husband was jealous of the attention Summers paid to her. She reassured him by saying, "If I was going to have anything to do with a man, I wouldn't have anything to do with an old man, but I would pick a young man."

After the murder, the Bollingers traveled to Napa, where Alfred pawned Summers's watch for ten dollars, adding it to the hundred-and-ten dollars he had stolen from the victim's body. He then sold the dead man's horse and wagon for fifteen dollars near Sacramento. Subsequently, the Bollingers lived with Mrs. Tulley until Bollinger's arrest on June 27, nearly a month later.

Relieved at the arrest of her husband, Eva declared, "I have nothing against Bollinger. Even though he did threaten to kill me if I told on him. He is suffering for that. Everybody seemed to look at me with suspicion on the street and I couldn't bear to see him worrying so. I'm glad the awful secret is off my mind." Although referred to as the "traitor-wife" by the *Oakland Tribune*, she believed her husband shouldn't hang, saying, "The penitentiary is bad enough."

Mrs. Bollinger's past marriages provided more newsworthy fodder than her husband's crime. Alfred Bollinger was not only Eva's fourth husband, but, in fact, he was her fourth *murdering* husband. In a tearful interview with the *Oakland Tribune* on July 16, 1924, under the headline, "Mrs. Eva Bollinger of Marysville Tells Her Harrowing Experiences as Bride of Men with Blood Lust," she related her torrid marital past and the existence of a fifteen-year-old daughter who "lives a tranquil life in a convent . . . but I shan't tell her name! She shall never know, if I can help it, what disgrace I have suffered." Vera, the daughter, stayed ignorant of her stepfather's crime, as well as that of her own father's.

Called the "strange little woman," Mrs. Bollinger couldn't understand why all of her husbands turned into killers. She surmised, "All men aren't that way. I've just had bad luck."

In the meantime, Bollinger pleaded not guilty, claiming self-defense, but he did not take the stand. After a short deliberation, the trial jury found him guilty of first-degree murder. His attorneys immediately filed an appeal to the California Supreme Court. The following day, Eva issued a statement to the newspapers, charging her mother with the deed of turning in her son-in-law: "My mother asked me the cause of my illness and I broke down and told her of the secret weighing on my heart. I was taken to the hospital then and my mother, whom I thought was my friend, blabbed to the officers. If she'd only kept her mouth shut, all this wouldn't have happened."

Before transferring to Folsom to await the outcome of his appeal, Alfred hatched a plan to escape from the county jail. Officers found a sharpened scissor blade, as well as a handful of cleaning lye. They theorized that Bollinger planned to stash the lye in his coat pocket, along with the handmade blade. Upon entering the court-room, he would throw the lye into the face of the sheriff to blind him. Then he'd stab the deputy sheriff in the back, grab his gun, and shoot his wife and the district attorney before escaping. Bollinger obviously did not have the opportunity or the gumption, as his plot did not materialize.

While awaiting the Supreme Court's decision, Eva wrote letters to the warden asking about the appeal. In one letter dated two days after sentencing, she pleaded with him. "Dear Mr. Warden is thair [sic] any thing I could do under the Sun to save his life [sic] My Husband is a good man and to take his life is afful [sic]. Can't the Death penalty be changed to life imprisonment?" She sent a letter in January of 1925 asking for any knowledge of the appeal and inquiring why "Mr. Bollinger don't [sic] write to me." Warden J. J. Smith responded that he had no answers to her inquiries. In July 1925, Mrs. Bollinger learned of her husband's fate via the newspapers. Alfred lost his appeal and a judge set aside October 9 for his execution.

On the morning of his execution, Bollinger chatted freely with guards as he ate the usual condemned man's breakfast of eggs, ham, griddle cake, and coffee. He made no statement on the scaffold and died "gamely" at 10:21 A.M.

Mrs. Eva Bollinger became Mrs. Eva Williams one week after her husband's execution. Several months later in an interview entitled, "Four Husbands Were Murderers, Hopes No. 5 Isn't," she said, "My luck has turned at last." She added that her newest mate, Calvin Williams, knew all about her tumultuous past and remained optimistic she would not turn him into a murdering man.

WHAT MADE HER HUSBANDS KILL?

In January of 1926, an article appeared in the *Zanesville Signal* entitled, "The Amazing Case of the Girl Who Married Four Murderers and How the Curse of the Gypsy Has Followed Her, Like an Avenging Fate, All Her Life."

As a young girl, Eva Chester read the Greek myth *The Three Fates*, the story of three goddesses who wove the story of everyone's life. Clotho saw people's lives on the fabric of her loom. Lachesis stood guard and determined who should be given a long life and who should not. But young Eva focused on the third fate, Atropos, or "The Inevitable," who broke off the "thread of life." Through her life, Eva never forgot about the story, and when she was seventeen and living in a convent, the story took on a new meaning.

The nuns organized a picnic along the Sacramento River where Eva and a few others wandered into a wooded area and came upon a gypsy camp. An old gypsy woman stood and stared at the girls. Eva recognized her immediately as "The Inevitable." The woman spoke to Eva, saying, "Daughter of Fate. Companion of woe. Wife of slayers! For your flouting of the Gypsy may the cup of fury be your portion. I see you marrying once, twice, thrice—four times. I see you standing before the altar and the sign of spilled blood is upon the forehead of each husband! And the fifth...."

Terrified, the girls ran from the gypsy camp. The incident left Eva shaken, but she refused to believe in the old woman's omen. A year later, Eva had a peculiar dream—the face of the dreaded Atropos appeared in front of her, shrieking and howling. The next day, she met her first husband, Charles Neff. Together they had a daughter named Vera.

They lived blissfully happy until Neff lost his job and started drinking. He went north to British Columbia to find work. He often wrote to Eva, expressing excitement for his family to soon join him. However, Neff became involved in a saloon brawl and hit a man with his fist, killing him. "It's the gypsy curse," Eva surmised. Neff went to prison for eight years and, in that time, urged Eva to divorce him and move on. She reluctantly complied.

After four years, the "Wife of Slayers" met Roe Damon, a tough, hard-working, and often jealous woodsman. Yet Eva described him as gentle and affectionate. As their marriage progressed, so did his violent temper and intense moods. Eva recalled going away for an overnight visit and leaving Vera with Roe. That night she dreamed once more of "The Inevitable." "I woke up with her screams in my ears," she said. Eva rushed home, where she learned from two neighbors that Damon had mistreated her daughter.

Eva took Vera and left him. The next day, Damon bludgeoned one of the neighbors to death with a hammer, put a bullet through the other, then shot and killed himself.

Eva denied the power of the curse, but still feared it, vowing to never marry again. It wasn't a promise she could keep. She soon married "Handsome Jim" Mellarkey, a "laughing, singing, jovial Irishman." He began "to have black days when he sat silently, plunged in deep thought," Eva recalled. Then he made a confession. As a young man, he shot and killed another man in a saloon over money and had spent seventeen years behind bars. Despite his admission, he and Eva remained married until he died in 1923. Eva made no more resolutions to outwit Fate. When she met the kind and loving Alfred Bollinger, she immediately consented to his marriage proposal after three weeks of courtship.

According to the article, "He had his own curious code of conduct. He never drank, nor smoked. He never swore. He worked hard and provided a better home that she had ever known before. He seemed to her very near ideal and she loved him more than she [had] loved the others." Eva had no idea that it would fall upon her shoulders to turn her fourth murdering husband over to the authorities when he hacked Alex Summers to death.

A week after Alfred Bollinger died on the scaffold, Eva married Calvin Williams, but still remembered the old crone's words: "Four times I see spilled blood, and the fifth….." As of 1926, the last date on record, Williams stayed on the good side of the law.

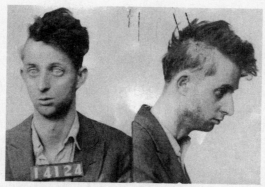

"They say I killed a policeman, but he's alive. . .He comes to me at
night and laughs at me."
—Felix Sloper, 1926

53. Felix Sloper, June 25, 1926

Felix Sloper spent most of his twenty-nine years committing robberies and
moving in and out of California's state prisons. His home life offered little in
way of support. One of six children, Sloper had an alcoholic father and a mother
who ran off with another man, earning her the nickname "Sloper the Eloper" in
one newspaper.

By the early 1920s, "Lone Wolf" Sloper had mastered stealing cars and selling
bootlegged liquor. In February of 1924, Sloper, along with Thomas "The Owl"
Griffin, held up the Clovis State Bank, netting more than thirty thousand dollars.
Police apprehended Griffin over a year later. His actions earned him a life sentence
at Folsom. Sloper escaped and wasted no time in planning another daring
robbery—this time, he'd go solo.

California Supreme Court justice J. Seawell called Sloper's plan "a well-considered
scheme . . . calculated to succeed." In April 1924, Sloper parked his newly purchased
car in a vacant lot. He then stole two cars, switching the license plates, and drove one
to the Mercantile Trust Company Bank in San Francisco. Armed with a loaded .38
Colt U.S. Army revolver, Sloper entered the bank and ordered the manager and two
employees, the only people in the bank at the time, to put their hands up.

As the tellers filled Sloper's bag with cash, the bank manager discreetly stepped
on a floor button which alerted the adjacent store to the robbery. Irritated by the
incessant ringing, the storeowner opened the adjoining door and told the manager
to turn it off, then departed. Carrying thirteen thousand dollars, Sloper raced to
the front door. Outside, sat his running automobile. He planned to drive to the
vacant lot, retrieve his new car, and abandon the stolen one.

It may have worked had Officer George Campbell not been patrolling the area and heard the alarm sounding. Like the storeowner, however, he didn't suspect that a robbery was in progress. Gun holstered, he entered the bank and came face-to-face with Sloper, who fired two shots. The first shot knocked off the officer's hat; the second struck his abdomen. Remarkably, Campbell still managed to wrestle Sloper to the ground and subdue him with the help of bystanders.

When arrested, Sloper admitted participating in about twenty robberies in the area. Sloper maintained that he "didn't aim to shoot" Campbell. "I am sorry that I shot you," Sloper told the dying officer, "but I had to shoot you in order to get away." George Campbell called Sloper a coward and died shortly thereafter.

Sloper and his attorney hoped pleading insanity would save his life, citing several family members, including his father, who suffered from mental illness. The jury disagreed. Awaiting appeal, Sloper plotted escape from the county jail. First, he fashioned a bludgeon from a broom handle with nails driven into it. Then, somehow, he made it to a window on the sixth floor of the jail with a rope made from bed sheets, where he planned to "hook on to a passing airplane or else fly down to the street." This earned him a stint in solitary confinement.

Six weeks later, he began a hunger strike. "I want to die," he told reporters after refusing food for nearly ten days. Sloper, described by the *Fresno Bee* as "emaciated, ashen-pale and glassy-eyed with shear fear," began muttering about ghosts. "They are after me—they are going to murder me. I don't want to live. They say I killed a policeman, but he's alive. He's here now. He isn't dead. He comes to me at night and laughs at me. He's going to kill me."

Months later, Sloper tried another tactic. Allegedly having stolen coal oil from a fellow prisoner, Sloper tried to set himself on fire, but a jailer overpowered him and extinguished the flames. When his appeal was denied, Sloper appeared for sentencing, where he insisted his victim continued to haunt him, saying, "He ain't dead yet. He ain't dead yet, I tell you." Judge Harold Louderback granted Sloper an insanity hearing, but determined that the condemned man's "realization of impending death and a frenzied fear is all that is the matter with Sloper." Before Sloper's transfer to Folsom, jailers discovered gruesome sketches on his cell walls depicting men being hanged or shot. Reportedly, a jailer asked Sloper about the gun he had drawn. "If I had it here, I'd use it on you," Sloper replied.

Standing on the scaffold on June 25, 1926, Sloper repeatedly muttered, "Burn me up if you want to. Go ahead and burn me up." Seconds before Warden J. J. Smith gave the signal to drop the trap, Sloper said, "Let 'er go. Spring it." When Sloper's sister, Evelyn, claimed his body, she defended him, saying, "My brother was insane, not only at the time he shot the policeman but had been for months before. I tried every way in my power to convince the authorities that he was not responsible for the crime . . . he grew to manhood without the affection needed by any normal boy and it preyed on his mind, finally resulting in complete mental breakdown."

SLOPER'S COMPANIONS

Leo Brennan, William O'Brien, and Thomas "The Owl" Griffin spent a decade robbing homes and businesses, often getting away with tens of thousands of dollars. Brennan, called a "super-bandit" by the press, robbed a home in 1920, fetching $22,000 for himself. Arrested in 1922, he escaped by sawing through jail bars and crawling through a sewer pipe. He later returned to prison after wounding a police officer, but he wouldn't stay long. On November 15, 1926, Brennan, O'Brien, and Griffin escaped from Folsom, clinging to the undercarriage of a truck. Four days later, authorities found Griffin dead from exposure and dehydration.

Griffin had earned his moniker while in school. He delivered newspapers at night and his teacher often caught him dozing off in class. She began calling him a night owl, and the name stuck. Police had hopes that Griffin had revealed to Brennan and O'Brien where he hid the $31,000 from the Clovis job. The money, however, never turned up. But authorities did arrest O'Brien in May of 1928 after he killed a clerk in a robbery. He committed suicide while awaiting execution. Brennan returned to the prison in November 1928 and was eventually released in 1939.

"I am not afraid. I am ready to go. Seems funny, though, that this is my last day on earth."
—Charles Peevia, on the scaffold, 1926

54. Charles Peevia, August 27, 1926

On March 29, 1926, police found eighty-year-old former slave John Scott dead from a bullet wound that severed his jugular. Authorities couldn't understand who would kill an elderly man with no known enemies and with only a dollar in his pocket. They discovered that Charles Peevia, whose real name was said to be Henry Gafford, had stolen a vehicle and left the ranch where Scott and he worked. Scott's son-in-law had hired Peevia to help Scott with the chores.

The description issued by authorities described Peevia as a "Mexican Negro" who "walks erect and speaks fluent Spanish." Captured in Aberdeen, Washington, where he was working for a circus, Peevia was returned to Bakersfield. "I've got to plead guilty, because I know that I am guilty," Peevia told the judge. He had a long list of previous convictions, including assault with intent to commit murder when he attacked a woman with an ax in 1922. He explained to the judge that he unintentionally killed Scott as they struggled over possession of the shotgun, after Peevia "couldn't stand the old man nagging at me."

Sentenced to death, Peevia spent his final night dancing the Charleston and eating watermelon and pork chops. The following morning, he shook hands with the warden and said, "I am not afraid. I am ready to go. Seems funny, though, that this is my last day on earth." Appearing unconcerned and brave, he died on the Folsom gallows on August 27, 1926.

"I am innocent. Please cut this
noose into thirteen pieces and give
one to each juror and the judge
who convicted me."

—Ray Arnold, on the scaffold, 1927

"It's terrible. I don't see how I can
stand it. It's torture. Why can't I be
hanged now, and have it over with?"

—Edward Sayer, the day before his
execution, 1927

55. Ray Arnold, January 28, 1927,
56. Edward Sayer, February 4, 1927

Twenty-seven-year old Arthur Muller committed suicide on November 6, 1924, less than a day after shooting Japanese storeowner Tamae Ninomiya in Penryn, California. "Please remember I am innocent," he wrote in a letter to his wife Irene. "You know who put me where I am, but I never turned yellow in my life and I won't squeal." In a separate letter to his father, Muller fingered twenty-four-year-old Edward Sayer for the killing. He also named Ray Arnold, a twenty-eight-year old mechanic, as an accomplice. Muller ended his letter to Irene with, "Watch baby. Hope he gets a real father someday. I always said I would die with my shoes on."

Officers found Arnold cleaning his car outside his San Francisco apartment. When they searched his room, they discovered a revolver in the trunk with one bullet missing. Arnold denied involvement in the crime, but admitted knowing "Eddie" Sayer. Both men pleaded their innocence, claiming to have alibis. Investigators then found Muller's car—one Arnold had arranged for Muller to buy days earlier—on the side of the road out of Penryn.

After three days of jury selection, the prosecution presented its case—built mostly on eyewitness testimony—against the two young defendants. District Attorney Marshall Lowell offered his rendition of the crime to the jury. He proposed the three men committed several burglaries that first week of November. Two men would hold up a business, while the third waited in the car. At four o'clock on the afternoon in question, Muller and Sayer, both armed, entered Ninomiya's shop. Ninomiya stood behind the counter writing a letter. Her brother, M. Ikeda, had followed the men into the store.

Muller aimed his gun at the storeowner, while Sayer pointed his at Ikeda. According to Ikeda, Muller ordered Ninomiya to open the safe. Instead, she turned and ran toward the back door. Muller shot her in the back, killing her. The men fled, jumping into the getaway car and then drove out of Penryn. Along the road, they abandoned the car and went their separate ways on foot.

The state relied on two Japanese witnesses. Unable to speak English, an interpreter translated their testimony. One identified Arnold as the man behind the wheel, but it wasn't until trial, three months later, that he named Sayer as the other assailant. This second identification came as a shock, even for Lowell, who had interviewed this witness after the crime.

The defense supplied testimony from eight men who placed Arnold and Sayer in various places around Sacramento from about eleven in the morning to four in the afternoon on the day of the crime. Despite this testimony, the jury concluded Arnold and Sayer partook in the attempted robbery and murder and handed down a guilty verdict. Defense attorney George Connolly appealed, citing several judicial errors, with particular emphasis on the judge's instructions to the jury.

Regarding an alibi defense, the judged called it "capable of being and has been occasionally successfully fabricated; that even when wholly false, its detection may be a matter of very great difficulty. . ." Connolly felt the inference "stripped [the defendants] of all hope, and doomed them to conviction and death." He also believed the jury viewed the defendants' alibi testimony suspiciously.

Arnold and Sayer declined to testify. The judge implied to the jury that the defense's choice to keep their clients off the stand could be considered suppressed evidence—evidence adverse to the defense. Connolly objected to the implication, saying, ". . . these defendants were virtually charged with the suppression of evidence because they themselves did not testify."

The final court instruction Connolly cited in his appeal involved punishment. Connolly claimed the judge instructed the jury to decide the defendants' punishment: death or life imprisonment. Connolly stated, " . . . nowhere throughout this last and most important instruction of all, did the court instruct the jury as to the form of their verdict on the event that they should find the defendants innocent . . . The jurors . . . were convinced that the court believed that the defendants were guilty, and that the only thing left in their hands was the matter of punishment."

Nearly a year after the trial, in January 1926, the appellate court affirmed the lower court's verdict. Connolly immediately appealed to the California Supreme Court, citing the same judicial errors. In October, the high court agreed with the earlier judgment.

This devastating blow to the defense spurred an outpouring of support for the condemned men, and letters and telegrams flooded Governor Friend Richardson's office. It also marked the beginning of a desperate campaign involving Sayer's mental health, something his father Daniel had hoped to keep quiet. Without admitting guilt, Sayer's family and defense felt his questionable sanity could be their only chance to save him from the gallows.

Edward Sayer came from a prominent Denver family, the only boy of five children. Dr. Edward Delehanty of Denver wrote to California's newly elected governor, C.C. Young. He described Sayer as mentally unstable and "generally known in the community in which he lived as 'The Crazy Ed Sayer.'" Dr. Milton B. Lennon, who examined Sayer prior to sentencing, felt Sayer "was doomed by a fatal heredity," offering that Sayer's mother, Margaret, had a "marked psychopathic trend." Lennon went on to say, "In the present patient, Sayre [sic], it is quite clear to me that he had a bad heredity and was born with a permanent defect in his moral sphere. He is no more responsible for his deficiency than he is for the color of his eyes or any of his other physical endowments."

Ben B. Lindsey, the juvenile court judge in Denver who had Sayer in his courtroom in 1921, told Governor Young, "I do not hesitate to say that this boy is of that type of mental defectives [sic] who certainly should not be executed for the crime with which he is charged." Former Denver county district attorney Philip Van Cise called Sayer "peculiar" and recommended psychiatric treatment. A previous employer called Sayer "inattentive," "listless," and "childish," and he claimed to have observed him buying and wearing women's undergarments.

Fear of disgrace had prompted Daniel Sayer's initial silence about his son's sanity. He never imagined the jury would convict his son of the murder.

Arnold's execution date of January 28 neared with no indication that Governor Young would interfere. Sayer's execution would be the following Friday, on February 4. Arnold's young son, in the custody of Arnold's father, anxiously awaited Young's decision. The governor issued a statement on January 27, holding the defendants equally responsible for Ninomiya's death, "as though they [each] had actually slain the deceased with their own hands."

Upon hearing his fate, Arnold said, "If they want to kill me, all right. I am ready to die. I would die gladly if I thought my death would aid in putting an end to capital punishment. Sayer and I are innocent. The guilty ones are those who prosecuted us for a crime we did not commit."

Warden J. J. Smith allowed the two men to share a cell on Arnold's last night. Together, they listened to music from a phonograph and talked, the last time the friends would speak to one another. The next morning, Arnold handed Smith a letter he had written to Governor Young making a plea for his comrade Sayer.

Sayer sat in his death cell and listened as the guards led his friend to the gallows. Arnold flicked his last cigarette away as he mounted the scaffold and faced the approximately fifty spectators, tightly squeezed into the small death chamber. "I am innocent," he told them. "Please cut this noose into thirteen pieces and give one to each juror and the judge who convicted me." Seconds later, Arnold dropped through the trap. When doctors cut down his body, newspaper reporters swarmed Sayer's cell, eager for a statement. The condemned man, with a tear-stained face, showed them a picture of his wife Grace and three-year-old daughter Barbara. He also shared a letter he had written to Arnold's parents, praising their son for his loyalty and generosity.

Sayer couldn't help but discuss the penalty he too would face. He stated:

LETTER FROM EDWARD SAYER TO THE PARENTS OF RAY ARNOLD

Poor Ray is gone and oh, how I miss him. I feel heartbroken. He was such a loyal, true, faithful and generous pal of mine. I am not old in years, but in many ways I am old in experience. And I've never met a fellow who had such admirable principles and morals as Ray. He is every inch a man, and certainly a son of whom to feel proud. I am surely proud to declare he is a friend of mine. The stupid, hypocritical, bigoted portion of society will gloat in smug self-righteousness by endeavoring to cast stigma on Ray's name. But who care for either their plaudits or denunciations. We who know him love him, and that's what counts. I feel that you know how deeply I concede and sympathize with you both, and although you are his parents, it seems that my grief and sorrow are almost as profound as your own. For two companions that have undergone such trials and tribulations as Ray and I have, we had become very closely attached to each other. I also wish to extend sincere thanks to you for all that you have done for me. You both have done as many things for me as you had for Ray and such devoted kindness can never be forgotten, much less repaid. I am quite overcome with conflicting emotions and I find it impossible to grasp sufficient composure to write a worthy letter, but I hope you will accept this little note in the spirit in which it is written. God bless you all, I wish with all my love and gratitude as your son's best pal. –Ed

Society uses the New Testament as a symbol and lives by the old, "An eye for an eye, a tooth for a tooth." Of course society—composed of so-called civilized people—are really ashamed of capital punishment. If not, why do they swing a man in a little hell-hole, hidden away behind barriers of stone? Why don't they march him out in the open, where everyone can witness the hanging? Let the people see one hanging; then there would never be another. Really, fellows, it isn't the actual act itself which bothers one. It is the suspense—the living death they consign you to . . . Really, it's like a dream—what I have come to now. And the hell of it is I have to die for something I didn't do. The tough part is for the wife and baby. Always our Barbara will be known as the daughter of a man who was hanged. A lifelong stigma for them.

As Sayer's date of death neared, Mr. and Mrs. Daniel Sayer knew all hope of saving their son dwindled. They thanked Warden Smith for his kindness, telling him, "Our paths may sometime cross again outside in this little world of ours and I want to always consider you among our friends." Days before the execution, District Attorney Lowell even offered to recommend life imprisonment to Governor Young, if Sayer would agree to plead guilty. Sayer refused. He continued to rely on his family's pleas for clemency. "Maybe it is hopeless going ahead thinking that somehow, some way, a fellow's friends can hold back the law," he said. "But even if it is hopeless, it is the only thing to relieve the maddening thought of the gallows, the noose and—God—the torture and disgrace to my wife and baby girl!"

On the day before his execution, the *Oakland Tribune* described Sayer's anguish, "Edward Sayer faced the most heartbreaking ordeal of his life—that of saying good-bye to his father, mother, his wife, and three-year old daughter, Barbara." The condemned prisoner cried as he paced his cell. "It's terrible," he moaned. "I don't see how I can stand it. It's torture. Why can't I be hanged now, and have it over with?" He spent the day with relatives and when Warden Smith asked him for any requests, Sayer replied he wanted ice cream, which he received. In the final hours before his execution, Sayer wrote letters to his family, including a poem for his mother.

As he mounted the gallows on February 4, 1927, Sayer leaned heavily on the arm of prison chaplain Reverend Michael Hogan. "I can only repeat that I am innocent," Sayer remarked. "I am being hanged by the state for a crime I did not commit. It is not for my own life that I care. It is for my old father and mother and my wife and baby. They will suffer a living death. In punishing me the state also punishes them."

As Edward Sayer's body swung from the rope, his daughter, unaware of her father's fate, sat on the floor of her grandparent's home, playing with her dolls. Her grief-stricken mother collapsed, knowing that at 10:06 A.M. her husband would be put to death. According to a *Modesto News Herald* reporter, Governor Young seemed "visibly distressed" as he dictated a telegram just before the execution took place, to Governor Adams, explaining why he couldn't interfere with the law.

156

Soon after the execution, Young received telegrams from angry citizens. "I tell you this much," one read, "if you stop breathing soon, my thoughts did it with the curse I putt [sic] on you and your children's children." Another read, "Extreme torture of the worst kind should be meted out to you the rest of your life." Although denouncing him, newspaper editors took a less threatening approach and publicly criticized the governor for his lack of interference, calling it a "grave injustice."

The next day, at the request of the Board of Prison Directors, Warden J. J. Smith resigned. The board called it an overall "reorganization of the state prison system," as San Quentin warden Frank Smith also resigned. "Jack" Smith left Folsom after thirty-seven years of service, saying he would "take a long anticipated vacation." Of all the executions that took place while he was warden, Smith found Sayer's to be the "most difficult to perform."

Smith, as he promised the condemned man he would, presented to the prison board Ray Arnold's last request to have a piece of his noose sent to each juror and the judge. They flatly refused to honor such a request.

"When you play the crime game you are gambling with death. If you lose it is up to you to be a good loser."
—Willard C. Shannon, 1927

57. Willard C. Shannon, May 4, 1928

Willard Shannon befriended Harold Lage and his wife and two young children. The Lages, however, knew him only as Walter Leslye. Shannon was a con artist with a long history of fraud and forgery.

Shannon needed a fast car and Lage, an auto salesman, agreed to take him on a "demo run" in a Lincoln touring car. Shannon, posing as a mine manager, paid for the car with a bogus check. Lage insisted they go to the bank, and when the check bounced, Shannon promised cash. All the young salesman had to do was drive Shannon to Jackson to collect payroll from a mine sale. Lage agreed.

On New Year's Eve, 1927, Lage said goodbye to his family and left with Shannon. Witnesses placed Lage and Shannon in Jackson, California, in the foothills of the Sierra Mountains near abandoned mining shafts later that day. Then checks signed with the salesman's name turned up at Baer's Clothing Store and the Hotel Victoria. A check from Lage's employer—a Christmas bonus—was used as payment. Soon, his wife received a telegram. "I am accompanying officials on inspection tour throughout southern California and Arizona. Having wonderful time. Be home in a few days. Harold." The telegram had been sent to the Lage's previous address.

Authorities soon suspected Lage hadn't written the checks and guessed the automobile salesman was dead—they just didn't know where to look. Police conjectured that the twenty-six-year-old had most likely met a grisly end, and based on descriptions from those who knew him, police pegged Shannon as the suspect. They recognized the forgeries as Shannon's work, work that had landed the twenty-seven-year-old Shannon in prison three times previously.

In the meantime, Shannon assumed the dead man's identity, using Lage's checks and business cards. One person wrote to the *Reno Evening Gazette*, opining, "If Shannon has really been using checks made out to Lage and has been calling himself by that name in a region where all the authorities know him as Shannon, it indicates that he is not a man of much intelligence." Even so, Shannon managed to elude law enforcement at every turn, even after being spotted in Bakersfield, San Francisco, and Sacramento. He was also brazen enough to take Lage's car to a repair shop in the early morning hours of January 7, have repairs done, and pay his bill with one of Lage's checks.

After meeting Shannon on January 31, Mr. and Mrs. Carl Derichs contacted police with a detailed story. They had accepted a ride from him when their car broke down. The couple had been explaining their car troubles to a clerk at the Merced Hotel in the town of Merced, when Shannon offered assistance. "He gave me his card which read, W. H. Lage, Edward Lowe Motors Company, Stockton," said Mr. Derichs. He and his wife described piling into the Lincoln and how Shannon drove recklessly, shooting around curves and traveling at a high rate of speed. Shannon was animated, jovial, and friendly, showing the couple all the points of interest in the Yosemite Valley, an area he seemed to know well.

Shannon made one stop, reportedly to see his half-brother at a hotel. Telling the couple to stay in the car, he returned an hour later and resumed the sightseeing tour. Mrs. Derichs told authorities they only paid the entrance fee into Yosemite; otherwise "the stranger would accept no money from us on the trip." Days later, Mr. and Mrs. Derichs read newspaper reports describing Shannon and called police.

On January 8, authorities found Lage's body at Pioneer Hill, near Jackson. He had sustained two gunshots, one through his neck and the other in his left temple.

The back of his head had also been smashed. The killer had dragged the body a short distance to some bushes, laying the victim's overcoat, hat, and left shoe next to him.

The authorities pieced together Shannon's motive from a letter another automobile salesman received two months earlier. Using an alias, Shannon contacted John Ross asking to test drive a new sedan. He stated he owned a gold mine and expected to receive a large sum of money for its purchase. Ross would be generously compensated. Suspicious, Ross refused Shannon's offer.

Police determined Shannon had at least two accomplices, but that Shannon alone engineered the plot to commit a seventy-five thousand dollar robbery of two Calaveras banks. They believed the men killed Lage for his fast car. Sheriff Joe Lucot confirmed this after learning the Pine Grove district and the Moore Brothers Mine had planned to sell for seventy-five thousand dollars in cash. Shannon knew of the impending deal. Lucot surmised that when Shannon murdered Lage, his accomplices deserted him and balked at following through with the plans.

For the next few weeks, Shannon eluded police. Another editorial appeared in the *Reno Evening Gazette* discrediting Shannon's intelligence: "Premeditation is obvious. Yet it was a stupid, cruel crime just [as] such a person of the mental development ascribed to the suspected man might be expected to commit for he left a trail as broad as the Carson-Reno highway."

The following day, on February 9, police in Salt Lake City arrested a Harold Riley on a Denver-bound train, as he sat in a Pullman hiding his face behind a newspaper. Initially, authorities didn't realize they had the elusive Shannon. They had arrested him for stealing checks from Walter E. Ware, a Salt Lake architect, cashing one for four hundred and twenty-five dollars to purchase clothes and a train ticket. While he was in district court pleading guilty to forgery, Utah authorities received a picture of Shannon from Lucot. Fingerprints confirmed his identity.

"My God, you win," Shannon said when he saw his picture. He admitted being a part of the mine robbery, but denied killing Lage, saying, "It was one of my companions." Shannon claimed his two accomplices set out to commit robbery and wanted to take Lage's car from his garage, but the victim interfered and was shot. His accomplices transported Lage's body to the mountains and hid it. Shannon claimed, "I knew I had to get out, so I took the car and beat it as fast as possible."

Shannon begged to avoid California: "Because if I go back there now the sentiment will be so strong against me; I will have no chance to escape the death penalty. If I can serve ten years here, this may cool down and I may have a chance." However, Governor C. C. Young wasted little time drawing up requisition papers for Shannon's extradition.

While awaiting his trip to California, Shannon spoke candidly with officers and the media. He blamed the "high cost of entertaining modern girls" for his predicament, explaining that while attending the University of California he began spending heavily: "I was trotting out some coeds and I had to be able to spend or drop out of the show. That's the way it is nowadays and any young fellow that can stand the gaff and stay straight is a wonder." While trying to "keep up the pace with these girls," he ran short on money and turned to forgery.

Shannon soon presented a different version of the crime. After he and Lage arrived at the mine, he turned Lage over to his "pals." Upon returning, the pals claimed something went wrong and they had to kill Lage. Shannon said he "bawled them out," gave them money, and took off in Lage's car. He admitted sending the telegrams to Lage's wife, Avis, in an attempt to keep officers off his trail. "I want to say about that trick that I'm mighty sorry for it. Of course, there was no intention of killing Lage, but that does not help her. I am very sorry about that, although it doesn't do any good now," Shannon said. "I'm a crook, but I'm not a killer and if they hang this job on me, they'll be hanging it on an innocent man." He steadfastly refused to name his accomplices, insisting, "Nobody will get their names out of me."

Authorities soon determined Shannon had worked alone. Shannon insisted he didn't kill Lage, but acknowledged his involvement in the crime: "When you play the crime game you are gambling with death. If you lose it is up to you to be a good loser. What's my advice? Stay straight if you can and if you can't—well, do your stuff and take your medicine." He even suggested the governor's reward money be given to Lage's widow, who he said deserved it more than anyone.

Just before his trial, Shannon gave a third version of the circumstances of the crime. This time, he admitted he shot the young car salesman. He said he drove Lage to Jackson, where his pals told him "the game was up" on the job. Shannon had to get rid of Lage and told him to stay in the car. He promised to go to the mine and get the money to pay Lage. Apparently, Lage grew suspicious and followed.

When he came upon Shannon and his associates, Lage pulled a gun on the three of them, threatening to take them to the Jackson authorities. A scuffle ensued, resulting in Lage's accidental shooting. Claiming self-defense, Shannon pleaded not guilty and awaited trial. Jailors felt he might try to take his own life, so they denied him a razor. The *Fresno Bee* remarked, "[he] presented a grotesque appearance with his auburn hair." The paper also described Shannon as cheerful, singing hymns and strolling about his cell, where he constructed a hangman's noose of string and hung it from a bar.

Mrs. Lage, visibly distraught during the trial, sat a few seats from Shannon. Her young children played happily in a corner of the courtroom. To some reporters, Shannon appeared indifferent to his situation, while others saw him smiling at times throughout the trial. Taking the stand, Shannon once again changed his story. This time, he claimed he was hiding in some bushes when his "two confederates" shot Lage. "I didn't kill him," Shannon cried weakly. He said after the murder the three men picked Lage's pockets and stole bank checks. "I figured I'd be blamed for the crime anyway," he carped. Referring to the earlier versions and admissions, Shannon said, "I had no intention of anyone believing that was the truth at the time I did tell it."

His flimsy defense and constant change of stories didn't sit well with the jury. After thirty-five minutes of deliberation, the jury found Shannon guilty of first-degree murder. He showed no emotion at the verdict, but laughed openly as he tried to console his sister, who sobbed on his shoulder. Shannon still refused to name his alleged accomplices.

After sentencing, Shannon, smiled and joked with officers while they transferred him to Folsom to await execution. In the meantime, Shannon's attorneys filed an appeal, stating authorities obtained the original confession illegally and based the verdict purely on circumstantial evidence. His attorneys also asserted a violation of Shannon's rights when Amador County failed to impanel women on the jury. At the time, officials deemed the courthouse "improperly equipped" for women, considering it "unwise and inexpedient" to impose jury duty on women. The defense had never objected during jury selection, nor contested this "violation." Shannon's defense also claimed he didn't receive a fair trial because Amador County residents were "highly incensed over the tragedy" and had an "adverse attitude" toward Shannon. But again, the defense had never motioned for a venue change.

In November 1927, Shannon lost his appeal. He filed another, claiming evidence against him came from the prosecuting officer, not by a grand jury. In April 1928, the court denied this appeal. His attorney asked for a thirty-day reprieve to submit recently found evidence, but Governor Young refused.

The night before his execution, Shannon listened to "The Sidewalks of New York" repeatedly, constantly smoking cigarettes. He nervously awaited death. The next morning, his last meal consisted of toast, strawberries, and chocolate.

The warden, guards, and various newspapermen were among the thirty-five witnesses to attend Shannon's hanging. In the past, Folsom wardens sent invitations to executions, inviting as many as two hundred people. "I can't understand why they want to see such a thing," Warden Court Smith said after witnessing his first hanging, adding, "As far as I'm concerned, there won't be any idle curious to witness the last few minutes of a man's life on earth. No man is entirely bad when he has but a few moments to live."

Smith did not ask Shannon for last words. He had discontinued this practice as well, deeming it "entirely unnecessary and only prolonged the agonizing moments of the condemned murderer as he stood on the gallows with the noose around his neck, waiting for the trap to spring." Ray Arnold's "melodramatic" speech on the gallows had prompted the change.

As for Shannon, he protested his innocence to the end. In their last conversation, Smith said to Shannon, "Be brave. Do you think you will be able to go through it all right?" Shannon replied, "I'm ready to go. Good-bye." He died on May 4, 1928, nine minutes and fifty seconds after the trap sprung.

"All right, boys. Let's have it over."
—George Kuryla, on the scaffold, 1929

58. George Kuryla, January 25, 1929

On November 1, 1928, George Kuryla lost his job as a miner for the Central Eureka Mine near Sutter Creek in Amador County. His boss, Elmer Guerrard, fired him for "high-grading," or stealing specimen ore. Kuryla denied the accusation and resented Guerrard for "blacklisting" him from other mining work.

After leaving the mine, Kuryla purchased a gun. He returned the following evening and waited for Guerrard to come out of the foreman's office. When Guerrard emerged, Kuryla shot and killed him. Kuryla then went to the hotel where he had been staying and told the owner to call the police because he just killed a man. Minutes later, police arrested Kuryla.

Refusing counsel, Kuryla insisted on pleading guilty, telling the court he was ready to pay with his life. He hoped, however, that the plea would earn him a life sentence. The judge thought otherwise. When Kuryla begged for clemency, Governor C. C. Young agreed with the judge, saying, "To recognize such a plea on its face would be to set a dangerous precedent which would know no bounds. I have read the transcript of the case. When Kuryla announced his intention of pleading guilty, the court warned him of the possible consequences of his act. There is nothing to indicate that any promise was made to Kuryla that he would escape the death penalty should he plead guilty. On the contrary, there was not."

While on the scaffold, Kuryla took one last puff off a cigarette and asked Warden Smith, "Are any of my friends from Amador County here?" When Smith answered no, Kuryla said, "All right, boys. Let's have it over. Warden, please tell my friends I am sorry." Setting the record for the shortest stay on death row, Kuryla hung from the noose on January 25, 1929.

"I don't know what made me do it but I did it."
—Harrison Randolph, 1928

59. Harrison Harvey Randolph, February 8, 1929

On November 29, 1928, Ralph Hunnicutt discovered his mother's body in a closet, with a rag stuffed in her mouth. A strip of her apron wound around her neck. Unbeknownst to Ralph, she had also been raped. The *Fresno Bee* described the forty-three-year-old mother of six as a "comely matron" who had recently separated from her husband George and moved from Oildale to Bakersfield weeks earlier. The paper reported, "The woman's clothing was torn to threads. In the kitchen of the house [were] the remnants of a cigarette which the intruder is believed to have smoked before or after he committed his revolting crime."

Overturned furniture showed Ms. Hunnicutt put up a strong fight, but eventually she succumbed to strangulation. Clothing belonging to her sons was missing, as well as a rifle. While searching the kitchen, police discovered that Hunnicutt may have known her attacker. Dishes on the table indicated she had served food and tea to someone. Fingerprints on a teacup gave investigators a name: Harrison Randolph.

The twenty-four-year-old Randolph had a long criminal history, dating back to 1916 when he was charged with a series of thefts at the age of twelve. In June 1928, he had been paroled from Folsom after serving his third term in a state prison. One month later, he offered to help the Hunnicutt family move into their new home. Being alone at the time, Ms. Hunnicutt allowed Randolph into her house. Together, they ate apricot pie and grapes and sipped on tea.

Police arrested Randolph at his grandmother's house in Tranquility in Fresno County. He told police Ms. Hunnicutt asked him to move furniture for her, but had given him food first. After eating, she showed him around the house, arriving at a large closet. "I don't know what made me do it but I did it," Randolph told police. "While there without any reason whatsoever, I choked her into unconsciousness, then first tied her with an electric extension cord, later changed it for a piece of rag, also putting a gag in her mouth. The rag came from an apron in the bathroom." Although he wouldn't admit it, evidence showed he had raped Hunnicutt, as well.

Randolph told investigators he took clothing from the sons' rooms, and he took a rifle that he later sold for $7.50. Mr. S. Taterosian, a rancher living north of Bakersfield who purchased the rifle, brought it to the sheriff and identified Randolph as the seller. Randolph pleaded guilty at his arraignment, but, when his day of sentencing arrived, asked to change his plea to not guilty by reason of insanity. His attorney said his client had once been struck in the head with an ax. The judge refused his request for a change of plea.

Randolph stated in court that he wasn't a "murderer at heart" and that he grew up poor and fatherless. Although he gave no motive for the crime, Randolph expressed remorse, saying he would "undo the crime," even if it wouldn't save him from the death penalty.

Randolph spent his final days writing letters to family and friends, apologizing for being a burden to them. His mother, Blanche Straks of Lincoln, Nebraska, wrote letters to Governor C. C. Young hoping he'd commute her son's sentence. She also urged Dr. A. L. Jones, superintendent of the Nebraska Society for the Friendless, to contact the Long Beach branch of the society on Randolph's behalf, but this didn't sway Young.

Heard murmuring a prayer, Randolph walked directly to the trap door of the scaffold, where he died seconds later on February 8, 1929.

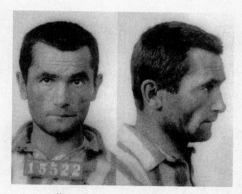

"No, I am not afraid to die."
—Paul Rowland, refusing to speak with a priest before his execution, 1929

60. Paul Rowland, September 27, 1929

Paul Rowland killed his best friend in prison. Rowland told Warden Smith's secretary, Bernard Huse, that the incident was a "personal affair." The two evidently shared a sexual relationship. On October 15, 1928, Rowland, a German native, approached Elgar Morrison in the yard by the horseshoe pits. He stabbed Morrison in the side and the five-inch, prison-made knife pierced Morrison's lung, spleen, and stomach. Rowland walked away into the crowd of convicts, while fellow inmates took Morrison to the prison infirmary. He died four days later from an infection in the wound.

Immediately taken to solitary confinement, Rowland expressed remorse to District Attorney Neil McAllister. Rowland stated he gave Morrison twelve packs of cigarettes and that he had come to collect the debt. He said Morrison kicked him, so he pulled out his knife and stabbed him in an effort to defend himself. However, witnesses testified that Rowland simply walked up to Morrison and, without a word, stabbed his best friend to death. Rowland told the jury that he never meant to actually kill Morrison.

After being found guilty and sentenced to death, the judge asked Rowland if he had a statement. Rowland replied, "I have nothing to say now—I didn't have a fair trial." Rowland had a long history of committing burglaries, dating back to 1915 at the age of 22. In a statement to Warden Smith, secretary Barnett Huse noted, "[Rowland's] mentality seems to be low and he has an apparently bad criminal tendency, especially to commit burglaries."

After an unsuccessful appeal, Rowland stood on the scaffold on September 27, 1929. He began to speak, "I have something of interest to tell—" when the trap sprung, sending Rowland's message to the grave with him.

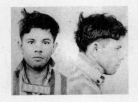
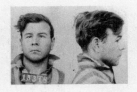

61. Anthony Brown, January 3, 1930
62. Roy Stokes, January 3, 1930
63. Walter Burke, January 10, 1930
64. James Gregg, January 10, 1930
65. Eugene Crosby, January 17, 1930

On Thanksgiving Day in 1927, a thousand convicts gathered in the auditorium to watch one of the latest Hollywood films, "Ankles Preferred." Certain holidays brought a departure from monotonous prison life. Men could enjoy a movie, along with an elaborate turkey dinner—a welcome reprieve from the usual bread and beans.

Six convicts[1] forewent the festivities and opted for plans of their own. Armed with a .45 colt, a hatchet, and various knives and razors, they began rounding up guards and trustees, locking them in a cell in the Back Alley. "The prisoners stripped us down to our underwear, searched us thoroughly, took our money and allowed us to dress again . . . We had nothing to eat but were handed a cup of hot chocolate," said guard Emory Campbell. For the next twenty-one hours, the captives of the inmates endured total darkness, hearing only the rapid pulse of machine gun fire and inmate screams.

The convicts set their sights on the warden's office in the administration building. After months of planning, they knew exactly how they'd gain access.

---

1. Anthony Brown, serving fifteen years for robbery; Roy Stokes, serving five years for burglary; Walter E. Burke, serving five years for robbery; James Gregg, serving a life sentence for murder; Eugene Crosby, serving five years for robbery; Albert Stewart, serving fourteen years for forgery.

The group approached guard James Gorhanson, who stood watch at the hospital door. With a prison-made knife pressed to his back, he had no choice but to obey the rogues. He led them to the switchboard office, which separated them from the prison yard and administration building.

Once here, the convicts counted on finding the key to open the inner and outer gates. However, Warden Court Smith had removed the key the previous day, "gambling on a hunch" about an escape plot. "There had been indications for months," Smith said, "that something of the sort would be attempted. And, Thanksgiving Day, when we allow prisoners a certain latitude, when discipline yields a little to the spirit of the day, was set as the time." Smith explained that a young convict, "never mind his name," phoned that morning, warning of an impending riot. Smith alerted his captain of the guard, who was unable to caution all of his men in time.

The warden's foresight in removing the key frustrated the convicts' plan, inciting panic. Taking guards Neil and Gorhanson hostage, they marched the men to another inner gate, which opened to a tunnel. At the tunnel's far end, an outer gate accessed the yard. Meanwhile, a trustee named George Baker had been led into the tunnel from the outside, and there he waited to enter the main cell house.

Anthony Brown used his gun to compel Neil to order another trustee to unlock the gate. (Only two months earlier, guards caught Brown digging a tunnel of his own beneath a large pile of granite near the quarry.) Pointing weapons at their backs, the convicts shoved the guards through the inner gate, a situation that gave Neil a split second to slam the gate closed in the convicts' faces. Furious, Brown fired two shots into the tunnel. The first one struck Neil in the leg, the other pierced Baker's chest, killing him instantly. Wounded from several razor cuts and a blow to the head from the hatchet, Gorhanson escaped through the outer gate along with Neil, thanks to help from a guard.

Without hostages or a gate key, the escapee band needed a new plan. They raced to the auditorium, intending to blend in with the large crowd of prisoners. From there they confronted guard Roy Singleton, who likely held the keys. When Singleton denied having them, five men pounced, stabbing him numerous times. Guard Bernard Deely came to his co-worker's aid, but sustained several stab wounds himself. "Knives were flashing so rapidly I couldn't tell who held the knife that killed Singleton," recounted Deely. Of Singleton's murder, Deely reported, "The five men closed in on him as he tried to fight them off with his cane—the only weapon a guard is allowed to carry. There were five to one and he didn't stand much of a show against them." Albert Stewart, struck Deely over the head with a club. He and his murderous cohorts threw Deely and four more guards into the cell with the other captives.

In charge only since March, Warden Court Smith immediately appealed to Governor C. C. Young for outside assistance. Young enlisted more than five hundred troops of the state militia, a machine gun company out of Yuba City, one hundred members of the Sacramento police force, and a field artillery unit from Stockton. It wasn't long before the 40th Tank Corps from Salinas soon rolled up to the iron gates, armed and ready to quell the impending riot.

The warden's secretary, Barnett Huse, made a dash across the yard. A shot rang out from the library, striking Huse in the leg. Presumably fired by Brown, this shot is said to have started the volley of bullets that continued for hours. The machine gun company showered the prison with gunfire, the cacophony barely drowning out prisoner screams. Canisters of tear gas flew into the library, flooding it with suffocating plumes.

A member of the militia then saw a piece of paper flutter to the ground. A note, written in blue crayon, was addressed to Warden Smith. "Warden, please do something else except to kill so many innocent men. Give us a chance. There is no harm to your affairs. We cannot open the door on account of the few whom you want. Signed CRAL." A white flag soon billowed from a window of the cell block. Although both sides ceased fire, the convicts refused to surrender. Prison engineer and guard Ed Bathurst soon found another note. It identified five ringleaders who were nearly out of ammunition. Bathurst volunteered to liaise between the rioters and the authorities to negotiate a surrender.

The convicts allowed prison physician Proctor Day inside the gates to tend injured prisoners. Day described Gregg and Brown as "the worst hardened pair I have ever seen. They picked up the wounded men after the fight and dumped them in the corridor near the hospital without the slightest show of emotion. Throughout the siege, they ruled the other convicts without mercy." Day reported six dead convicts, three more dying, and seventeen injured. He also relayed the convict's threat to kill the six guards held hostage if authorities launched another attack.

Aware of their losing battle, the riot instigators released four of the guards the next morning, including seventy-five-year-old librarian Atone Messich. And they agreed to unconditional surrender.

In the end, eleven prisoners died, including trustee Baker, while seventeen were injured. During the riot, entrance gate guard Charles Gillies, who had worked at the prison for thirty years, suffered a heart attack and died. Sacramento Deputy Sheriff Harry Murphy also died from appendicitis after refusing to leave his post outside the prison during the riot.

"The boys all realize they will likely get the death penalty," said Smith. "And, with the exception of Stokes, they all appear to be sorry for the whole affair." Roy Stokes had arrived at Folsom only months earlier, convicted of burglary. Shortly before the riot, a search of his cell revealed an arsenal of weapons and drugs. Fellow prisoners testified in front of the coroner's inquest that, although five of the convicts attacked guard Singleton, Stokes administered the fatal stab wounds.

One inmate reported Stokes wiping the blood from the knife and referring to it as "Singleton's lifeblood."

The coroner's jury determined that Brown killed George Baker and shot secretary Huse, which instigated the machine gun fire that swept the prison, killing the ten other prisoners. "Every one of the six convicts who led the Folsom riot is as good as hanged already," District Attorney Neil McAllister declared. All six would be charged with Singleton's death.

Editorials appeared in the papers, one opining that the "intolerable conditions" caused the men to revolt. Others disagreed, saying, "These vicious murderers are entitled to no more consideration than so many rattlesnakes."

In January, Brown and Crosby pleaded not guilty by reason of insanity. Gregg, Burke, Stewart, and Stokes pleaded not guilty. It took five days to select a jury, whose members subsequently listened to both guards and inmates testify. Neither group could clearly convey the convicts' movements, yet several witnesses concurred that all of the defendants, except Crosby, simultaneously attacked Singleton.

No one could have predicted what would happen next. Albert Stewart, the forger of the group, took the stand for the defense. To the shock of his co-defendants and attorney, Stewart pinned the blame on the other five men: "I would like to tell my story. Tony Brown was the actual instigator of the riot . . . He told me he had a gun and was to use it on the warden in an effort to get away. I told Brown I was willing to help if no violence would be used. Each of the other five convicts gave me their word of honor that they would not use violence in making their getaway—that the weapons would be used only to intimidate whoever tried to stop them."

The defendants and their attorneys erupted, jumping to their feet and objecting to Stewart's statements, but the judge accepted the confession. J. J. Henderson, council for Brown, called for a recess and court briefly adjourned. Henderson called Stewart a "craven creature" who had waited for his chance to take the stand and attempt to "free himself of all connection with the riot and the murder and jeopardizing the lives of his fellow men." When testimony resumed, Stewart said Brown and Stokes stabbed Singleton, while Burke beat him over the head with the hatchet. He said he didn't see Gregg or Crosby strike the guard.

Previously known as the "Penman," Stewart quickly earned the moniker "The Squealer." Officers kept him in isolation for the duration of the trial. After several weeks, the jury found all six men guilty of first-degree murder, but recommended life imprisonment. Gregg was already serving life for murdering Constable George Boyle in Kingsburg three years earlier, and so, in fact, the sentence actually amounted to virtually no punishment. Gregg's arresting officer called him one of the most dangerous men in California, adding, "Possessed of plenty of nerves when he sees a chance, Gregg would kill his own mother if she stood in [the] way of his ends . . . Undoubtedly, the man should be hung if he was connected with this attempt. Two lives have been taken by him when he was sent to Folsom the last time, and he should have been hung then."

The verdict outraged McAllister and the public. One editorial read, "Justice was mocked and the law treated with an almost infinite contempt . . . the verdict is both idiotic and criminal." The district attorney announced another jury's chance to send the men to the gallows, this time for the murder of convict George Baker.

In April, the second trial commenced. The defense tried to impeach Gorhanson's testimony, alleging discrepancies in his story to the grand jury. Judge J. F. Pullen allowed the testimony. Then an elderly juror became ill and eventually passed away. The search for another jury began. The following month, the six men faced a new trial and again pleaded not guilty. Stewart continued to blame his fellow defendants, now specifying Baker's murder in his testimony.

The jury found Brown guilty of murdering Baker and found his co-defendants, including Stewart, guilty of complicity. They all finally received the death penalty. Stewart's conviction caused the other five men to break out in laughter and pig squeals, mocking the "stool pigeon," who would go down with the rest of them. During sentencing, Brown asked to be the first to go, but the judge denied him. The others remained quiet. Stewart would be sentenced later, pending a review of his role in turning state's evidence.

While awaiting the outcome of the men's appeals, J. J. Henderson received evidence charging that jury foreman T. A. Andrews had acted improperly. He had allegedly visited the courtroom during the rioters' first trial. He even sat next to Burke's mother, Florence Cleghorn, telling her, "they [the jury] will never convict them on that evidence." Andrews claimed he had been in the courtroom "only five minutes and didn't know what it was all about." The judge denied Henderson's motion to grant a new trial.

In the meantime, Albert "The Squealer" Stewart escaped the noose when his sentence was commuted to life.

After the affirmed judgment from the higher court, Henderson turned his attention to saving Eugene Crosby. Henderson stated, "Gregg on behalf of himself and Brown, Burke and Stokes, implored me to do something on behalf of Crosby. As Gregg expressed it, Crosby 'just happened to be there and was unfortunately drawn into the proceedings on Thanksgiving Day 1927.' The only thing that could be held against Crosby is he refused to turn state's evidence on being given that opportunity by the officials, the same as Stewart did." Crosby, arriving at Folsom in early 1927 on a burglary charge, became known as the "Poet Burglar," after several of his poems made their way to local newspapers.

Crosby left his mark on the wall of his county jail cell where the men awaited trial. The poem was written about Stewart, who was also known as Dick Saunders:

> Judas betrayed Christ, his Master,
> And having hanged himself in abject shame.
> Dick Saunders, the traitor, should,
> Like Judas, do the same.
> We staked our all for freedom
> And shook death's own grim dice.
> Then Saunders turned, as did the
> Worm, and let us pay the price.

Governor Young refused to grant clemency to Crosby, who was scheduled to be the last of the five hanged. On January 3, 1930, Anthony Brown got his wish after all, and mounted the gallows first. According to the *Ukiah Republican*, Walter Neil, "the guard who was crippled for life" by Brown's bullet, escorted the condemned man to the noose. Neil reportedly "asked for the privilege." Brown tossed away his cigarette butt before guards strapped his arms to his sides. "All right, Warden," he said grimly, "let's make it snappy." The night before, Brown wrote to Mrs. Cleghorn, thanking her for her kindness and interest, as she had visited the men regularly. Stokes took his place on the scaffold after Brown. He had written to his mother, claiming to be ill and that it was "best that he go now." Smith complimented Stokes on his letter. Stokes replied, "Oh, that's all right. I'm not much of a letter writer, but I wanted her to know that I appreciate all she has done for me." Stokes looked at the gathered witnesses and remarked, "My God, Warden, you got an awful bunch here today." With that, Stokes fell through the trap.

On the following Friday, snow fell and unusually cold weather accompanied the executions of two more rioters. James Gregg and Walter Burke spent their final evening dining on an elaborate meal and writing letters to family. Burke gave his mother a poem penned by Crosby, its lines urging his family to "keep on smiling," "forget the past," and expressing regret for "the tears I have caused you."

Burke puffed on a cigarette until the black cap covered his head. "The executioners moved quickly," said the *Oakland Tribune*. "Before he was aware of what was happening, the condemned man was half shoved through the trap. His neck was broken instantly by the fall. It was, according to prison officials, a 'perfect hanging.'"

Smith led Gregg down the long corridor to the death chamber. Gregg turned to the warden. "I want you to know I hold nothing against you. I played the game and lost." Both Burke and Gregg, like their two cohorts before them, refused religious consolation, an apparent pact among the five men.

On January 17, Crosby smoked his last cigarette as Captain of the Guard Clarence Larkin led him to death chamber. Crosby, who, according to the others, "kept still because he didn't want to queer us," left his final words in a poem to his mother:

> This old world seems all against us
> But say, it's not the end

For the clouds will someday brighten
If our courage does not bend.
You think that we are hardened?
That we're a sinful lot?
Look in our hearts and you will find
A little tender spot.
That spot is for our mother.
We've taken all her joy
All mothers know the anguish
Caused by a wayward boy.
So let us grin at this old world
And never say we're down
We are then men whom God forgot
We'll smile though others frown.

Crosby held his hand had out to Smith, saying, "Shake, Warden. I'm not going to break down." It was rumored that Smith and other prison officials thought Crosby's death sentence unjust. In accordance with Crosby's request, Smith turned his body over to the Veteran's Welfare Board to rest in the Presidio burial grounds.

Once desperate to save his own life, Stewart experienced a change of heart and now welcomed death. "Mine is the hell that Milton describes . . . the anxious soul alternately tossed from the ardors of hope to the petrifying rigors of doubt and dread . . . To prolong it would be folly," Stewart wrote to Superior Court Judge Malcolm Glenn. The courts granted his request to die, but nearly a year later, with his execution set for March, 1931, "The Squealer" had another change of heart and decided he did not, in fact, wish to die. After reviewing Stewart's new request, the California Supreme Court, in a highly unusual move, recommended by a four-to-three vote to commute his sentence back to life imprisonment.

Officials transferred the lifer to San Quentin after he received threats for turning against his co-conspirators. A year later, Stewart begged to be sent back to Folsom. "I'm no rat," he told San Quentin's warden, James Holohan. "Maybe some convicts will think so and will stick a knife in me, but anything is better than this awful solitude. Put me out there. I haven't much to live for anyway." He got his wish.

Stewart laid low until 1941, when, at the age of forty-eight, he applied for clemency from Governor Culbert Olson. He had served twenty "solid years" and suffered from heart trouble. Unsuccessful with Olson, Stewart appealed to the State Supreme Court in 1944, stating that when Governor Rolph commuted his sentence to "imprisonment for his natural life," he didn't indicate whether Stewart could apply for parole. The majority of justices agreed and Stewart won his freedom—at least for the next two-and-a-half years.

Arrested on forgery charges in 1947, Stewart returned to Folsom to serve out his life sentence.

"The verdicts are just as they should have been. They will not bring my husband back to me, but they may save [an]other woman's husband from a similar fate."

—Emma Carey, wife of the victim, 1930

"Warden, I wish you a long and prosperous life. I hold no ill feelings against anyone."

—George Davis, on the scaffold, 1930

66. Alfred Boss, December 5, 1930, 67. George Davis, December 5, 1930

Alfred Boss and George Davis entered the Arata Brothers grocery store in Sacramento on November 18, 1929, armed with revolvers. "Everybody be quiet and put your hands up!" one of them yelled. After securing four hundred dollars, Boss and Davis ran from the store. Clifford Carey, a twenty-year-old employee, ran after them, urging other employees to help. Boss turned and fired a single bullet at Carey, striking him in the head and killing him instantly.

Boss and Davis fled to an apartment owned by three female acquaintances, where they divided up the money. After an intense two-week search, police received word the men were staying at a hotel in Albany, Oregon. Officers surprised Boss as he came down the stairs to the lobby. Boss surrendered and led the way to Davis's room. Each suspect carried a pistol and their car contained additional guns and ammunition, as well as an ax.

With his hands cuffed in front of him, Davis sat and calmly smoked a cigarette. He spoke in a cool and even voice, boasting, "If we had come down these stairs into the lobby together, things would have been different." If apprehended together, the men had agreed to shoot their way to freedom. Boss and Davis were returned to Sacramento to face trial, where both men pleaded not guilty. Hester Wilcox, one of the women in the apartment where Boss and Davis hid, testified the men admitted to the robbery and murder, with one saying, "Well, we had to shoot to get out." Others corroborated her story. The defense then surprised the jury by not offering any testimony at all. Neither Boss nor Davis took the stand.

When the jury foreman read the guilty verdict, the defendants showed no reaction. The *Woodland Daily Democrat* reported, "They were perhaps the least affected, outwardly, of any persons in the courtroom." Mrs. Emma Carey, wife of the murdered clerk, reacted with solemn joy. "The verdicts are just as they should have been," she said. "They will not bring my husband back to me, but they may save [an]other woman's husband from a similar fate." Eight months after her husband died, Emma gave birth to a boy and named him after his father.

Basing his appeal on the fact that it was Boss who killed Carey, Davis claimed to be a "victim of circumstance." Four of the seven California Supreme Court justices upheld the lower court's decision, citing Davis's previous felony charge. Silently passing his partner's death cell, Boss mounted the gallows on December 5, 1930, his thirty-second birthday. A cigarette hung from his lips until the moment the executioner pulled the black cap over his head. Boss left behind two children, both unaware of their father's fate.

Twenty-five minutes later, after doctors had declared Boss dead and cut down his body, guards led Davis to the gallows, with his arms strapped to his sides. He looked at Warden Smith and said, "Warden, I wish you a long and prosperous life. I hold no ill feelings against anyone. I'm sorry I can't raise my arm to shake hands with you." He looked down at the seventy witnesses and said, "Goodbye, men. Good luck to all of you."

ONE MOTHER'S TRAGEDY

Nora Hopkins, Alfred Boss's mother, buried her fifth child, the only one who lived past boyhood. She had experienced the loss of many loved ones during her adult life. She lost her husband, Alfred's father, when Alfred was only thirteen months old. A month later, Nora's mother-in-law passed away. Seven months later, her father was tragically killed when struck by a train. Her own mother, whom Nora cared for in her home, died next. As she struggled to raise Alfred on her own, Nora promised her dying brother, Columbus, that she'd care for his six children. Another relative also gave Nora her three children to look after.

Nora said, apologetically, "If I didn't give Alfred the care he should have had, it's because I didn't have the time." When Alfred was twelve years old, Nora married Herman Boeing. This is when Alfred began his crime career by stealing candy, and he soon landed in a reform school. Eight years later, Boeing died from an accidental shooting while duck hunting. Two years later, Nora married Mark Hopkins. Soon thereafter, she learned her only living son faced the death penalty. Nora was supportive of her son to the end, saying:

> He says he never did it and he's not going to tell them now that he did it. And if they're going to hang him, he wants them to get it over with. And I don't believe he did do it. Why they never had a witness who could identify him. But we're poor, and it just seems as if poor people shouldn't be in this world, anyway. Anyhow, my shoulders are broad and the Lord wouldn't be giving me all this trouble if he didn't give me the strength to bear it.

PART VII: 1931–1937

Folsom Wardens: Court Smith, March 1927–April 18, 1936

Clarence Larkin, April 18, 1936–November 20, 1937

California Governors: Clement C. Young, January 4, 1927–January 6, 1931

James Rolph, Jr., January 6, 1931–January 2, 1934

Frank Merriam, January 2, 1934–January 2, 1939

After a decade of prosperity and opportunity, the United States fell into despair. The Great Depression blanketed the country and brought unemployment to a quarter of the workforce. Farmers in the Midwest suffered a one-two punch when severe drought and dust storms threatened or ruined their livelihood. Because of California's thriving agricultural industry, 200,000 Midwestern and Southeastern farmers packed their meager belongings and headed west, only to receive hostility in their new home. California farmers had no desire to share the state's land by giving it to these "Okies" and "Arkies."

Many desperate citizens across the country "road the rails," hoping to find a better place. It's estimated that 600,000 people hitched rides in boxcars during the 1930s. The increases in prostitution and suicide suggested that some felt they had few, if any, survival options. Prohibition ended in 1933 and, for many, alcohol provided solace from the uncertainty, although alcoholism rates increased accordingly.

Franklin D. Roosevelt's New Deal promised more jobs in the early 1930s. His newly formed Civilian Conservation Corps (CCC) provided almost two million jobs to young men, while the Works Progress Administration (WPA) kept public art projects alive. Families gathered around their radios and listened to Roosevelt's "Fireside Chats," which attempted to reassure Americans that the economy was recovering.

Meanwhile, overworked and underpaid labor workers had had enough. In July 1934, the "General Strike" in San Francisco marked the first time a major U.S. port was completely shut down. The International Longshoremen's Association demanded more control over hiring and better pay and hours. When employers tried to open the docks to unload ships, strikers clashed with 1000 police, forcing a four-day strike which ended with sixty-four injuries and two deaths. The following year, the Wagner Act passed, creating a National Labor Relations Board to protect workers' rights to form unions.

Despite the turmoil of the Great Depression, Californians still had reasons to celebrate. The Bay Bridge, the world's longest steel bridge at 8.25 miles, was completed in 1936. A year later, the Golden Gate Bridge opened to vehicles and pedestrians. In 1935, San Francisco opened City College, its first two-year public college. Today, it boasts over 100,000 students enrolled at various associated campuses, making it the largest community and junior college in the country. The movie *It Happened One Night* entertained moviegoers in 1934 and, a year later, two of every five Americans filled movie theaters to see *The Bride of Frankenstein*, *Dracula*, and *King Kong*.

Folsom Prison experienced continued overpopulation and the Board of Prison Directors made several recommendations to Governor Rolph, including making Folsom a maximum security prison, segregating youthful first-time offenders, and funding an institution for the "criminally insane and feeble-minded." In 1936, Captain of the Guard Clarence Larkin became warden and began installing plumbing in the older buildings, established the prison's first two-way radio system, and oversaw completion of a new cell block. His term as warden ended when he was killed during the September 19, 1937 riot, now known as "Bloody Sunday." That same year, legislation approved execution by lethal gas, replacing eighty-six years of death by hanging. Those responsible for Larkin's murder were some of the first to experience San Quentin's new gas chamber.

"I'm tired of living anyway—I hope the rope doesn't break."
—Fred Mott, on the scaffold, 1931

68. Fred Mott, July 17, 1931

Carrying a .32 automatic Colt behind his back, Fred Mott walked into the Jackson-Bell radio store on Market Street in San Francisco to confront Jay Douglas Thomas, the informant responsible for sending him to Leavenworth on drug charges. Having previously been a drug dealer, Thomas and his wife Grace became narcotic informers for the feds. They turned Mott in.

Thomas sat with Grace in a small office in the store. Mott walked in, leveled the gun at Thomas and fired one shot, killing him. Mott fled across Market Street and jumped on a streetcar. An employee of the radio store followed Mott out of the store and located an officer, who pursued Mott. Detective Sergeant Desmond soon caught up with the streetcar and approached Mott, who stashed the gun under the car seat. "He squealed on me," Mott said, "I'm a hop peddler and he and his wife were my customers. They turned me in and I did a year and a day in Leavenworth prison."

Mott's long criminal history included two previous felony charges, one for shooting at a military official. "It was just mischief, and in New Hampshire there people do anything they want," Mott explained. Having been dishonorably discharged from the Navy on two occasions, Mott was considered by the military as weak-minded, paranoid, and a constitutional psychopath.

At his arraignment, Mott pleaded not guilty by reason of insanity, but later he changed his plea to not guilty due to self-defense. He told jurors that he came to the shop on a "friendly intention" to meet Thomas and "let bygones be bygones." However, Thomas confronted him and said, "You son of a bitch, have you been telling people around that I am an ex-convict and informer?" Mott claimed

Thomas then reached under his desk for a gun, but Mott shot first. Mott said he didn't remember anything about being arrested, saying, "I was in a daze."

Found guilty and sentenced to die, Mott filed an appeal, but due to his two previous felonies the higher courts could not intervene. Mott begged Governor James Rolph, who had blocked fifteen executions, to grant him clemency. "Please grant me a reprieve," Mott pleaded. "I am innocent. I hang tomorrow at Folsom." Rolph, who would experience his first hanging since taking office, couldn't interfere. Rolph said, sympathetically, "What can I do? These things hurt me, too."

Mott wrote to his attorney instructing him to donate $235, his worldly fortune, to the Shriners' Hospital for Crippled Children in San Francisco. On July 17, 1931, Mott thanked Warden Court Smith for the "good eats" and said, "I'm tired of living anyway—I hope the rope doesn't break . . . be sure you get it on right." And, so saying, Mott went to his reward.

"Say goodnight to the boys."
—Wilbur McCabe, on the scaffold, 1931

69. Wilbur McCabe, July 24, 1931

Out on parole after serving six years at San Quentin for robbery, Wilbur McCabe entered the Los Angeles University Club on July 16, 1930, shortly after midnight, intending to rob it. Armed with a gun, he gave night clerk Henry P. Miller a note demanding he put money into a bag and hand it over. "You are stuck up. Don't put your hands up or dare make a sign. If you try to make signs to anyone, you will die," McCabe had written. A night watchman passed by and saw McCabe and Miller, but thought nothing of it and continued on his way. Miller, who had been cleaning his fingernails with a penknife as McCabe approached, refused McCabe's demands and slashed McCabe's face several times with the knife.

McCabe shot Miller in the chest and abdomen and fled with blood pouring from his face. Police followed McCabe's bloody trail twenty blocks to his home, where they found him in the bathroom washing the blood away. Police took

McCabe to the hospital, where the critically injured Miller identified him as the shooter. Miller died the following day.

McCabe pleaded not guilty by reason of insanity. His defense charged police "with unfair methods in forcing a confession from him when he was still weak from loss of blood." McCabe also claimed to have been intoxicated when arrested, but witnesses who dressed his wounds didn't corroborate this. McCabe told the jury that he and Miller planned the robbery together. McCabe claimed Miller was a "moral pervert" and the two "engaged in numerous acts of depravity." According to McCabe, Miller lost his nerve and lashed out, making McCabe shoot in self-defense.

With no evidence to support McCabe's claim of Miller's collusion in the crime, the jury seriously doubted this account and found McCabe guilty. The appellate court denied McCabe's appeal. When asked by Warden Court Smith if he had any final requests, McCabe requested a head of lettuce, which he received. He said he hadn't spoken to any of his relatives in twenty years and that "they do not know about me and I do not want them to learn what has happened to me." He told the warden to "say goodnight to the boys," and within minutes, on July 24, 1931, McCabe fell through the trap.

 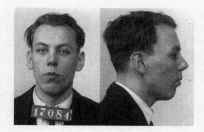

70. William Hudson, October 2, 1931, 71. Robert O'Neill, October 2, 1931

Armed with guns and knives, William Hudson and Robert O'Neill drove around Los Angeles in a stolen car looking for a "soft spot" to hold up. They decided on Henry Kraus's malt shop on Vermont and 9th Avenue. It was three days before Christmas, and the streets were crowded with shoppers and early evening traffic.

Thirty-year-old Deputy Marshal Perman C. Calderwood was driving home when he saw the robbery in progress. Calderwood pulled over and ran to aid Kraus, who had tackled O'Neill to the ground. Calderwood arrived just as Hudson fired shots that struck Kraus in the back. The deputy tried to subdue Hudson, who drew a knife and plunged it into his back.

According to the *Oakland Tribune*, Calderwood's brother William happened along the scene, totally unaware of his sibling's involvement until he "elbowed his way to the center of the group of spectators and found the dead man was his brother."

The two holdup men escaped, leaving Calderwood dead and Kraus seriously injured. In his haste, O'Neill dropped a dry cleaning bill with his name and address. Police arrested him within a few hours. Initially, O'Neill refused to name his companion, but eventually he signed a confession and implicated Hudson, although it wasn't until February 7 that police found and arrested Hudson in Salt Lake City.

Tried together, the men pleaded not guilty. Due to damaging testimony from witnesses and Kraus, the jury found them guilty. The two men had hoped that an appeal would result in a life sentence, but as their execution date of August 7 neared, they heard nothing from their attorneys. In fact, their defense council had not submitted the appeal as promised. O'Neill penned a letter to Warden Smith, who sent it to Governor Rolph. O'Neill and Hudson requested the opportunity to write their own statements to the higher court.

The governor criticized the "apparent laxity of the lawyers" and issued a reprieve. In the meantime, the rogue attorneys wrote to Warden Smith claiming their clients had agreed not to appeal. They also asked to witness the execution of their one-time clients. Smith denied their request to witness the executions. In September, Chief Justice William Waste, concluding that the men were "fairly tried and convicted of a vicious and cruel murder," upheld the lower court's decision.

On October 2, 1931, twenty-five-year-old Hudson, who refused to reveal his true name and "disgrace his family," murmured a "farewell" before falling through the trap. Twenty-one-year-old O'Neill slept very little the night before, and he died less than half an hour after Hudson.

"Won't you look at the Scales of Justice and see how uneven they are—hear the cries to even them—to let me live."
—William Henry Burkhart, in a letter to Governor James Rolph, 1930

72. William Henry Burkhart, January 29, 1932

On March 23, 1930, William Burkhart purchased a Ford coupe, using a fictitious name and a bogus check. The following day, he quit his job as a bookkeeper for the Los Angeles Gas & Electric Corporation and paid for the first month's rent on a bungalow apartment, again using a fake name and a bad check.

That same evening, he lured his former wife, Ann McKnight, a dancer and movie extra, to the new home. He claimed he wanted to reconcile. McKnight had secured a divorce months earlier after a short marriage filled with physical abuse on the part of Burkhart. According to Burkhart, the two saw one another many times following the divorce in an effort to mend their relationship.

At around seven, the pair left in the coupe and returned about three hours later. Burkhart knocked on the door of Mr. and Mrs. James Thompson, his new next-door neighbors. They were playing cards with another couple, Mr. and Mrs. King, and invited Burkhart in. He asked for a match and remarked, "I have been drinking, you might think I am stiff but my wife is stiffer. I will make myself acquainted tomorrow."

Burkhart left, only to return moments later. He looked at James Thompson. "May I speak to you as a friend?" Thompson replied, "Surely," and went outside with Burkhart. Mr. King followed the two. Burkhart led them to a sidewalk at the rear of the apartment where they saw McKnight lying on the ground. He asked the men to help him carry her to his car, claiming she was drunk and had passed out. Thompson knelt down, felt for a pulse, and said she didn't look drunk. Burkhart responded with, "Well, she always acts that way when she gets drunk."

Thompson told Burkhart to bring his car closer and he'd help him. When Burkhart left to move his car, Thompson and King went inside and called the police. They returned to find Burkhart dragging his ex-wife's body along the sidewalk toward the coupe, leaving a trail of blood in her wake. Burkhart also had blood on his clothing.

Officers arrived and one remarked, "We better call an ambulance."

Burkhart lit a cigarette and replied, "There is no use; she is dead."

When asked if he had been drinking, Burkhart replied yes, and he added that his wife was "dead drunk." Officers noted that Burkhart didn't appear intoxicated, and a subsequent stomach pumping yielded little alcohol. However, police did find a fully loaded .38 caliber Smith and Wesson revolver in Burkhart's pocket.

"Well, that gun was fully loaded, and I had not fired any shots," Burkhart contended while being questioned at the police station. "You can't prove I shot my wife."

"Is your wife shot?" asked the officer. Up until this point, no one had mentioned her cause of death.

Burkhart backpedaled, saying he heard it from officers. He then said, "She is a great kidder. She is around here someplace."

The interior of the Ford coupe revealed blood and bullet holes. Ann McKnight had apparently been killed inside the vehicle, shot in the arm and chest and three times in the back. She had been dead at least two hours. The ballistics report showed that Burkhart's gun had been recently discharged, and at least one of the bullets in McKnight's body had come from a .38. Then officers discovered more.

"You had sexual intercourse with your wife after she was dead, didn't you?" asked the officer. Burkhart hung his head and didn't reply.

At his arraignment, Burkhart pleaded not guilty by reason of insanity. However, at trial he dropped the insanity clause and pleaded not guilty. Joy Haskins, McKnight's sister, testified that when Burkhart attempted to see his wife on two previous occasions, he stated, "By God, I will have her. She is my wife and if I can't have her nobody else shall because I will kill her first." He also allegedly said, "I have made up my mind that if I cannot have her nobody else will if I have to spend the rest of my life in the penitentiary."

Burkhart didn't take the stand to testify on his own behalf. Based on witness testimony and the ballistics report, the jury found Burkhart guilty of premeditated murder. Showing no emotion at the verdict, he merely said, "I hope Joy is satisfied now."

Burkhart appealed and sent several long letters to Governor James Rolph, claiming he had no recollection of the night he killed his wife. He blamed a "spree" of drinking alcohol and taking morphine tablets that day. Burkhart claimed, "I was riding around and I didn't know who I was with, where I went, or what I did. My mind is blank as to what happened that evening. The next I remember I was in jail terribly sick and dizzy."

He accused McKnight's two sisters of turning her against him and for convincing McKnight to get an abortion shortly after the two married. Burkhart said of his sisters-in-law, "Those who were responsible for my grief, I trust, they have learnt a lesson and won't ruin another happy married life." He also denied making threats to kill his wife: "I loved my wife with all my heart and soul—like she loved me. Her love to me was liking [sic] to that of my Mother—as sacred, it was Heavens [sic] last gift, which I will always cherish . . . The pleasant dreams of her have lingered sustaining me these miserable days; she has never left me."

Burkhart also asked the governor to spare his life for the sake of his parents, saying, "No wonder they have aged and gotten feeble. God only knows how much misery they have suffered—more than their share, I know."

Burkhart's mother, Sarah, wrote to William Waste, California Supreme Court justice, begging for clemency: " . . . how can I do with out [sic] his sweet letters and the father who is so old he is helpless as I have talked to you [sic] are a man of a heart and will [sic] all in your power to save his life and as I told you his wife is gone and it will not bring her back but it will make so many sad hearts so happy just to know he lives."

Even Joy Haskins asked the governor to consider life imprisonment for her sister's killer, but only because of Burkhart's mother, who came to appeal to her daily. Haskins wrote, ". . . for the sake of his aged mother, I will be willing to signe [sic] some [thing] for life sentence, but not to help him get out in a few years."

McKnight's brother disagreed, asking Governor Rolph to allow the execution: "This is not the case of a man inflamed by liquor killing the thing he loved, as may be stated by those who wish you to commute his sentence, but a case of a man using liquor as an excuse for doing something he had planned to do a year before . . . he seemed to delight in abusing her much the same as some people do with a little kitten that can't fight back."

Nearly a year after the murder, the California Supreme Court upheld the original decision, ruling, "The jury's implied finding in this case that the killing was the product of an abandoned and malignant heart [and] was premeditated finds ample support in the record, and warranted the infliction of the death penalty." By this time, Governor Rolph had issued Burkhart five reprieves.

Attorney and former superior judge Carlos Hardy opted to take Burkhart's case, promising to produce evidence supporting his new client's claims of insanity. However, Folsom Prison physician Dr. P.W. Day reported that the condemned man's "emotional reactions are good" and he "does not show any delusions, hallucinations, or abnormal mental processes."

After being given his sixth reprieve, on the eve of his execution, Burkhart said, "You're kidding me," as he finished off one of the two cigars he requested as a final privilege. In fact, three of Burkhart's reprieves came the night before his scheduled execution. However, the California Supreme Court again denied his appeal and Rolph had to let the law take its course. The justices cited Burkhart's two previous felony convictions as part of their decision to uphold the sentence. They also opined that Burkhart, "possibly abnormal, is not suffering from the kind of insanity recognized by state law as being of that nature which renders one incapable of knowing the results of his own voluntary acts and which does not deprive him of the ability to know the distinction between right and wrong."

The war veteran spent his final night writing letters to his mother and sister, and he went silently to his death on the Folsom prison gallows the following morning, January 29, 1932.

James "Sunny Jim" Rolph

Rolph served as San Francisco's mayor from 1912 to 1931, making him the longest serving mayor in San Francisco history. Because of his gregarious and charming disposition, residents called him "Sunny Jim." He became governor of California in 1931, and he was never shy about his distaste for the death penalty. He issued at least one reprieve to every condemned prisoner, some receiving as many as nine. Many Californians criticized Rolph for his stance, saying, "It bespeaks again an emotional instability and a shocking lack of a true understanding of the responsibilities of his high office" and "Governor Rolph's weakness for granting reprieves to murderers is one that he ought to cure. This is no time for placating criminals." Rolph did, however, favor a bill making execution mandatory for slaying police officers. "Our policemen must be protected," he announced.

Rolph looked for reasons to issue reprieves. He issued one when an execution date landed on a bank holiday. "I have reprieved money," said Rolph, "and I can reprieve a human life, which is more than money." He also told the press, "You just couldn't hang a man on his birthday. And, I couldn't permit a death sentence to be carried out next Friday—St. Patrick's Day." He defended his stance. "We've got to give him at least one reprieve. I haven't failed to give an extension to a doomed killer so far. They're at least entitled to that much. [One] can't blame them if they try to escape the noose." Rolph also angered residents when he endeavored to save a man who shot his unfaithful wife: "I'm not inclined to let men hang when their crimes involve infidelity of their wife and breaking up of their home." Then, in 1933, when a San Jose police officer was killed and suspect Clyde Johnson was dragged from jail by a mob and lynched, Rolph condoned the hanging, calling it a "fine lesson to the whole nation." He even promised to pardon any of those convicted of the lynching. "Sunny Jim's" once adoring subjects now called him "Governor Lynch." The negative publicity and fallout from his comments took a toll on his health and Rolph suffered several heart attacks in early 1934. He died in June, but not before issuing more reprieves from his hospital bed.

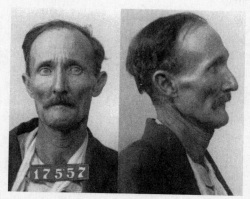

"Get your gun and go ahead and shoot me. I'm ready to go right now."
—Thomas Walker to officers after he killed his victim, 1931

73. Thomas Walker, August 19, 1932

There is no woman going to double-cross me and get away with it," Thomas Walker said to officer T. W. Johnson on November 13, 1931. Moments earlier, Walker had bludgeoned girlfriend Anna Garcia with a hammer before stabbing her thirty-eight times with a butcher knife. Garcia shared her home, where the murder occurred, with her thirteen-year-old son and washed clothes as a means of support. The *Fresno Bee* noted, "The condition of the house indicated that the woman was orderly and industrious, a matronly housewife and thrifty."

Garcia and a neighbor, Mrs. Goodman, sat in the backyard when Walker asked Garcia to come inside the house. After ten minutes, Goodman went inside and heard Walker yell, "You double-crossed me!" Garcia screamed and Goodman ran from the house to call police. Officer Robert Powers found Walker standing in the doorway, a razor in his hand. "Get your gun and go ahead and shoot me. I'm ready to go now," Walker shouted. When Walker refused to let go of the blade and threatened to slice his own throat, Powers shot Walker in the arm. Walker dropped the razor. "I shot quick to save him for the hangman's noose," said the officer. After subduing Walker, Powers found Garcia suffering from several large stab wounds. She died shortly after arriving at the hospital.

Walker, described as the "vagabond lover of the 350-lb woman" by the *Fresno Bee*, pleaded not guilty by reason of insanity. His court-appointed attorney insisted upon his making the plea, although Walker wanted to plead guilty. The *Bakersfield Californian* described Walker at his trial: "With his lean, hollowed-cheeked face covered with a beard, the slayer resembled strikingly the paintings of John the Baptist done by the early Italian school. He might have been a model for Giotto.

Judge Lambert called him before the witness stand and Walker stood outlined like an angular, attenuated scarecrow against the gray rain-swept window pane."

Walker told the jury he had witnessed Garcia drop something in his coffee. After drinking it, he became violently ill, which convinced him Garcia tried to poison him with what he called "carbolic acid." When he confronted her, she allegedly said, "What can you do about it?" While never apologizing for his deed, Walker told the court, "My life ain't worth anything after doing a thing like that; what is my life worth? I ain't crazy, insane, I won't stand to be double-crossed, if I lose my life, I won't stand to be double-crossed, I am that kind of man."

The jury returned a guilty verdict and the judge obliged Walker's wishes by sentencing him to death. His attorney, Raymond Henderson, said, "The guilt of the defendant was so well established that it would be frivolous to appeal the case."

The prisoner himself declared, "I am satisfied to let the law take its course." Governor James Rolph disagreed, believing Walker had to be insane. "Every friend this man has—even his attorneys and relatives—seem to have forsaken him," said

RAYMOND W. HENDERSON

When the judge appointed Henderson to be Walker's attorney, Henderson had been practicing law for fourteen years. What set him apart from other attorneys was that he was blind. After graduating in 1904 from UCLA, Henderson, who was self-taught in the law, went on to pass the bar exam in 1917. Henderson made his own notes in court using a perforated metal strip through which he pricked holes on heavy paper using a punch. When he addressed the court, he'd often run his fingers along the paper. Henderson was not only a public defender, but he also represented those involved in American Civil Liberties Union cases, often lobbying on behalf of the disabled, the elderly, and the poor. He provided much of his work at no charge. He became a leading figure in Kern County, championing for the blind, and he was instrumental in getting legislators to authorize pensions for the needy blind.

In 1932, Henderson won the Socialist nomination for assemblymen in the county, promising to help farmers become more independent from banks by creating co-ops, lightening the tax burden on the poor, and developing unemployment insurance. Although he did not win election, he continued to fight against social injustices. He condemned the Kern County Board of Supervisors's support of the burning and banning of John Steinbeck's *The Grapes of Wrath*. Dr. Newell Perry of the California School for the Blind called Henderson "a reformer, with poetry in his soul and literature in his stylus. Raymond came to the organized blind movement in his maturity from a long background of experience in other causes. He brought to it a notable array of personal abilities, a high degree of professional skill, a fine spirit of humanity, and the enrichment of wide and intensive activity." Henderson passed away in 1945 at the age of 64.

Rolph. "I'm not going to let him hang until he has exhausted every possibility of beating the noose." His other attorney, Jay L. Henry, applied for clemency on Walker's behalf, something Walker himself refused to do. In the application, Henry called his client "constitutionally inferior" and "mentally low," and he characterized Walker's behavior as "paranoid dementia praecox," a mental disease involving systematized delusions.

Rolph submitted Henry's findings to chief Supreme Court justice William Waste. In the meantime, Rolph issued Walker five reprieves he never asked for. When the Supreme Court refused to interfere with the execution, it left Rolph with no choice but to permit the execution. Walker leaned on the arm of the prison chaplain as he walked to the gallows. "God will be with you," the priest said. "I hope He will," replied Walker. "Warden Smith has been good to me." Walker died minutes later.

"But I won't give her name. I won't hide behind a woman's skirts."
—Peter Farrington, 1932

74. Peter Farrington, March 24, 1933

On April 29, 1930, veteran police officer John Wesley Malcolm came upon a robbery on Pier 26 in San Francisco. According to the *San Mateo Times* and the *Fresno Bee*, Malcolm initially mistook the scene as a "movie stunt." One man sat in a car as two others pointed their guns at Maurice Murphy and Max Kahn, Stevendore and Ballast Company's paymaster and office manager, respectively. The two company officers held the entire $3,200 payroll. A small crowd of laborers watched helplessly from an adjacent platform. Without drawing his gun, Malcolm approached. One of the robbers yelled, "Here comes a cop! Give it to him!" Malcolm took two bullets to the chest and died on the site, as the three men escaped with the money in a roadster.

In mid-June, police found a man in Tacoma, Washington, fitting the description of Malcolm's killer. They arrested Peter Farrington, known as "Little Spud," and put him in a line-up. Chris Clausen, the port captain who witnessed the shooting, walked straight up to Farrington and identified him as the shooter. The other two assailants were never found. At trial, Farrington pleaded not guilty. Several eyewitnesses gave testimony that directly implicated Farrington in the crime.

Farrington's defense hinged on an alibi he wouldn't divulge. "I don't want to bring her name into this case. But I was with her in Stockton when the state claims I shot Malcolm during the holdup," Farrington said. "But I won't give her name. I won't hide behind a woman's skirts."

When the guilty verdict was read, Farrington never flinched. His sister-in-law, however, jumped up and screamed curses at the jury. Farrington appealed the verdict, but in August 1931 Farrington lost his appeal. Due to continued promises from defense attorneys to produce an alibi, Governor James Rolph issued Farrington seven reprieves over the course of nearly two years. Farrington also earned reprieves when each of his subsequently scheduled execution dates coincidentally fell on a bank holiday, St. Patrick's Day, and his birthday.

In January 1933, Farrington and two other death row inmates, John Fleming and Glen Johnson, sawed through the bars of their cells with files, but they were caught before they could flee. Evidently, the men acquired the files via the prison library. Warden Court Smith surmised the "blades might have been concealed in books which had been re-bound in the prison binery [sic], operated with convict labor." Rolph acknowledged this stunt hurt Farrington's chance of executive clemency.

Before mounting the gallows, Farrington shook hands with the chaplain and a guard, and said, "I can always shake hands even after losing a fight." Standing on the scaffold, he instructed the guard to "let 'er go."

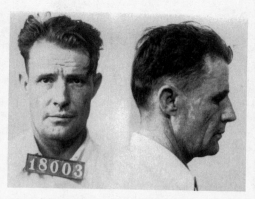

"You seem to be taking it harder than I do."
—John Fleming, to the witnesses of his execution, 1933

75. John Fleming, November 17, 1933

Fifty-four-year-old Amos Leece and his wife stopped at Midway Service Station and Roadhouse in San Bernardino County on May 21, 1932. There they encountered John Fleming and his girlfriend, Peggy O'Day, who happened to be a prostitute. Both Fleming and O'Day had been drinking most of the day. When Leece and his wife went inside to pay for the gas, O'Day asked him to buy her a drink. He refused and O'Day cursed at him. Leece responded, "I think you are a cheap, chippy whore." Leece and his wife returned to their car. While Mr. Leece was retrieving the crank from the trunk to restart his car, Fleming approached and demanded that Leece apologize for insulting his girlfriend.

Leece refused, even repeating the remark to Fleming, and then he walked back into the barroom to speak with owner Charles Adcock. "[Charlie,] what kind of place are you running here, that a fellow can't come here without being insulted?" Leece left the barroom, shoving Fleming out of the doorway, as he returned to his vehicle. Three gunshots resounded. Charlie and another patron rushed outside to find Fleming standing over Leece's prone body, holding a .45 caliber revolver. Fleming fled to one of the roadhouse's bedrooms and hid in a closet, where police eventually found him. Fleming, a card dealer on a Long Beach gambling ship, pleaded not guilty to the murder of Leece by reason of insanity.

The defense tried to show that Fleming acted in self-defense when Leece attacked him with the car crank, but Mrs. Leece refuted this claim. O'Day's testimony provided little help, as she had been intoxicated at the time of the incident and could offer few clear details.

Found guilty, the "four-time loser" awaited the outcome of his appeal at Folsom, where, in January of 1933, he attempted a break. Along with fellow death row inmates, Glen Johnson and Peter Farrington, Fleming sawed through the bars of his cell using a file that had been hidden in the bindings of books from the prison library. The men were apprehended before they could flee from the cell block.

Fleming lost his appeal, although one justice, J. Langdon, dissented, calling the testimony of Mrs. Leece, the only witness to the shooting, "conflicting, incomplete and exceedingly indefinite." Langdon also called Leece the aggressor and took little stock in the testimony of the witnesses who were frequenters of "the bootleg place and prostitution house."

Standing on the scaffold, Fleming surveyed the crowd and said, "I'm sorry to have caused all this trouble. You seem to be taking it harder than I do."

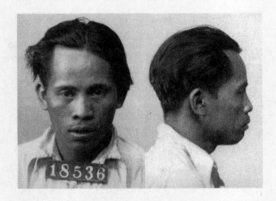

76. Dick Villion, December 1, 1933

On September 20, 1932, Dick Villion and four other Filipinos entered a gambling hall owned by Wong Sun. Armed with guns, the men began grabbing money out of drawers and from the gambling tables. During the melee that followed, Sun received a bullet in the chest and died immediately. According to the *San Mateo Times*, the men filed into two cars and fled. Within hours, police apprehended Joe Corpus, one of the gang members, in the backyard of a home belonging to an off-duty police officer.

Unwilling to take the rap, Corpus struck a deal by divulging the whereabouts of his companions. Police arrested three of the others, including Villion, the following March, but they never found the fifth bandit. Villion's fellow gang members all pleaded guilty and received life sentences, but Villion pleaded not guilty. Corpus told the jury that Villion instigated the robbery and shot Sun. Villion claimed that an employee of the gambling house shot at him, but hit Sun instead.

Found guilty, Villion faced the death penalty. While awaiting transfer to San Quentin, Villion and four others attempted to make a break from the Santa Clara County Jail using a wooden makeshift knife, but deputies discovered the knife on Villion. After threats erupted between Villion and his fellow gang members, authorities transferred Villion to Folsom, instead of to San Quentin.

According to one newspaper, Governor James Rolph, "[maintaining] his unsullied record of granting every doomed man at least one reprieve," issued Villion his first reprieve. "We've got to give him at least one reprieve," the governor said. "I haven't failed to give an extension to a doomed killer so far. They're at least entitled to that much. Can't blame them if they try to escape the noose."

Rolph granted Villion another reprieve after Villion's attorneys promised to submit strong evidence supporting their client's claims. However, neither the attorneys' promise nor the governor's reprieve were enough to save Villion. On December 1, he bid "adios" to his fellow inmates on death row before mounting the gallows.

77. Glen Johnson, January 19, 1934

At approximately 9:00 P.M., Mrs. Andrew Bell heard someone knocking on the door to her house. Having been asleep, she ignored it, until she heard someone fumbling with the door knob. She opened the door to find two men with flashlights. Her screams frightened away the would-be intruders and woke her police officer husband. Andrew Bell immediately summoned fellow officers. They soon received a call from neighbor Harry Darling, reporting that two men were now entering another neighbor's home.

Officer Mervyn Reardon, Bell, Darling, and two other officers surrounded the home. Its owners were away for the night. Searching the house, Bell spotted a hand resting on top of a box in a closet. The hand belonged to Benjamin Moore, one of the two intruders. Handcuffed, Moore said he didn't know where his companion had gone, but Reardon soon caught sight of him as Glen Johnson emerged from behind a large radio, a gun in each hand, and began firing at his pursuers.

A gunfight ensued. Bell and another officer were injured, while Reardon and Darling received fatal gunshot wounds. During the mayhem, Moore broke loose. Officer Lotus stopped him with a bullet, killing him. Johnson dropped to the floor after taking three bullets to the stomach.

Charged with the murders of officer Reardon and civilian Harry Darling, Johnson pleaded not guilty by reason of insanity. His defense attorney attempted to prove he was merely taking refuge in the house, not burglarizing it, and contended Johnson didn't have "an intent to commit murder." The attorney asked for a manslaughter charge instead of a murder charge. However, contradictory evidence hurt Johnson's claims, as it seemed to show that he had clearly rifled through the house.

Johnson was found guilty and, while awaiting the outcome of his appeal in Folsom Prison, he participated in the ill-fated break attempt, along with fellow condemned men Peter Farrington and John Fleming.

The higher court subsequently affirmed the earlier judgment. Governor Frank Merriam refused to issue Johnson a reprieve. He had a policy of denying clemency to any convicted cop killer. On January 19, 1934, Johnson muttered goodbyes to fellow death row prisoners as guards escorted him to the gallows. When asked if he had any final words, he gave no reply.

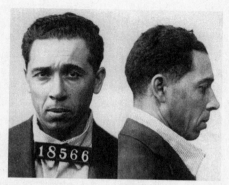

"**Well, the deputy sheriffs that brought me from Arizona said I cut his head off, and I know I didn't do such a thing, because I don't remember it.**"
—Daniel Harris, 1933

78. Daniel Harris, July 6, 1934

Daniel Harris wandered the streets of Crockett, California, on a winter day in December 1932. His train to Vallejo wouldn't be leaving for another hour. He watched jeweler Harry Whited place items in the display window of his shop. Sixty-seven-year-old Whited then stepped away from the store. Once Whited rounded the corner, Harris entered the store through the unlocked door.

After finding the cash register empty, Harris began shoving watches and rings and other jewelry into his pockets and turned to leave. Harris later remarked, "I started to go out of the store then and I passed the cash register again and I happened to think of the money again. So then I went to the safe."

As Harris looted the safe, Whited returned. Harris retreated to the back of the store, hoping to find an exit; Whited followed, yelling at the intruder. Harris recalled, ". . . he tried to grab hold of me and I fought him off. I knocked him down, I believe, first; he hung on to me though." Within minutes, Whited lay dead, his throat slashed. His nearly severed head had also sustained five fractures. Harris wiped his bloody hands on a curtain, cleaned the safe of the remaining cash, and fled. A customer later found Whited's body in the back of the store.

The *Richmond Daily Independent* called Whited "one of the best known and most respected citizens of Crockett," a man who belonged to the Lions Club, the Masons, and the advisory board of the Boy Scouts, and who participated in numerous public movements.

Harris boarded a train to Sacramento and, once there, he threw the pocket knife he used to kill Whited into the river. From Sacramento, Harris traveled south, leaving "a glittering trail of gems," according to the *Fresno Bee*, which authorities discovered in several pawn shops from the East Bay to Los Angeles.

Finally, hungry and penniless, Harris made his way to Phoenix. How he spent the ill-gained money is unknown, as he eventually had nothing to show for the stolen jewels. Harris resorted to stealing again, and police finally nabbed him for stealing buns off a bakery cart. When authorities realized their man wasn't just a petty thief, they confronted Harris with photos of Whited's body.

Harris responded to his arrest, saying, "Well, the deputy sheriffs that brought me from Arizona said I cut his head off, and I know I didn't do such a thing, because I don't remember. I know I did it, because afterwards I didn't examine him there, but I was covered with blood and had blood all over everything. . . ."

Harris insisted Phoenix Undersheriff William Veale told him that if he just admitted to the killing, he'd avoid the death penalty. Harris claimed that "[Veale] said, 'If you want to save your life, you just make a clean slate of it.'" He continued, "So after they had promised to save my life, why I thought well the best thing I can do is tell the truth anyway, so I did and I took them to all the places where I had pawned things and sold them in Los Angeles and on the way up I stopped at Fresno and showed them where I pawned things, sold them rather."

In spite of making a not guilty plea, Harris admitted killing the elderly jeweler. "I am guilty and I expect to pay for it," he told the court—a statement he would later deny making. Remarkably, after eleven hours of deliberation, the jury came back without a verdict. Harris would face another trial, and again he would enter a not guilty plea.

During his second trial, Harris chronicled his twenty-year criminal career, one that began at the age of sixteen, just months after his mother passed away. The half-Hispanic teen found it difficult to be raised by his Caucasian stepfather, whose other children were fair-skinned and blonde. Harris knew he was different and was treated as such.

Ester Flores, a woman who cared for Harris as a young boy, testified that Harris didn't play with the other children. He lacked intelligence, something she felt responsible for after dropping him as a baby. She noticed he had trouble grasping and learning things that other children learned easily.

Harris rarely found steady employment, his ex-con status working against him. In and out of Folsom and San Quentin for burglary, forgery, and receiving stolen goods, Harris routinely pleaded guilty, was imprisoned, and then was released early for good behavior. "He was definitely not a mean, vicious person," said Jeanine Hammer, a descendant of one of Harris's half sisters. "As an adult, by all accounts, he had a warm and good natured personality and was great with the younger children in his extended family. He just never seemed to get a break in life."

The second jury found Harris guilty, with no recommendation of leniency. Just before sentencing, however, Harris changed his plea to not guilty by reason of insanity. Judge C. W. Miller allowed Harris an insanity hearing, but Harris and his attorneys failed to furnish sufficient proof to result in a favorable insanity ruling.

Harris filed an appeal, and he was optimistic about his prospects for clemency. "I'll never hang," he told the press. In the appeal, Harris's attorneys cited several judicial errors and contended that District Attorney Hoey's statements of immunity to Harris were prejudicial and dishonest. The California Supreme Court justices disagreed with Harris's defense and denied his appeal, ruling, "[Finally] it should be said that herein demonstrates beyond any doubt that appellant was guilty of a most cruel, cold-blooded murder. There can be no question in the mind of the one who reads it that there are no circumstances which would have justified the jury affixing anything less than the extreme penalty of the law."

According to the *San Mateo Times*, Harris offered himself up to scientists for experimental purposes, saying he'd be of "more aid to science alive than dead." With no support for his request, Harris accepted his fate, even forgoing an application for clemency to Governor Merriam. Harris made a terse statement: "I have nothing to say. Let's get it over with as soon as possible."

On July 6, 1934, Harris became the first condemned man to mount the stairs into Folsom's new execution room, situated in a triangular space between the new annex and the old cell building. The permanent death house replaced the previous method of erecting the scaffold for each hanging.

"I remember hitting her but I didn't know she was dead. After I struck her I just walked out and shut the door . . ."
—Walter Lewis, 1934

79. Walter Lewis, August 3, 1934

Mrs. Wright called the police when her sister, Ernestine Halliday, failed to show up for a party. When officers arrived, Mrs. Wright decided they should check with Walter Lewis, a man to whom she rented a "shack" at the rear of her home. Fifty-two-year-old Lewis lived there with his girlfriend, whom he referred to as his wife.

Finding the door locked, the police forced their way in and found Halliday lying dead in a pool of blood on the bed. Her head had been smashed in by an ax. The bloody weapon leaned against the wall. Court documents said Halliday, "a colored girl about thirty years of age, small of stature, partially crippled, of good moral repute and unmarried," could have been raped.

Police arrested Lewis a month later in March 1933 at a hobo camp near El Centro, California. In a confession, Lewis said Halliday came to his shack and he told her, "My wife had quit me." In his statement, Lewis continued:

> She (Halliday) said she would be my girl. And she said that she would come to see me twice or three times a week. She told me how much she cared for me. There was no argument nor fight nor nothing and I was just drunk and knocked her in the head with an ax. I remember hitting her but I didn't know she was dead. After I struck her I just walked out and shut the door . . . I kept the axe setting in the closet. I just walked over and got it and struck her with it.

While awaiting trial, Lewis attempted to escape from the county jail, along with Dick Villion, by burning a hole in the wooden ceiling with a candle. The plan failed when deputies discovered them. At his arraignment, Lewis pleaded not guilty, and during his trial he argued he was intoxicated at the time of Halliday's murder; however, several witnesses refuted his claim. Found guilty and sentenced to death, Lewis appealed, but the higher court deemed that "the killing was wilful [sic], deliberate, and premeditated, or that it was committed in an attempt to perpetrate rape."

Lewis died on the Folsom gallows on August 3, 1934.

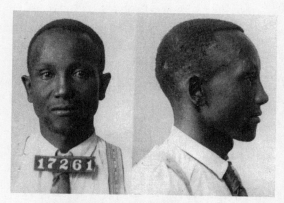

"This is just where I want to catch you."
—Pat Nobles to his victim, 1931

80. Pat Nobles, November 23, 1934

Pat Nobles and his wife Luberta had been separated for several months. On March 29, 1931, Nobles found Luberta engaged in conversation with Walter Vones on the front porch of her house. "Here comes my husband," Luberta said to Vones, "you better run."

"This is just where I want to catch you," Nobles told Vones, and he chased Vones to a neighbor's backyard where he slashed Vones's throat with a "sharp instrument."

Nobles then ran down the block, chasing Luberta. He pulled her down to the ground and inflicted several flesh wounds. Luckily, a sixteen-year-old boy subdued Nobles by hitting him over the head with a large piece of wood.

Nobles pleaded not guilty to murdering Walter Vones. During trial, the district attorney asked Nobles whether he had ever been convicted of a felony. Nobles replied no. He also denied having served time in a Texas prison. The prosecutor then produced notarized documents contradicting Noble's testimony. Even though the judge instructed the jury to ignore the documents, Nobles felt the jury had taken them into account. The jury found him guilty.

Governor James Rolph made several unprecedented visits to Folsom to speak with Nobles—deemed the "giant negro" by the press—about his case, determined to gather evidence to warrant life imprisonment. "I'm not inclined to let men hang when their crimes involve infidelity of their wife and breaking up of their home," the governor said. He issued Nobles a record nine reprieves, but by April 1934, Rolph's ill health forced him to retire from his executive post. Two months later, he died. The new governor, Frank Merriam ignored further requests for clemency. According to the *Modesto Bee*, Nobles's subsequent execution, on November 23, 1934, "took place in the twinkling of an eye."

"There is so much crime in the world today[,] one must pay the price for any mistakes."
—Mike Lami, on the gallows, 1935

81. Mike Lami, January 11, 1935

At approximately 3:00 A.M., Mike Lami climbed through the window of an unoccupied apartment on E Street in Sacramento. The adjoining apartment belonged to his estranged wife, Hasner, and their two children. The couple had been separated for over a year, and, several days prior, Hasner had Lami arrested for "failure to provide" for the children. In retaliation, the rug peddler lay in wait with a butcher knife until he heard his wife enter the bathroom four hours later.

The Lamis' nine-year-old daughter, Lamia, heard her mother's screams and rushed to the bathroom. There she saw her father pick up his hat and run out the back door. Her mother lay in a pool of blood, the result of several stab wounds. Lamia's stepbrother, Jack Joseph, called an ambulance, but Hasner never regained consciousness.

Mike Lami took refuge at a friend's house, where authorities soon located him. When police arrived, he attempted to stab himself to death, but failed in the effort. He admitted to the killing, but claimed to have been drunk when he stabbed his wife, although arresting officers found no evidence of alcohol on Lami. At trial, where he pleaded not guilty, Lami blandly remarked, "Sure, I stabbed her."

Lami testified that on April 2, 1934, the day before the crime, he came to see his daughter and Hasner refused to let him in, but she "permitted a Greek to enter the house." This made him jealous and angry.

Lami and his defense attorney relied upon his Muslim upbringing as justification for the killing, saying that his wife's "treason and open defiance of marital vows was worse than murder." Many letters from various Arab organizations and supporters poured into Governor Merriam's office. One letter read, "Owing to the fact that his wife was intimate with another man, and that Lami is a very religious man, steeped in the beliefs of his race, and believes that because [of] his wife's intimacy with the other man she destroyed, dishonored, and dis-respected [sic] her marriage vows."

Before his execution, Lami wrote a letter to Warden Court Smith, saying, "I wish to thank you kindly for my good treatment here at Folsom and also thank Governor Merriam for me. I realize he could not help my case any. There is so much crime in the world today[,] one must pay the price for any mistakes."

On January 11, 1935, "With a smile on his lips and a pleasant goodbye," according to the *Salt Lake Tribune*, Lami mounted the gallows.

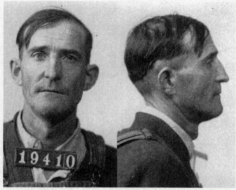

"I don't mind the hanging, but it's a hell of an idea to swing me on Groundhog Day. I'm going to ask for a quart of whiskey just before the necktie party."
—Harold Bieber, 1934, after sentencing and his mistaking the day of his execution as Groundhog Day

82. Harold Bieber, February 1, 1935

On November 18, 1934, Jim Tritely called police to report a disturbance, stating that his girlfriend, Lena Blair, had been "scratched." In fact, she had been stabbed in the side. Police did not investigate, ostensibly because Blair and her two siblings had been arrested for disturbing the peace once before. In the morning, a doctor was summoned, but forty-nine-year-old Blair had been dead for at least three hours.

Blair lived with her brother, Harold Bieber, their mother, and their mother's husband. Bieber told investigators that Blair had disobeyed him by seeing Tritely, a man he had warned her against. After a search, Bieber found her hiding under Tritely's bed, wearing only her underclothes. Bieber later stated, "She was cussing me and then began throwing her fists in my face. I shoved my knife toward her as she step [sic] outside and left it sticking in her side." Bieber's stepfather brought Blair home, where she later died.

Bieber refused counsel, demanding he be put to death right away, but the court insisted on appointing Bieber an attorney. "What's with them, anyway?" he asked an officer. "I said I wanted to plead guilty and get it over with and they try to make me wait. I don't care if they hang me."

Much to the dismay of his mother and his sister, Grace Miller, Bieber insisted on the gallows, saying:

> I pleaded guilty to first-degree murder and asked the judge to hang me because it is what I deserve. My philosophy where murder is committed is a life for a life. I'm ready to take my medicine any time. The only regret I have is because of my mother. I didn't attend the funeral of my sister because I didn't want to hurt my mother seeing me there in custody of several policemen. I'm going to walk up the stairs to the noose, probably a little shaky—but not afraid.

In a letter from Grace Miller to Governor Merriam, she begged for leniency, saying, ". . . it is killing my mother and our doctor says she will not survive if he goes to the gallows." Miller claimed Bieber killed Blair in an effort to protect her from Tritely, who planned to take Blair with him to "run a white slave house in Fresno and [her] brother wanted her to behave herself but she wouldn't listen to his plea's [sic]."

Bieber wrote a different letter to Merriam, stating that he was "guilty of cold-blooded murder and I do not want any reprieve or any change in my sentence as I will pay the death penalty and then the people will be satisfied with a life for a life." In the end, Bieber did apply for clemency, but he did so to appease his family: "I believe in a life for a life and am applying for commutation on the representation of my sister who wishes me to do so for the sake of my mother." Unmoved, Merriam ignored the application.

Before he realized his error, Bieber had strongly objected to the date of his execution being on Groundhog's Day. Ironically, the forty-one-year-old Bieber did not make it to see Groundhog's Day, but he gave no air of fear as he stood on the gallows, facing a crowd of curious spectators, on February 1, 1935. He died minutes later.

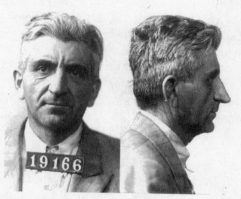

"I feel that my time has come, so I am ready to pay the penalty."
—Tellie McQuate, after receiving his death sentence, 1933

83. Tellie McQuate, May 24, 1935

Tellie McQuate stood on the shore of San Diego Bay and watched sailors on a U.S. Navy ship pull two bags from the water. McQuate had thrown those bags into the bay on the previous night, and he had returned to make sure they weren't floating. Unfortunately, they were. He then left to go see a show.

The servicemen aboard the *U.S.S. Langley* made a gruesome discovery. Inside the bags they had retrieved were the severed limbs of a woman, later identified as seventy-four-year-old Mrs. Ella Straw. When McQuate read in a newspaper that police suspected him, he immediately took a taxi to Los Angeles, paying for the ride with money he had stolen from Straw.

A wealthy "eccentric," Straw owned a house on Eighteenth Street in San Diego, as well as three rental properties. She often befriended those who were down on their luck. McQuate was one such person, and he had lived with Straw in a relationship as husband and wife for the past year and a half. She knew him as Thomas Jones.

Seven months later, a police officer spotted a man sitting on a bench in Los Angeles. He held a strange package that turned out to be a garden hose loaded with BB shot. The man told the inquiring officer he needed money and planned to use the makeshift weapon to rob people. He let the officer in on another secret. "I might as well kick in," he blurted. "You'll make me anyway when you trace my record. Yes, I'm wanted for killing an old lady in San Diego."

According to McQuate's confession, on October 8, 1933, he and Straw visited a market where he conversed with another woman. This made Straw infuriated and jealous. They continued arguing at home and decided to take naps in

201

separate rooms. At one point, he passed her door as he went to the kitchen, and she continued to yell at him. McQuate confessed, "We quarreled and kept on, and I was in bed and she was in bed and we kept on chewing the rag . . . I stood by the bed a minute and there was a hammer laying [nearby] and I picked up the hammer and hit her, and I hit her harder than I thought; I didn't intend to kill the woman and I hit her a harder blow than I figured."

McQuate related that following his attack on Straw, he ate breakfast, worked on the yard, and went to town. For six days, Ella Straw lay unconscious in her bed, while McQuate slept in the other room. The autopsy later revealed that she had an "exceedingly thick skull." Six blows to the head did not kill her. Dismembering her did, however. McQuate divided her body parts and placed them into two bags. Then he borrowed a car from a dealership, saying he wanted to "show his wife" the car. He drove to the bay and threw the bags into the water. The next morning he returned, hoping the bags had sunk.

In his guilty plea, McQuate said, "I feel that my time has come, so I am ready to pay the penalty." After receiving the death sentence, he appealed, claiming the murder wasn't premeditated. The higher court disagreed, citing a portion of his original statement where he said he had grown tired of Straw and refused her marriage proposal.

As he approached the steps to the gallows, he asked the guards to release their grip on him. "I want to walk up those steps alone, Warden." He made no other comments, and twenty witnesses watched McQuate fall through the trap on May 24, 1935.

"There will be two people buried tomorrow."
—Anastacio Bermijo, to his second would-be victim, 1933

84. Anastacio Bermijo, May 31, 1935

Anastacio Bermijo and Felix Villasor farmed as partners on a tract of land near Hood, California. In May 1933, Bermijo left for a month, but rumors circulated that he had taken more than his share of the farm proceeds with him. When he returned on June 7, Bermijo went to Villasor's new home in Walnut Grove, where Villasor lived with his wife and three children. As Villasor and his wife prepared dinner, Bermijo walked in, and accused his former partner of spreading the rumor about him.

As Villasor dried his hands on a towel, Bermijo drew a gun and shot Villasor in the back, directly below the right scapula. Villasor picked up an ax in an effort to protect himself and his wife, but Bermijo fired again, striking Villasor. Bermijo ran from the house, and the wounded Villasor attempted to follow, but he collapsed in his wife's arms and died. According to Mrs. Villasor, Bermijo returned to the house, aimed the gun at her, and said, "There will be two people buried tomorrow." Bermijo's gun misfired and the bullet lodged in the house's exterior wall.

Several witnesses testified that Bermijo spoke freely about killing Villasor for days leading up to the murder. Bermijo denied this and insisted Villasor came at him with the ax first, forcing him to shoot in self-defense. Found guilty and sentenced to pay the ultimate penalty, Bermijo appealed, but to no avail. He died on the Folsom gallows on May 31, 1935.

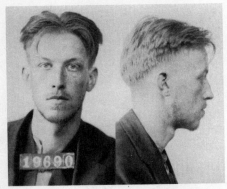

"The monkeys and parrots drove me crazy and I did not know what I was doing."
—Aldrich Lutz, after confessing to murder, 1935

85. Aldrich Welsford Lutz, June 21, 1935

Sixty-two-year-old Frank Angermeier was the superintendent at Mount Shasta's Snowman's Hill, a winter resort lodge near Dunsmuir in Siskiyou County. He met nineteen-year-old Aldrich Welsford Lutz at a restaurant Angermeier owned in Dunsmuir. The older man befriended the unemployed dairy worker, and on March 20, 1935, he hired Lutz to help tend the resort. The following morning, Angermeier lay dead on a trail leading to the lodge, a bullet wound in his head, his pockets turned out.

Police arrested Lutz in Bend, Oregon. He had stolen Angermeier's car. While in the Deschutes County jail, Lutz paced his cell and rambled on about Angermeier's pet monkeys and parrots chattering the prior night. "The monkeys and parrots drove me crazy and I did not know what I was doing. I did not sleep any that night and in the morning about seven o'clock when Angermeier was walking down the trail to the place where I was staying, I took a .38 revolver and pulled the trigger and shot him." Those who knew Lutz in his hometown of Portland, Oregon, considered him "a little queer" and "backwards."

After being sentenced to death, Lutz applied for clemency, then changed his mind and wrote to Governor Merriam stating he no longer wanted a stay of execution. He spent his final night writing letters to friends and family, slept very little, then ate a hearty breakfast in the morning. He walked firmly to the scaffold, appearing cool and collected. He died, on June 21, 1935, exactly three months after killing Frank Angermeier.

"Well, I tried to beat the rope."
—Harry Garcia, following a failed suicide attempt, 1935

86. Harry Garcia, July 10, 1935

On October 7, 1933, Harry Garcia approached Juan Garcia, who was of no relation, in the prison yard. He grabbed his arm, whirled him around, and stabbed him just below the heart. Thirty minutes later, he approached Stanley Price as he ate a sandwich and listened to the World Series game on the radio. Garcia "uttered an ugly epithet and plunged a long-bladed knife into the chest of Price before he had a chance to rise from his sitting position." Garcia wiped the blood off the knife and disposed of it.

While Price died immediately, also from a wound under the heart, Juan Garcia lived long enough to name Harry Garcia as his assailant. Garcia pleaded not guilty by reason of insanity and made the strange declaration that he wanted his victims "to get that out of their heads that they meant to kill me." Several prisoners who witnessed the killings said the attacks were unprovoked, although the three men had years of "bad blood" between them.

After the jury found Garcia guilty of murder in the first degree, Judge Dal M. Lemmon set Garcia's execution for Wednesday, calling Sacramento County's long-standing tradition of performing executions on a Friday "silly."

Garcia's execution marked the first time Folsom Prison executed an inmate on a day other than Friday[1]. Days before his scheduled execution, Garcia attempted to "beat the rope" by slashing his wrists. Captain of the Guard William Mitchell saw a trickle of blood coming from under the door of Garcia's death cell. He rushed Garcia to the infirmary where doctors treated his wounds, allowing the state to finish the job on July 10, 1935.

---

1. There is no recorded explanation why executions in the United States took place only on Fridays. Historians believed that after Christ's crucifixion occurred on that day, ecclesiastical courts began fixing Friday for legal executions. The custom continued in England and was brought to the United States.

"I was willing to die if necessary to save him from hanging."
—Frances Hall, wife of George Hall, 1936

87. George Hall, March 27, 1936

Thirty-one year-old U.S. customs agent Ernie Ballinger was patrolling the Canadian border at Seattle Heights, Washington, when he stopped a south-bound vehicle for inspection. He found two Thompson submachine guns, six automatic pistols, and a large amount of narcotics stashed in the Ford coupe. Before Ballinger could call for backup, George Hall, one of the eventual suspects, struck him over the head, knocking him out. The other, unnamed, suspect helped throw Ballinger into the trunk of the car.

One hundred twenty-five miles later, the two men dragged Ballinger from the truck, and forced him to listen to the suspects debate whether or not they should "bump him." Eventually, they threw Ballinger back into the trunk and drove to Medford, Oregon, five hundred miles from his place of capture. There, they transferred him to another vehicle, presumably driven by Hall's accomplice, who handcuffed Ballinger to a tree on a remote ranch and brutally beat him. A farmer discovered Ballinger and alerted authorities.

In the meantime, Hall stopped in Drain, Oregon, where he picked up an unsuspecting hitchhiker, Paul Newcomb. The men continued south toward California. When Hall and Newcomb reached Eureka, police immediately spotted them. Forty-one-year-old Stephen Kent of the newly formed California Highway Patrol (CHiPs) took part in the lengthy car chase that ensued. Held hostage in the speeding vehicle, Newcomb made several attempts to grab the car keys, and eventually he was able to pull the emergency brake, forcing the car to a sudden stop.

Officer Kent and sheriff's deputy Lester Quigley approached the car. Hall had been released from San Quentin only a year earlier and he had no desire to see the inside of a cell again. He opened fire on the two officers, killing them instantly. He shot forty-three-year-old Quigley three times and Kent once.

Newcomb bolted from the vehicle into a nearby drugstore where he gladly surrendered to authorities. Hall fled down the street, emptying his gun at pursuing officers as he went. Sheriff Andy Calkins and his son Charles, a deputy, chased Hall, shooting him in the legs during the pursuit.

Authorities suspected Hall had participated in the kidnapping of Denver resident Charles Boettcher in February 1933, the previous month. During questioning, Hall denied involvement. Even though Hall's known associates were suspects in the infamous kidnapping, police couldn't link Hall to it. Described as a "handsome blonde with blue eyes," Hall did admit to kidnapping the customs agent. Speaking of Ballinger, Hall stated, "I cracked him on the head [and] put him in the car, but [I] did not make the trip to the California line with him. Ballinger will identify me, but he will not tell that I brought him to the line or tied him to the tree." He also claimed that he used Ballinger's gun to kill Kent and Quigley. "I'm all through. If the boys [the crowd gathering in front of the jail] want me, I am willing to go."

Hall entered a plea of not guilty and trial was set for mid-April. Hall admitted to killing the two lawmen, but claimed not to know they were officers. He also said Kent reached for a gun. Newcomb, exonerated of any wrongdoing, contradicted Hall by testifying that Kent announced himself as an officer and was clearly dressed in an officer's leather jacket, cap, and wore a badge. After a thirty minute deliberation, the jury found Hall guilty. Judge C. J. Luttrell sentenced him to death. The California Supreme Court affirmed the lower court's decision in February 1934. Hall appealed his case two more times, again to the California Supreme Court, and once to the Ninth Circuit Court of Appeals. He argued that he had not been given the due process of law and his attorneys claimed their client should have been allowed to plead not guilty by reason of insanity. Hall also complained of being denied a change of venue when he felt he could not get a fair trial in Eureka.

During his wait at Folsom prison, several Los Angeles bank robbers, arrested for attempted robberies, claimed to fund Hall's defense and constant appeals. Authorities were certain Hall belonged to the notorious bank-robbing "Mutt and Jeff" gang. California residents, apparently tired of waiting, responded to Hall's lengthy appeals process by lynching Clyde L. Johnson for murdering Police Chief Jack Daw. Citizens of Siskiyou County saw the lynching as a clear protest against the delay in executing Hall. The gang money could only take Hall's case so far. Eventually, he exhausted all legal efforts to obtain a new trial.

During his three-year confinement at Folsom Prison, Hall's wife, Frances (a.k.a Ann), often visited him. On March 8, Mrs. Hall arrived by taxi for her regular visit. She ordered the driver to wait. After receiving an anonymous tip, prison guards suspected Hall's wife might help him escape. As a result, the visit occurred in a room across from the office of the warden's secretary, Barnett Huse. A glass pane separated the pair at the table.

The forty-page text mentioned in the introduction of this book, that accompanied the mug shots, gives an interesting and unexpected account of Mrs. Hall's visit. The unknown author paid particular attention to her appearance:

She was pretty; brown eyes that were large, innocent, one would unhesitantly [sic] declare; a bit wistful as though from much introspection; appealing eyes. And her hair, worn in the accepted fashion, was ever neatly arranged, shining with careful attention. Her skin, perhaps, told most. It was flawless. High cheek bones accentuated the slight hollowness of cheeks which, some thought, indicated a latent tubercular condition. "She was dainty," one guard commented and the description is an apt one, she was. Assuredly, she would be the last person chosen, so far as appearance and behavior went, as the consort of a "killer" of Hall's type.

The visit ended without incident and guards escorted Hall toward his "death" cell. A nervous Mrs. Hall started down the corridor toward the secretary's office. Loud enough for her condemned spouse to hear, she said to the guard beside her, "I'm going into the secretary's office; [I'm] going to ask him if I can see George next week." At this, Hall broke from his two guards and ran to his wife. "Give me that gun," he said to her. According to the text, officers were well aware of Hall's capabilities:

Knowing Hall, they felt certain that, if the slightest opportunity presented itself, he would make a bid for freedom, and that any, or all who, unfortunately, stood in his pathway would be brushed aside as callously as one would brush aside a house fly.

Elsie Kent, to Governor Rolph

I am Mr. Kent's sister. Steve made a home here in Yreka for me and my baby, [and] the other man Mr. Quigley also lived with us. Since that dreadful night when I heard and counted the shots that took Steve out of this world so suddenly and so needlessly, his friends by the hundreds have asked why hasn't Hall been hanged. Just because he must have some gangster money behind him will the law finally find some excuse to let him go free? He took two lives in cold-blood and bragged that he did not get more, why should the law allow him to keep on living ten months, almost a year since he murdered them, being an expense to the State and to his County.

I did not have the honor of meeting you personally but I was at Santa Barbara a year [ago] with Steve at the Traffic Officers Convention and I had the pleasure of hearing you talk to the boys.

I would like to tell you also how much I approve your attitude taken concerning the San Jose lynching. That is what should have taken place up here and I hope [it] will if Hall is ever given a new trial.

Would it be asking too much, Governor, to have you look into the case and if you have any power over the case to have it brought to a head and have something done? I know it won't bring my brother back but it would be some consolation to me and to my parents back in Nebraska to know that justice had been dealt out to his murderer.

Huse, hearing the commotion, leapt from his chair and over his desk. The only lethal weapons allowed at Folsom Prison were in the possession of the guards not inside the prison walls, but outside—in the towers above the yard. Huse, no doubt feared the worst:

> It was at this point, this tense moment, that Mrs. Frances Hall belied her right to the appellation of "Gun Moll." She did not react as would have cigar-smoking, cussin [sic], hell-raisin' Bonnie Parker—who smilingly went to death with her paramour, Clyde Barrow—but reacted as was to have been expected. She fumbled, grew nervous, hesitated for an interval in trying to abstract the gun from her purse, and in that little moment of time Huse, the warden's secretary, grappled with the enraged Hall and was wresting about the office, striving to keep him from within reach of the woman who still fumbled with her bag.

Huse had the advantage of treaded footwear. Hall wore the soft-soled shoes issued to condemned prisoners, which slipped on the highly waxed linoleum floor. This helped Huse dominate the struggle, keeping Hall from gaining access to his wife. Mrs. Hall, in a debilitating state of nervousness, could not extract the weapon. She dropped her purse during a futile attempt to hand it to her husband. The bag slid beneath Huse's desk.

Guards arrived, as did Albert Mundt, clerk of the Board of Prison Directors, who heard the scuffling from his office. Mrs. Hall now began pulling at her clothing:

> She was dressed in a shirt-waist skirt affair. Mrs. Hall's hand still fumbling about her waist band, detecting the handle of a revolver protruding from an elastic girdle about her waist. It was a .45 calibre [sic] weapon with one shell under the hammer and a clip, fully loaded, in magazine. When the handbag was picked up, from under the desk, it was found to contain a .32 automatic, fully loaded, with a shell under the hammer.

While Mrs. Hall struggled to produce the weapon, Mundt pulled a gas-billy from Huse's desk, and administered a blow to Hall's head. This subdued the prisoner and caused tears to swell in everyone's eyes. It was all over. Guards returned Hall to his cell while his wife sat quietly in Warden Court Smith's office.

> Of medium build, she was, 'tis true, but there was about her a neatness of clothing, of hair, of hands and of general appearance altogether out of keeping with the generally accepted conception of "Gun Moll."

When Smith told her how foolish her actions were, she replied, "Well, there was a chance. Anyway, we would have died together." This would have been likely had they escaped. The tower guards at the front gates would have quickly ended their liberty quest. Inside the waiting taxi were two boxes of shells for the guns she smuggled in, suitcases of clothing, and nearly two hundred dollars. When questioned, Mrs. Hall said she had rented a house in south Sacramento and there, as recorded in a suicide pact, the two would "have died together."

The night before her preliminary hearing, Mrs. Hall admitted to Chief of the State Bureau of Identification Clarence Morrill that she and her husband had planned to kidnap the warden and Huse and use them as shields to escape unscathed. Such a plan proved successful in the 1903 prison break where thirteen prisoners took Warden Wilkinson and other officials hostage and used them as human shields against the tower guards.

Investigators also learned the Halls had developed a code they used in letters between them. The senseless paragraphs contained hidden meanings that baffled authorities. They also determined the escape had long been in the works. A Sacramento gunsmith revealed he sold two guns to Mrs. Hall a year earlier.

The twenty-three-year-old stenographer was unmoved and stoic at the preliminary examination, where she was granted a day's delay. Townspeople packed the courtroom, eager to get a look at the two-gun toting wife. Some intimated that her husband's death would be delayed once again to allow him to testify at her trial. Only Governor Frank Merriam could offer a reprieve, and he refused, saying he didn't see how Hall could help his wife.

On March 27, 1936, a large crowd, including peace officers, gathered at the prison to watch the cop killer forfeit his life. Frances Hall had not seen her husband since the ill-fated escape attempt and she wept hysterically in her jail cell. She clutched a farewell letter from her husband. On that day, Hall, devoid of his usual bravado, went to his death without a word, unaware of the outcome of his wife's legal affairs.

Less than twenty-four hours later, Mrs. Hall presented herself in court, "dressed in a black, tailored suit, finished with a fur scarf. She wore flat-heeled black oxfords and a gray felt hat." She pleaded guilty. The court sentenced her to one-to-five years in the Tehachapi institution, an all-women prison south of Bakersfield, California.

District Attorney Otis Babcock said, "It was a foolhardy act and was fraught with danger of sacrificing lives. Mrs. Hall's objective was to save her mate. She was not of the criminal type and there was no gang working with her." Authorities buried George Hall in the prison cemetery. A single wreath, the last tribute from his wife, lay over his grave.

Many editorials in the newspapers declared that Mrs. Hall got what she deserved. Others felt she had suffered enough, her misguided love causing her strife. A. R. O'Brien, editor of the *Ukiah Republican Press* and director of the state Board of Prison Directors of California, said: "Ann Hall is down in the hills of Tehachapi. She's just a number there, but hers was not, as District Attorney Otis Babcock correctly said, 'a case that demanded the exacting of the last pound of flesh.' Ann Hall had an almost unbelievable supply of one of the biggest virtues in the world—Loyalty. She misplaced its use, it is true, but that was a mistake of the mind, not the fault of heart. One wonders why fate threw Ann Hall, and all her loyalty, a murderer?"

Mrs. Frances Hall was paroled on July 1, 1938.

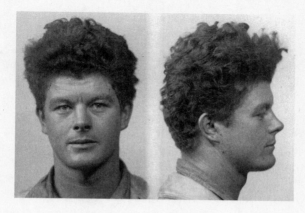

"I performed what some people would call drastic out raged[sic] justice . . . I
was just one unfortunate in the present day whirl pool [sic] of life."
—Earl Budd Kimball, in a letter to Governor Frank Merriam, 1936

88. Earl Budd Kimball, May 22, 1936

In August 1935, two mountaineers searched for hides and cattle rustlers near
Emigrant Gap in the Sierra Nevada region, northeast of Sacramento. They
discovered a body floating in stagnant water at the bottom of an abandoned mineshaft. A letter lying nearby on the ground bore the name of James C. Kennett, a
retired businessman from Chicago, who had come to the area two months earlier
to learn the mining trade and to "improve his health." Not having received word
from him, Kennett's ex-wife had reported him missing.

But the body was not Kennett's. The unidentified remains were that of an adolescent
male, not a fifty-five-year-old man. The victim had suffered two rifle shots to the head.
His skull was smashed. A description of the discernible features coincided with those
of a red-haired youth who had been seen in the area the previous weeks. Placer County
sheriff Elmer Gum had arrested twenty-one-year-old Earl Budd Kimball for "illegal
possession of venison," as well as having a concealed weapon. It came as a surprise
when officers found another letter with Kennett's name on it in Kimball's pocket.

Authorities figured Kennett's body would turn up in the same location as the
other body. Initially, Kimball denied knowing either the victim or Kennett, but
overwhelming evidence soon prompted a confession. Kimball had met Kennett
on a train in May or June of 1935, and he had tempted the Chicagoan with stories
of plentiful fishing and abundant gold. They agreed to share a cabin. Kennett
purchased supplies and groceries. Unimpressed with the output of both fish and
gold after a couple of weeks, Kennett demanded Kimball pay for his share of
expenses. They fought and Kimball moved to another cabin.

At that time, Kennett went fishing with another prospector who had borrowed
Kimball's rifle. Kennett returned it to Kimball, but later Kimball came to the cabin

211

and the two argued. Kimball said, "I come over with my rifle and by golly, we just got into a fight, [which] ended up with somebody getting hurt." Kimball claimed that Kennett came after him with a knife. "I'm a straight shooter," said Kimball. "I don't like being double-crossed." He shot Kennett twice in the back and finished him off with a blow to the head with an ax. Wrapping the body in a blanket, Kimball dragged it to the mineshaft and shoved it in.

Sure enough, Kennett's body surfaced in the same mine where the other victim's body had been found earlier. In the meantime, Kimball, "the giant ex-sailor," boasted that he had killed at least twenty-five other men, giving reporters names and apparent locations of the bodies. One sheriff's deputy said, "Well, we know he's killed two men in a pretty brutal manner and we have the bodies—who can say there aren't more? Maybe it will solve some of the strange disappearances that have been going on."

Sheriff Gum suspected Kimball in the murder of Fred Realing, caretaker of a mining camp. After Realing went missing, Kimball applied for the man's job. The sheriff also surmised Kimball figured in the shooting death of a rancher near Loomis, as well as the murder of a Sacramento service station attendant.

The next day, Kimball denied being a serial killer. "Sure, I killed Kennett and the red-head—I had reason to kill them, didn't I? But the other twenty-five—I told them all that stuff out of devilment to get some bananas and cigarettes. Well, I said I'd give them a real story for some bananas and something to smoke. I gave the story all right—it's all a lot of baloney." He later wrote in a letter to Governor Merriam, saying, "I told the newspapers the most of my false storys [sic] because I could get apples and oranges, grapes, cookies. And I had a wolfish apitite [sic]." Despite the surprising accuracy of details Kimball gave about other disappearances, Gum called Kimball's boastful confession "a lot of hooey." Kimball also told reporters he slaughtered calves and sheep to drink their blood, earning him the nickname "Werewolf of Fulda Flat" and "Panther Man."

Kimball enjoyed the media attention, reading as many newspaper articles about himself as he could. Gum put an end to the interviews, saying, "Sorry, but Earl saw his last reporter yesterday. He likes publicity and dotes on what the boys are writing about him."

In the meantime, a woman identified the remains of the red-haired victim as her son, Virgil Smith. Clothing, other belongings, and a chipped tooth were consistent with descriptions from Mrs. Smith and other relatives. Seventeen-year-old Virgil had served a term at Whittier State Reform School and then ran away from a ranch near Porterville in June. His heartbroken mother was particularly proud of the honor scholar medal the Kiwanis Club awarded Virgil for his rehabilitation effort at Whittier.

Shortly after Kennett's murder, on or around July 1, Kimball had met Smith on a train. Kimball only knew Smith as "Red." Smith moved into the second cabin with Kimball, but things quickly soured between the pair. According to Kimball, Smith made off with his rifle, and when Kimball caught up with him, Smith pointed the gun at him. They walked back to the cabin. Kimball later explained his actions in court, "After that I happened to get the drop on him, folks, this young man, and I performed justice in my own way, making a long story short, this is the way it was, Gentlemen of the jury." Kimball said he asked Smith for a cigarette. When Smith handed it over, Kimball stabbed the boy in the side with a knife, finishing him off with two bullets to the head. Smith's body joined Kennett's in the abandoned mine.

Kimball pleaded not guilty by reason of insanity, but his attorney tried to show Kimball had acted in self-defense. As officers led Kimball from his cell at the county jail to the courthouse, they found that the "Werewolf of the Sierra" had stashed a fourteen-inch piece of pipe in one of his boots. Kimball remained manacled to an officer for the duration of his trial. During jury selection, Kimball made several remarks regarding jury members such as, "Sure, he's a stool pigeon, too," and "Aw, nerds." Kimball also appeared eager and forthcoming on the stand, giving expansive testimony and often using the expression "jiminy crickets." At one point, he said, "Gee, the courtroom is full."

An Erroneous Execution

On April 6, 1935, attorney Richard F. Bird learned from a newspaper that his client had been executed at 10:02 the previous morning at San Quentin Prison. Nineteen-year-old African American Rush Griffin had been convicted, along with William Smith, for the shooting death and robbery of thirty-year-old University of Southern California medical student Laurence Leonard Lyon. Smith received a life sentence, while Griffin, the shooter, was given the death penalty. Bird quickly launched an investigation and during a search of the Los Angeles County Clerk's office, Bird's appeal—that he filed two months previously—was found in the clerk's desk, apparently forgotten. The appeal would have automatically stayed Griffin's execution. Despite contradicting witness testimony, Bird stated that he was "positive" that Griffin's plea of self-defense would have resulted in his death sentence being commuted to life imprisonment. During the investigation, it was also revealed that San Quentin officials were notified twice of the pending appeal; the first being a letter dated January 29, days after Griffin's conviction, and then a certified copy of the same information was delivered to and signed by the acting warden. Curiously, both notices were filed away and either ignored or forgotten. After the discovery of the error, the appeal was immediately filed with the state Supreme Court, but chief justice Emmett Seawell said that pursuant to the California Code of Civil Procedure, the high court could not consider the case; to do so would be an "idle act." After a two-week suspension, the negligent clerk was reinstated.

This "legal blunder" prompted Los Angeles Assemblyman Augustus F. Hawkins to prepare a bill, dubbed the "Fool Proof" Law, requiring death sentences to be automatically appealed to the state Supreme Court. Today's automatic appeals process is the direct result of Rush Griffin's premature death.

Kimball testified he had suffered a kick to the head by a mule at the age of five and his grandfather had lived in an insane asylum. Having attended school through the seventh grade, Kimball said, "I couldn't learn nothing [sic]," and he claimed that school officials wanted to "get rid of me so they passed me out of the seventh grade—I dragged one of the teachers down the stairs." Kimball's parents abandoned him as a child, sending him to live with various relatives and a family acquaintance, Ina McArthur, when he was fourteen. McArthur later wrote to the governor asking for clemency: " . . . I never saw anything quite so pitiful. A boy raised to that age, just like some wild animal or something wild that had just grown up by its self [sic]. He had absolutely no training of any kind." She added that there were some "very strange things about that boy . . ." Regarding his defense, McArthur said Kimball grew up with few belongings and he fiercely protected [those he had]. "I can understand how he happened to kill."

A jury found him guilty after thirty minutes of deliberation. Kimball wrote to Governor Frank Merriam, not asking for clemency, but to explain, "I did kill two men because I was agitated to unto a [sic] abnormal plight. I performed what some people would call drastic out raged [sic] justice . . . I was just one unfortunate in the present day whirl pool [sic] of life. . . I have been stamped on, cheated, sqeazed [sic]—several other things."

After a common "death cell" breakfast of bacon, two eggs, cereal, and coffee, on May 22, 1836, Kimball appeared on the gallows, smiling and cheerful. "Hello, boys!" he said to the spectators. He followed with a "Goodbye" before the trap door dropped.

CLARENCE LARKIN BECOMES WARDEN

When the Board of Prison Directors reached a deadlock vote between electing Frank Esola, a former U.S. marshal, or Clyde Plummer, an investigator for the Los Angeles district attorney's office, as Folsom's warden, the Board appointed Folsom's captain of the guard, Clarence Larkin, to the job. On April 18, 1936, forty-five-year-old Larkin welcomed his new position, saying, "I've gone up step-by-step since I first came here 21 years ago, and it isn't very often a guard gets to the top." The convicts, who highly respected Larkin, cheered when they heard news. Guard Lieutenant W. J. Ryan called the demonstration "the most unusual spontaneous outbreak of enthusiasm he ever witnessed at the prison. Ordinarily, announcements of that kind are greeted by silence." Perhaps Larkin's towering presence earned him the respect. At six-foot-six, 260 pounds, prisoners saw him as a formidable authority figure. Earl Kimball's execution marked the first hanging Larkin would oversee as warden. Unfortunately, his reign over the prison ended on September 19, 1937, when an inmate stabbed him to death during a riot. Clarence Larkin is the only California warden killed while on duty. Clyde Plummer took over as warden, a position he held until 1943.

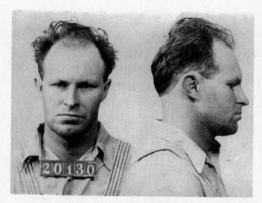

"Hanging is okay. It will clear up my debt."
—Elton Stone, January 1936

89. Elton M. Stone, June 12, 1936

On a foggy night in November, 1935, a quiet, dark figure waited alone in a parked car, one block from Walter and Dorothy Stammer's upscale home in the Fig Garden District of Fresno, California. It was nearly 8:00 P.M. The Stammers and their middle daughter, Delores, drove to the train station. Mr. Stammer was going to San Bernardino on business.

Elton Stone watched them leave. He got out of his car and crept to the front window of the home. He stayed for nearly five minutes, watching Mary, the Stammer's fourteen-year-old daughter, as she sat in a chair reading. The high school sophomore aspired to be an attorney like her father, and she was reading over a legal transcript.

Stone removed the glove from his right hand and placed his finger on the trigger of a .22 caliber automatic pistol. He took aim at the young girl. The one and only bullet he fired pierced the screen and window, striking Mary on the top of her head as she bent over the documents. The bullet lodged itself at the base of her brain. He watched her fall back into the chair and then slump to the side.

Stone quickly retrieved the discharged shell and hurried to the back of the house, where he placed the shell in his mouth and chewed it, rendering it unrecognizable. He threw it into the bushes. With the butt of his pistol, he smashed the window of the door and removed large shards of glass, which he threw into the shrubs. Stone reached inside, unlocked the door, and quickly ran to the music room, where he found Mary slumped in the chair. Blood soaked the chair and floor around her.

Stone picked up her limp body, carried her to a bedroom, and placed her on the bed. After he removed her clothing, he ran back to the music room and pulled the draperies closed, before returning. Stone carefully pulled the bedspread from underneath Mary's body and laid it on the floor. Next, he placed a pillow on the spread and dragged Mary's naked body to the floor, maneuvering the pillow underneath her hips.

But something nagged at Stone. It wasn't remorse or the fact that Mary's siblings, Joan, aged six, and Walter, Jr., aged two, were asleep upstairs. He left Mary's dying body, went out back, and searched the ground and bushes. He couldn't find what he was looking for.

Mrs. Stammer was nervous about leaving her daughter home alone for the first time, so she instructed Mary to lock the front door. Dorothy Stammer and her daughter Delores returned from the station about half an hour later and knocked on the door, expecting Mary to let them in. When no one answered, Dorothy became alarmed and ran to the back door. The anticipation was nearly more than she could stand. Bloody footprints led her through her home to a large pool of blood where Mary had been shot. According to the *Fresno Bee*, Mrs. Stammer found the front door wide open, with bloody and smeared fingerprints seen on one of the front porch pillars. Stone, however, later insisted he left long before the matriarch returned home.

Dorothy found her daughter's body where Stone had left it, naked except for her stockings. Blood pooled beneath her head. A doctor who was summoned assumed Mary had been beaten on the head with a blunt instrument. When an ambulance came, a dense fog had set in which caused a delayed arrival to the emergency room. Mary died two hours later without regaining consciousness.

During the early hours of the investigation, William Mortland, Jr., the youngest member of Sheriff Overholt's staff and a former Fresno newspaperman, stumbled on what he thought could be invaluable evidence. In the bushes, he found a single piece of glass from the back door window bearing the perfect imprint of a thumb. The Stammer home had swarmed with people and most viable fingerprints belonged to the Stammer family.

The glass was wet from fog, so he and his team decided to wait to dust the print. The following morning, Mortland hurried into the station to find the glass dry. He recalled, "The fingerprints were smudged, but the thumbprint was clear and sharp. It was not the full imprint such as is taken on prison records but the 'pattern' was all there and that is all that is needed to identify a thumbprint."

The young deputy photographed the print and added it to the other pieces of glass, placed together like a jigsaw puzzle. As exciting as this evidence was, it was still the *only* evidence. The existing methods for matching fingerprints involved the naked eye and endless stacks of fingerprint cards—a tedious endeavor. It would not be an easy job, so Overholt asked for the state's assistance. State officials sent Clarence Morrill, head of the State Department, and two others, Owen Kessell and Rodger Greene, to find the thumbprint's owner. The State Bureau of Identification considered more than one hundred thousand people capable of committing such a brutal crime.

The following day, on the 25th, an investigator discovered an overlooked clue when he pulled back the draperies: the bullet hole. Mary's cause of death was now clear. Authorities brought in dogs to track down the killer. C. M. Vanderburgh, an investigating doctor, said the killer "was some youth with degenerate tendencies and not an older person, as the latter type are not in the habit of carrying guns."

District Attorney Conway echoed his sentiment. He opined, "I can't help but think there is a boy in this—some youth with a twisted mind who knew this girl," as well as the Stammer family, and their home. Conway also brought in E. O. Heinrich, a nationally known criminologist from the University of California at Berkeley to pore over the evidence.

Meanwhile, Morrill and his team were more than willing to get to work, and they had help. Thirty-five men from the Fig Garden Men's Club adopted a resolution urging every boy and man living within a two-mile radius of the Stammer home be fingerprinted. Then, Fresno State College students proposed that all male students do the same, as well as all high school boys.

Soon, Conway announced a shift in the investigation, declaring, "There is a possibility that this whole thing was carried out by an older, cooler head." New reports surfaced that the killer may had been between the ages of thirty and forty. The fact that the Stammer children were not aware of their father's trip to San Bernardino until that evening was important. This, the officers said, appeared to rule out Mary's acquaintances. Mary had also been home all day and didn't have a boyfriend.

Morrill agreed that the killer might have been older: "All the evidence supports the conclusion the girl was murdered by someone who knew her and watched her for an opportunity to make the attack. It is more than a coincidence, in my opinion, that she was murdered the first night she had been left at home without the protection of an older person. Also, it appears sex is the only motive for the crime. I believe that the murderer is not far away from the Stammer home."

During the investigation, Conway and Overholt were haunted by two other unsolved attacks, both strikingly similar to the Stammer killing. In July 1934, Mrs. Bertha Blagg was raped and bludgeoned while she slept. Partially paralyzed and unable to speak, Bertha wrote a name on a piece of paper: Clayton Stone. When the fourteen-year-old Boy Scout and schoolmate of her two sons was cleared of all wrongdoing, the case became a mystery. Blagg died a week after the attack. Nina Gates Johnson, who also lived in the area, narrowly survived an attack in her bedroom in 1931. Conway and Overholt felt sure of a connection between the cases, but they were unable to put their fingers on it.

By January 1936, fewer than half of the Fig Garden neighborhood's residents had reported to Overholt's office for fingerprinting—one hundred and seventy-five males had failed to report. The sheriff issued a stern warning: "Suspicion will be cast upon any man or boy more than twelve years of age living in the district unless he reports here for fingerprinting." The warning worked. Within a week, the numbers of missing fingerprints on Morrill's list dwindled to thirteen names, listed on a piece of yellow paper.

Then Kessell received a tip from Mr. Boyer, a sixty-nine-year-old resident of the area. He gave Kessell a name—a name that happened to be one of the thirteen on the non-fingerprinted list: Elton Stone. The thirty-year-old Stone had not only been an inmate at San Quentin from 1931 to 1934, but he had also lived a few blocks from the Stammer home for nearly three years before his incarceration.

Kessell went to the Fresno County Identification Bureau, hoping to match fingerprints from any of the thirteen names with the index cards. He pulled Stone's prison record card with his fingerprints and sat down at a desk. After close examination under powerful magnification, Kessell knew Elton M. Stone was his man.

Fifty-two miles away from Fresno, in North Fork, California, Elton Stone lived and worked at an auto shop, a job he'd held since July 1934. He had a .38 caliber pistol hidden in his cabin and, in the event of his capture, he planned to "fight it out." When Undersheriff Jack Tarr, Kessel, and detectives John Ford and Jerry Mohler pulled up to the garage shop, Stone was outside. He remembered the pistol, but in the end gave himself up.

Boastful, Stone made a full confession. His motive? "When [Mr.] Stammer sees me he will know why I did it," Stone declared. However, Walter Stammer said he had never seen or heard of Elton Stone. Veteran investigator Charles Stone (of no relation) echoed the consensus of officers when he said, "He is hiding his true reason, his sadism, behind this trumped-up explanation." Elton Stone insisted he had not targeted Mary saying, "If [Walter] had been there, it would have been him and if [Dorothy] had been there, it would have been her."

Authorities didn't buy Stone's motive. If it was revenge, he logically would have fled after the shooting, not risked entering the home. Charles Stone didn't believe the slayer, stating that "I believe he prowled around the Fig Gardens, saw the Stammer girl on some previous occasion or several of them, and struck when he had the chance. The grudge business is just a half-baked excuse he is giving."

The investigation refocused on the other unsolved crimes, particularly the Blagg killing. Authorities discovered that Stone had lived three blocks from the Blagg home in 1929 and police had suspected him at the time. Stone also lived a few blocks from Nina Gates Johnson. When Deputy Sheriff W. H. Collins questioned Stone about the case, the victim's name slipped Collins's mind. Stone filled in the blanks. "Oh, they had just moved into that home, hadn't they?"

Collins pressed on. "Who?"

Stone replied, "The Gates."

When Collins asked him how he knew this, Stone smirked, "You keep on and you'll have the whole story."

Authorities began to think they had a serial killer on their hands. They drilled Stone on other unsolved murders, particularly that of two girls in San Diego.

Initially, Stone expressed bitterness over the "unjust accusations," complaining, "They are trying to hang every murder in the last five years on me. I didn't kill all those people." At other times, he taunted the police, dangling false promises of more information.

The Stammers identified a clock and some clothing found among Stone's belongings, thus linking him to at least one of three mysterious burglaries of their home, all occurring a few months before Mary's death. Watches and jewelry belonging to other Fig Garden residents showed up among his possessions as well.

Stone then offered to reenact the crime to which he confessed. He related stealing his employer's car and .22 caliber pistol and waiting outside the Stammer home. He claimed that after doing an "immoral act" to Mary, but "not raping her," he searched for the piece of glass he knew had his fingerprint on it. In the darkness, he couldn't find it, and he assumed the moisture from the incoming fog would erase proof of his presence. He admitted this was his one and only regret— failure to commit the "perfect crime."

Despite Stone's insistence he left before Dorothy's arrival, investigators suspected Mrs. Stammer's return had frightened Stone away. Stone also emphatically denied it was a sex crime, exclaiming, "If I had to do it all over again, I would do it a little differently. I'm a little sorry the girl is dead but there wasn't any sex in my mind when I killed her. I didn't care which of the Stammers I got. And I don't care what rap I have to take for it. I'd do the same thing again."

Stone's criminal career had begun at age fifteen when he stole a rifle and cash from a retired Sacramento fire chief who had taken in the troubled teen. Stone claimed his father and stepmother forced him to take part in burglaries; Lola Stone, his stepmother, said to be reputable and sincere, denied the accusation. After serving a year of his three-year sentence, Stone was paroled to a foster family, but returned to Preston after stealing a car in 1925. From there, Stone served time in San Quentin for burglaries and auto thefts.

Stone now faced a grand jury on a murder charge. After three hours of testimony and fifteen minutes of deliberation, the jury indicted Stone. He indicated he would plead guilty and "take my medicine." Conway was ambitious, saying, "We want this man hanged and hanged quickly. No dodging his just dues through an insanity loop." As hoped for, Stone pleaded guilty in front of Judge T. R. Thompson, who quickly sentenced Stone to death. Stone's stepmother sobbed audibly from behind him in the courtroom, her face shrouded by a black lace veil. Stone seemed resigned to his fate, stating, "I have caused you fellows a lot of worries. I pleaded guilty to get it over with for all of us."

The state wanted Stone dead as soon as possible, but a new state law compelling an automatic appeal stood in the way. This was required because Stone pleaded guilty and offered no defense testimony. An execution date could not be set until the State Supreme Court made a decision. That could take months, possibly over a year. Conway would be damned to see that happen. He could circumvent the automatic appeal if Stone's attorneys agreed to dismiss it, but they refused. In fact, one of his attorneys made a single bid for clemency since his client had waived his rights and confessed. The application was denied. Stone's case marked the first time in California that a defendant received an automatic appeal to his guilty plea, and the first time in Fresno County history that a defendant had been hanged on a guilty plea.

In the meantime, Stone toyed with officers, implying he would tell them about other crimes he had committed. Charles Stone didn't give into him, concluding, "These tentative promises he is making that he will reveal something further probably refers to some insignificant detail he has magnified into importance in his own mind. Other than that, he just wants to think up an excuse for degeneracy and there is none."

Two and a half months later, the State Supreme Court unanimously decided to let Stone hang. It was the fastest high court decision on record. Warden Clarence Larkin broke the news to the condemned man.

"That is fine, that is fine. Thank you for the information," Stone said. The date of June 12 was fixed for his execution, the earliest possible date. Despite boasting on numerous occasions that he welcomed the noose, Stone didn't want to die. He wrote to a Sacramento attorney asking what he could do to help obtain a commutation of his sentence, but the lawyer wouldn't get involved. Stone then tried to save his life by writing a two-line, handwritten statement to Chief Justice William Waste seeking clemency: "The public prosecuting attorney, defense attorney, and arresting officers were predajust [sic] against me even before my arrest." Waste ignored the letter.

On the eve of Stone's execution, Conway and other officers tried one last time to extract information about the other crimes from the doomed man. "I'm taking whatever I have on my mind with me tomorrow," Stone replied. "I won't turn up anything for you. I haven't a thing against any of you. I've just thought it over and I've decided I've got nothing to win or lose either way, so I'm not talking."

Regardless of Stone's refusals, Overholt and other investigators proclaimed Stone's guilt in the murder of Blagg and the attack on Nina Gates Johnson: "We are certain that Stone is the man in both cases. The fact that he would neither affirm or deny his guilt convinces us that he is guilty. We are prepared to write 'solved' to both the Blagg and Gates cases."

The next day, June 12, 1936, more than 180 people witnessed Stone shuffle across the gallows with his hands and arms bound and step on the trap door. "I want my people to forget about this as soon as possible," said Stone, who had not left any letters or final words for his family. Less than a minute later, the trap sprung. One man in the audience fainted. The "lust killer" took his motives for killing Mary Louise Stammer with him in death.

"i [sic] will be a man and a good man [if] you only let me keep my life if you plese [sic] sir . . ."
—John Berryman in a letter to Governor Merriam, 1936

90. John B. Berryman, August 14, 1936

Seventy-five-year-old turkey farmer John Grant hired John Berryman, a war veteran, to help on his farm. On the way to the farm, the men pulled up to a service station near the town of Wilton, California. According to the station clerk, Grant paid for the gasoline and opened his wallet in Berryman's presence. It contained between thirty and forty dollars.

At around 6:00 P.M., the men drove up to Grant's farm, where Grant introduced Berryman to his wife, Blanche. Grant said he had planned to retire for the night, but he wanted to replace a radio battery and he decided to head out again. Berryman drove since Grant had been drinking. They ran a few errands, including a stop at a radiator shop. There, the clerk noted that Grant, still noticeably intoxicated, displayed the money in his wallet.

The next time Blanche Grant saw her husband's automobile, it was around 8:00 P.M. The vehicle stopped at the end of their long driveway. A man step out of the car, hesitated for a moment, re-entered the vehicle, and "drove away at a rapid rate of speed." Fifteen minutes later, two women found Grant's body in the driveway where Blanche had seen the car stop. He died from a severe beating to his head, presumably from a tire iron. His pockets had been turned out.

Berryman showed up in Elk Grove, where he offered Martin Moritz two dollars and fifty cents to drive him to Sacramento where he claimed his wife was hospitalized. Moritz agreed and brought a neighbor along. When they arrived in Sacramento, Berryman didn't rush off to the hospital, but insisted the three men have some beer, and they obliged. When Moritz returned home and heard the news about Grant's death, he immediately phoned police, who arrested Berryman near the bar in Sacramento. Berryman claimed he had no recollection of Grant. His blood-stained pants suggested otherwise.

During his trial, Berryman admitted he and Grant drove around together. After drinking heavily, they struggled for control of the steering wheel. Berryman's defense counsel claimed that Grant fell from the car during the fight and Berryman didn't stop the car to check on him. Berryman insisted he never robbed the victim.

After less than an hour of deliberation, the jury found Berryman guilty of first-degree murder. A week before the execution, Albert Mundt, clerk at Folsom Prison, wrote to Judge T. N. Harvey in order to present information following a close examination of the case. He wrote, "While the evidence points to murder in furtherance of a robbery, it is illogical to assume that Berryman or anyone else would associate with a man during an entire day in the presence of witnesses, visit his home and converse with his wife, and then deliberately murder and rob him almost in his own front yard." He also pointed out that Berryman did not attempt to conceal himself in Sacramento, contending the condemned man thought Grant had only been knocked unconscious. Mundt urged Harvey to look into the case, saying, "I believe the facts warrant an investigation, particularly since a life is involved."

Chief Deputy J. Frances O'Shea wrote to Harvey about his prison interview of Berryman. Evidence contradicted Berryman's claims that Grant didn't have any money, and that the injuries were the result of falling from the vehicle. Harvey responded, "Apparently Berryman concocted the story he gave the Board in order to save his life, and there now appears no further reason for not carrying out the sentence imposed by the court."

Berryman wrote to Governor Frank Merriam, begging for leniency (as written in Berryman's own words): "When the government ask for help in the wars and then i went to war at his call and help out all that i cod and if he call I wood go if i cod now i am asking you to help me sir if you will plese and save my life and no Body will not have an trouble with me it is my last trouble with any Body so help me god as long as i lives . . ."

Berryman received a visit from his brother, Dalton, with whom he had served in the war and whom he hadn't seen in ten years. "I can die peacefully now," he wrote. "I have seen my brother and he said my family does not believe I could commit a murder." Shortly after that visit, on August 14, 1936, Berryman died on the Folsom gallows.

**"I intended to hit him, and after I saw he was out, I got scared, I
thought it was better to kill him."**
—Charles James, 1935

91. Charles James, August 14, 1936

On the evening of July 4, 1935, Charles James met truck driver Dave Jennings
and his assistant, John Shepler, at a pool hall in Isleton, Sacramento County.
They drank heavily and left around midnight for Santa Ana to deliver Jennings's
truckload of beer.

A few hours later, Shepler awoke to strange noises and witnessed James beating
Jennings with a crowbar. James told him, "Shut up or I'll give you some of it!"
Shepler ran to a nearby cannery and reported the crime. Jennings died of multiple
skull fractures, and his right thigh had been torn open after being run over by the
truck.

Police found James asleep in a farmer's barn and arrested him. They discovered
Jennings's watch and other personal belongings in James's pockets. James admitted
he killed and robbed Jennings, but he later recanted his statement, claiming he
feared a beating from the district attorney and the other officer if he didn't confess.
He testified that after waking up in the truck, Jennings wouldn't let him out. He
didn't want to go to Santa Ana, but Jennings allegedly told James, "Any time men
get in my truck, they do as I say." James also claimed that Jennings had called him
a "black son-of-a-bitch" and said, "You are going to Santa Ana, nigger."

James said he managed to switch the truck ignition off and they came to stop.
Jennings then exited the cab, came around to the other side, and began to pull
James from his seat. James grabbed a crowbar and struck Jennings three to four
times in the head.

After Shepler retreated, James tried to operate the truck, but lost control, sending it into a sandbank. James denied running over Jennings. After being found guilty, James appealed to the State Supreme Court, who affirmed the judgment. Folsom executed James on August 14, 1936, the same day as #90, John Berryman, making it the prison's fifth double execution.

FOLSOM'S BLOODY SUNDAY

On September 19, 1937, Warden Clarence Larkin and Captain of the Guard William Ryan were conducting interviews with inmates when seven prisoners, in a move reminiscent of the 1903 break, rushed the office. Armed with ten knives and two dummy guns carved and painted to look like pistols, the group of inmates immediately overpowered the two men. One threw a wire loop around Larkin's neck, while another stabbed him. Ryan was left to fight off five other convicts with his lead cane. He suffered several stab wounds. Guards Martin and Kearns rushed in, but both were no match for the group. Martin died after being stabbed. The convicts forced Larkin and Ryan out into the yard, ordering Larkin to free them. Tower guards shot and killed two of the convicts, but not before one of them stabbed Larkin several more times. The other prisoners were wounded by gunfire or clubs.

On September 24, Larkin died from his wounds. Ryan, who doctors gave a 50 percent chance, recovered. The five surviving convicts were found guilty of first-degree murder and sentenced to death. In 1938, they were the first men executed by lethal gas at San Quentin.

"If I chance to live I'd be a great man."
—Lloyd Dale to Warden Larkin, 1936

92. Lloyd Dale, October 16, 1936

Lloyd Dale, a well-known nomad, earned the nicknames "West Coast," "Coastline," and "Coast to Coast" after years of traveling the country. On September 7, 1935, Dale sat by a bonfire with other hobos in the railroad yards near Stockton, California. According to witnesses, he waved a razor in the air and warned the group to not mess with him. "Nobody wants to bother with me, monkey with me here," he ranted.

By midnight, everyone left the fire and Dale decided to find a boxcar to sleep for the night. Dale encountered Roderick Gordon, an officer working for the Western Pacific Railroad. Gordon allegedly shined his flashlight in Dale's face and hit him over the head with his gun, causing Dale to black out. The only thing Dale claims to remember is being a mile from the scene and deciding to get out of Stockton.

The following morning, police found Gordon's body, riddled with fourteen deep razor cuts on his upper body. They also found Dale's hat, bag, and bundle near the officer. Investigators didn't locate Dale until January, when he was arrested for trespassing in Niles, Ohio. The tips of Dale's fingers had been burned to avoid identification. The assistant superintendent of the Bureau of Investigations testified that when he attempted to get Dale's prints, Dale said, "no use of fucking around with my fingers, you have the right man."

Dale pleaded not guilty by reason of insanity. His defense established that Dale had previously been diagnosed with dementia praecox (paranoid type) and he had been sent to the St. Elizabeth Hospital for further testing. Doctors there concluded that "his worsening condition" disabled him "one hundred percent." The prosecution, however, assigned four expert witnesses to examine Dale. They concluded

Dale was sane. One of the experts acknowledged Dale suffered from dementia praecox, but concluded that it didn't affect his ability to know right from wrong.

As Warden Larkin escorted Dale to the scaffold, Dale told him the slaying of Gordon was "unavoidable" because the officer "kept getting in my way." Interestingly, Dale then told the warden if he had been given the chance, he could have been a great man. On October 16, 1936, Dale became Folsom's penultimate execution.

DEATH ROW SITS EMPTY

After the execution of Lloyd Dale, Folsom's death row sat unoccupied for the first time since 1926. Not since the 1927 Thanksgiving Day riot had the cells been that quiet. The cells remained empty for four months until Charles McGuire, Folsom's final execution, was sentenced to death in February 1937.

"I pulled a hold up in Sacramento last night. I had to plug a guy a couple of times when he put up a battle."
—Charles McGuire, 1936

93. Charles McGuire, December 3, 1937

On December 30, 1936, Charles McGuire and a companion known as "George" entered a Sacramento bakery and candy shop owned by Max Krall and Mina Hawky. McGuire, armed with a gun, approached Hawky. She asked what he wanted, but he didn't reply. Frightened, Hawky yelled for Krall, who came from another room located behind the front counter.

McGuire ordered Krall to raise his hands. Krall obeyed. According to Hawky, a German native, Krall and McGuire exchanged words, but she couldn't understand them. Krall then moved around the counter toward McGuire and his companion. As he did so, the robbers charged Krall. Hawky heard two gunshots, just before

McGuire and George ran from the bakery. Krall had been shot once in the chest and once in the back. He died within minutes.

The following day, McGuire boarded an eastbound train where he met fellow passenger Maynard Berry. The men talked and ate lunch in a restaurant during a stop in Roseville. According to Berry, the men ate soup as they read sections of the newspaper. McGuire suddenly threw down his paper and said, "Let's get out of here," and he immediately left the restaurant. Berry rejoined McGuire later on the train. On the ride to Colfax, McGuire asked Berry how much he thought he could get for the gun he carried. McGuire also divulged having used the gun to kill a man the previous night. He then wiped the shells and gun of fingerprints and threw the shells out the window.

When the train reached Colfax, McGuire kicked the gun down an excavated pit. Berry reported the entire incident to someone on the platform and Constable Thomas E. Stanley arrested McGuire at the next stop in Gold Rush. McGuire admitted he had shot Krall, but he claimed it happened during a struggle when Krall charged him. However, McGuire's account didn't explain how Krall received a bullet in the back.

McGuire claimed he was intoxicated at the time, but officers found no evidence to support his statement. During his trial, McGuire pleaded not guilty and answered questions vaguely, saying, "I can't recall," "I can't say for sure," or "I may have."

After thirty minutes of deliberation, the jury found him guilty. Following an unsuccessful appeal, on December 3, 1937, McGuire became Folsom prison's final execution.

DOWN COME THE GALLOWS

May 7, 1937, marked an end to California's tradition of the administration of swift justice by dangling its criminals from the end of a rope. Former San Quentin warden James Holohan had introduced the gas chamber bill in 1933, but Governor James Rolph, Jr., vetoed it, saying the gas chamber would be "experimenting with human misery." Holohan contended that lethal gas was more humane, "eliminating all element of violence." He added, "After all, the purpose of an execution is to remove the convicted person from the ranks of society. As long as this aim is accomplished, it should matter little how it is done." Governor Frank Merriam signed the bill and the practice of hanging, synonymous with justice in California since 1851, ended and Charles McGuire, sentenced before the law took effect, was the last to die on the Folsom gallows.

References

HANE

Application for Pardon, File #603, California State Archives; *People v. Hane*, 108 Cal. 597 (1895); *Harper's Weekly*, February 13, 1886; *Sacramento Record-Union*, June 1, 1892, June 2, 1892, June 3, 1892, June 6, 1892, June 9, 1892, June 10, 1892, June 24, 1892, June 25, 1892, June 27, 1892, June 28, 1892, July 8, 1892, July 14, 1892, May 2, 1893, May 4, 1893, May 5, 1893, May 23, 1893, May 29, 1893, July 7, 1893, December 17, 1894, December 12, 1895, December 13, 1895, December 14, 1895; *San Francisco Morning Call*, July 6, 1892; *San Francisco Call*, December 12, 1895, December 14, 1895, *Oakland Tribune*, December 12, 1895.

KOVALEV

Application for Pardon, File #270, California State Archives; *San Francisco Morning Call*, November 8–12, 1893, November 20, 1893, November 22, 1893; *San Francisco Call*, April 1895, June 27, 1895, November 5, 1895, February 20, 1896, February 22, 1896; *Sacramento Record-Union*, November 24, 1893, December 31, 1894, January 1, 1895, June 27, 1895, September 26, 1895, November 7, 1895, November 12, 1895, November 14–16, 1895, November 19, 1895; *Lowell Sun*, November 9, 1893; *Fresno Republican*, January 3, 1895, June 29, 1895; *Oakland Tribune*, January 9, 1895, January 10, 1895, June 26, 1895, June 27, 1895, September 21, 1895, November 16, 1895, November 18, 1895, February 21, 1896; *Reno Evening Gazette*, July 12, 1895; *San Francisco Examiner*, March 5, 1896; David A. Kulczyk, *The Temperance Family Grocery Store Murders*, 2008.

CRAIG

Application for Pardon, File #114, California State Archives; *People v. Craig*, 111 Cal. 460 (1896); *Fresno Republican*, July 26, 1894, November 24, 1894; *San Francisco Call*, July 26, 1894, July 27, 1894, June 13, 1896; November 16, 1894; *Sacramento Record-Union*, August 1, 1894; *Oakland Tribune*, June 12, 1896.

KAMAUNU

Application for Pardon, File #257, California State Archives; *People v. Kamaunu*, 110 Cal. 609 (1895); *Sacramento Record-Union*, May 8, 1894, May 9, 1894, September 24, 1894; *Hawaiian Gazette*, January 7, 1896, April 17, 1896; *San Francisco Call*, February 8, 1896, June 20, 1896; *Mountain Democrat*, May 30, 1896; *Oakland Tribune*, June 19, 1896.

HOWARD

Application for Pardon, File # 224, California State Archives; *People v. Howard*, 112 Cal. 135 (1896) *Fresno Republican*, August 28, 1894; *Oakland Tribune*, July 17, 1896.

ROBERTS

Application for Pardon, File #636, California State Archives; *San Francisco Call*, April 15, 1896, April 16, 1896, June 4, 1896, September 5, 1896; *Oakland Tribune*, September 4, 1896.

LOPEZ

Application for Pardon, File #277, California State Archives; *San Francisco Call*, April 5, 1896; *Sacramento Record-Union*, April 5, 1896; *Oakland Tribune*, May 21, 1897.

BERRY

Application for Pardon, File #42, California State Archives; *San Francisco Call*, May 20, 1897, May 23, 1897, May 25, 1897, May 28, 1897, August 14, 1897; *Fresno Republican*, May 20, 1897; *Oakland Tribune*, August 13, 1897. Sheila O'Hare, Irene Berry, Jessie Silva, *Legal Executions in California*, McFarland & Company, Inc., 2006.

RAYMOND/WINTERS

Application for Pardon, File #4842, California State Archives; *People v. Winters*, 125 Cal. 325 (1899); *Oakland Tribune*, November 17, 1897, April 8, 1898 *San Francisco Call*, November 18, 1897, November 19, 1897, November 23, 1897, November 27, 1897, November 29, 1897, January 12–15, 1898, January 20, 1898, February 14, 1898, March 3, 1898, March 4, 1898, March 20, 1898, July 11, 1899, December 9, 1899; *Fresno Republican*, February 13, 1898, *Fresno Morning Republican*, October 28, 1899.

BARTHELMAN

Application for Pardon, File #36, California State Archives; *People v. Barthelman*, 120 Ca. 7 (1898); *San Francisco Call*, November 4, 1896, November 5, 1896, January 28, 1897, February 11, 1897, March 11, 1897.

BELEW

Woodland Daily Democrat, November 9, 1897, November 10–13, 1897, November 15–20, 1897, November 22–24, 1897, February 4, 1898, February 7, 1898, March 29, 1898, April 10, 1898, May 3, 1898, May 12–14, 1898, June 16, 1898, November 7, 1899, January 7, 1901; *San Francisco Call*, November 10–13, 1897, November 15–24, 1897, February 4–9, 1898, February 11–12, 1898, February 24, 1898, March 9, 1898, March 30, 1898, April 6, 1898, April 14, 1898, May 14, 1898, June 17, 1898, November 22, 1898, November 26, 1898; *Oakland Tribune*, February 8, 1898, June 16, 1898.

PUTMAN

Application for Pardon, File #401, California State Archives; *People v. Putman*, 129 Cal. 258 (1900); *Reno Evening Gazette*, May 16, 1899; *San Francisco Call*, May 17, 1899, May 21, 1899, June 12, 1899, November 20, 1900; *Oakland Tribune*, May 22, 1899, November 19, 1900; *Fresno Morning Republican*, June 7, 1899, October 29, 1899; *Salt Lake City Tribune*, June 29, 1899.

MILLER

Application for Pardon, File # 231, California State Archives; *People v. Miller*, 125, Cal. 44 (1899); *San Francisco Call*, March 14, 1902, March 16, 1902, June 24, 1902, September 16, 1902, September 26–27, 1902; *Oakland Tribune*, September 26, 1902.

GLOVER

Application for Pardon, File #189, California State Archives; *People v. Glover*, 141 Cal. 233 (1903); *San Francisco Call*, June 12, 1902, June 15–19, 1902, September 9, 1902, October 1, 1902, December 3, 1902, February 4, 1904, February 7, 1904; *Mountain Democrat*, June 28, 1902; *Oakland Tribune*, February 6, 1904.

HIDAKA

Application for Pardon, File #207, California State Archives; *San Francisco Call*, October 23–24, 1902, March 1, 1903; *Reno Evening Gazette*, June 10, 1904; Sheila O'Hare, Irene Berry, Jessie Silva, *Legal Executions in California*, McFarland & Company, Inc., 2006.

LAWRENCE

Application for Pardon, File # 284, California State Archives; *People v. Lawrence*, 143 Cal. 158 (1904); *San Francisco Call*, September 6, 1902, *Ukiah Dispatch Democrat*, September 12, 1902; *Oakland Tribune*, January 22–23, 1903, October 8, 1904.

YOW

Application for Pardon, File # 359, California State Archives; *People v. Yow*, 145 Cal. 1 (1904); *San Francisco Call*, November 26, 1902, December 2, 1902; *Oakland Tribune*, December 2, 1902, March 10, 1903, April 3, 1903, April 22, 1903, January 6, 1905.

MURPHY/ELDRIDGE

Applications for Pardon, File #150 and File #308, California State Archives; *People v. Murphy*, 146 Cal. 502 (1905); *People v. Eldridge*, 147 Cal. 470 (1905); *Oakland Tribune*, July 27–28, 1903, July 31, 1903, August 3, 1903, August 18, 1903, August 24, 1903, September 4, 1903, September 28–29, 1903, October 4, 1903, October 9, 1903, October 17, 1903, October 26, 1903, February 24, 1904, February 27, 1904, March 24, 1904, March 28, 1904, February 2, 1905, May 13, 1905, July 14, 1905, August 17, 1910; *Reno Evening Gazette*, July 27, 1903, August 24, 1903, August 31, 1903, September 1, 1903, September 3, 1903, September 7, 1903, April 1, 1904, December 1, 1905; *Woodland Daily Democrat*, July 28, 1903, August 6–7, 1903, April 2, 1904, May 20, 1904, January 10, 1904, February 24, 1905; *San Francisco Call*, July 27, 1903, July 29–30, 1903, August 2–3, 1903, August 5–6, 1903, August 8–11, 1903, August 14, 1903, August 23–28, 1903, September 14, 1903, October 13–14, 1903, October 17, 1903, November 7–8 1903, November 15, 1903, December 1, 1903, December 9, 1903, December 12, 1903, February 3, 1905, November 14, 1905; *Daily Nevada State Journal*, August 14, 1903, August 27, 1903, August 30, 1903, September 19, 1903, October 6, 1903, February 2, 1905; *Amador Ledger*, December 25, 1903; *Modesto Evening News*, February 9, 1904, June 7, 1904; Jack Black, *You Can't Win: The Autobiography of Jack Black*, New York: Macmillan, 1926; Jim Brown, *Images of America: Folsom Prison*, San Francisco, Arcadia Publishing, 2008; Shelly Bookspan, *A Germ of Goodness: The California State Prison System*, 1851–1944, Nebraska: University of Nebraska Press, 1991.

EASTON

Application for Pardon, File #155, California State Archives; *People v. Easton*, 148 Cal. 50 (1905); *Woodland Daily Democrat*, November 3, 1904, November 5, 1904, January 10, 1905; *San Francisco Call*, November 3, 1904; *Oakland Tribune*, November 4, 1904, January 20, 1905, April 7, 1906; *Fresno Republican*, October 8, 1905.

GRAY

Application for Pardon, File #7058, California State Archives; *People v. Gray*, 148 Cal. 507 (1906); *San Francisco Call*, April 23, 1905, April 13, 1906; *Oakland Tribune*, April 13, 1906.

WEBER

Department of Corrections, Folsom Inmate Case File #6504, California State Archives; *People v. Weber*, 149 Cal. 325 (1906); *Woodland Daily Democrat*, May 27, 1904, February 23, 1905; *San Francisco Call*, May 27, 1904, May 29, 1904, November 11–19, 1904, November 22–25, 1904, November 28–29, 1904, December 3, 1904, December 11, 1904, December 22, 1904, February 7–8, 1905, February 10–11, 1905, February 15–19, 1905, February 21, 1905, March 18, 1905, Mach 25, 1905, April 13, 1905, July 6, 1905, December 13, 1905, June 22, 1906, June 25, 1906, July 17, 1906, August 25, 1906, September 27–30 1906; *Modesto Evening News*, November 11, 1904, November 15, 1904; *Oakland Tribune*, November 17, 1904, November 21, 1904, November 25, 1904, November 29, 1904, November 30, 1904, December 1, 1904, January 27, 1905, February 7, 1905, February 10, 1905, February 17, 1905, February 20, 1905, February 23, 1905, May 8, 1905, June 10, 1906, June 24, 1906, July 18, 1906, September 27, 1906, October 2, 1906; *Los Angeles Herald*, February 16, 1905, February 24, 1905, December 12, 1905, July 28, 1906; *Fresno Republican*, September 8, 1905; *Fresno Morning Republican*, September 5, 1906; Lewis Swindle, *The Story and Trials of Adolph Julius Weber*, Victoria, B.C., Trafford, 2002; Robert F. Rooney, *California State Journal of Medicine*, May 1908.

CIPOLLA

Application for Pardon, File # 117, California State Archives, *People v. Cipolla*, 155, Cal. 224 (1909); *Woodland Daily Democrat*, March 3, 1908, March 5, 1908, March 9, 1908, April 4, 1908, April 8, 1908, April 11, 1908, April 22, 1908; *San Francisco Call*, March 3, 1908, February 19, 1909; *Oakland Tribune*, April 30, 1909.

BENJAMIN

Application of Pardon, File #34, California State Archives, *People v. Benjamin*, 158 Cal. 158 (1910); *Woodland Daily Democrat*, October 6–9, 1909, October 13, 1909, October 20, 1909, November 8, 1909, November 17–20, 1909, November 22, 1909, August 25, 1910, October 28, 1910; *Fresno Republican*, October 7, 1909; *San Francisco Call*, October 7, 1909; *Los Angeles Herald*, October 8, 1909.

LEAHY

Application for Pardon, File # 203, California State Archives, *San Francisco Call*, May 10–11 1910, May 20–21, 1910, June 9, 1910, June 19, 1910, July 30, 1910, November 23, 1910, November 26, 1910; *Oakland Tribune*, November 23, 1910, February 8, 1911; 1910 California Census, Ancestry.com.

DELEHANTE

People v. Delehante, 163, Cal. 461 (1912); *Oakland Tribune*, February 16, 1912, March 4, 1912, April 7, 1912, October 19, 1912, December 6, 1912, July 24, 1921; *San Francisco Call*, February 17, 1912, March 5, 1912; James A. Johnston, *Prison Life is Different*, Boston: Houghton Mifflin Company, 1937.

OPPENHEIMER

People v. Oppenheimer, 156 Cal. 733 (1909); *Oppenheimer v. California*, 225 U.S. 718 (1912); *San Francisco Morning Call*, March 15, 1892, May 11, 1892, May 24, 1895, May 17, 1899, February 10, 1903, January 16, 1904, October 9, 1904, August 18–19, 1907, August 23–25, 1907, September 20, 1911; *Oakland Tribune*, May 13, 1895, May 21, 1895, August 17, 1895, September 30, 1898, May 16, 1899, October 28, 1899, August 16, 1907, January 26, 1910, February 13, 1910, June 3, 1913, June 11, 1913, May 29, 1921, June 5, 1921; *Los Angeles Herald*, August 30, 1908; *Fresno Morning Republican*, September 20, 1911; *Woodland Daily Democrat*, June 6, 1913; Thomas Samuel Duke, *Celebrated Criminal Cases of America*, San Francisco: James Barry H. Company, 1910; James A. Johnston, *Prison Life is Different*, Boston: Houghton Mifflin Company, 1937; Jake Oppenheimer, *Softening the Heart of a Convict*, San Francisco: Ed Morrell, 1912; George Wilbern, *The Human Tiger: The Story of Jacob Oppenheimer*, New York, Vantage Press, 1991.

RABER

People v. Raber, 168 Cal. 316 (1914); *Modesto Evening News*, July 9–10, 1913, October 24, 1913, February 16, 1914; *Oakland Tribune*, July 10, 1913, July 19, 1913, August 2, 1913, October 18, 1913, October 21, 1913, October 31, 1913, December 17, 1913, July 12, 1914, October 27, 1914, January 15, 1915; *Reno Evening Gazette*, July 11, 1913, December 19, 1914, January 15, 1915; *Nevada State Journal*, July 11–13, 1913, July 28, 1913, August 1, 1913, August 3, 1913, October 25, 1913, October 30, 1913, January 15, 1915; *Wisconsin State Journal*, July 17, 1913; *Des Moines Daily News*, July 20, 1913, August 17, 1913; *Woodland Daily Democrat*, August 2, 1913, August 8, 1913, October 24, 1913; *Ogden Examiner*, August 10, 1913; *Fresno Morning Republican*, October 15, 1913, October 18, 1913, October 24, 1913; *Racine Journal-News*, January 28, 1914.

CRECKS

People v. Creeks, 141 Cal, 259 (1904); *People v. Creeks*, 170 Cal. 368 (1915); *Daily Californian*, February 26, 1902; *Fresno Morning Republican*, October 17–18, 1914, October 24, 1914; *Oakland Tribune*, October 17, 1914, October 19, 1914, December 29, 1914, January 6, 1915, January 10, 1915; *Muscatine Journal*, October

17, 1914; *Nevada State Journal*, October 18, 1914; *Colorado Springs Gazette*, April 18, 1915; *Modesto Evening News*, August 27, 1915; *Woodland Daily Democrat*, August 27, 1915; Fallen Staff, Folsom Prison Museum website.

FOUNTAIN

People v. Fountain, 170 Cal. 460 (1915); *Oakland Tribune*, December 6, 1914, December 8, 1914, December 10, 1914, February 16, 1915, October 5, 1915; *Bakersfield Californian*, February 23, 1915; *Modesto Evening News*, December 7, 1914; *Woodland Daily Democrat*, September 10, 1915; *Mountain Democrat*, September 18, 1915.

B. HARRIS

Department of Corrections, Folsom Inmate Case File #218, California State Archives; *People v. Harris*, 169 Cal. 52, (1914); *Modesto Evening News*, September 27, 1913; *Bisbee Daily Review*, September 28, 1913; *Fresno Republican*, September 28, 1913, October 8–9, 1913; *Oakland Tribune*, September 28, 1913, October 2, 1913, October 7, 1913, November 12, 1913, December 31, 1913, January 12, 1914, October 8, 1914; *Washington Times*, September 28–29, 1913; *New York Tribune*, September 28, 1913, September 30, 1913; *Tacoma Times*, October 6–7, 1913, October 14, 1913; *Logan Republican*, October 9, 1913, *Los Angeles Examiner*, November 14–15, 1913, January 1–2, 1914; *San Francisco Chronicle*, January 1, 1914.

LOOMIS

Application for Pardon, File #9097, California State Archives; *People v. Loomis*, 170 Cal. 347 (1915); *Oakland Tribune*, August 18, 1914, August 23, 1914, November 12, 1914, November 15, 1914, June 6, 1915, November 5, 1915; *Colorado Springs Gazette*, April 18, 1915; *Lodi Sentinel*, September 14, 1915; *Woodland Daily Democrat*, September 16, 1915, October 30, 1915; *Berkeley Daily Gazette*, November 4, 1915.

BARGAS

Department of Corrections, Folsom Inmate Case File #9793, California State Archives; *Modesto Evening News*, July 12, 1915, January 21, 1916; *Oakland Tribune*, January 21, 1916; *Woodland Daily Democrat*, January 21, 1916.

UNG

People v. Ung Sing, 171 Cal. 83, (1915); *Mountain Democrat*, March 13, 1915; *Modesto Evening News*, February 18, 1916; *Oakland Tribune*, February 18, 1916.

WITT

Application for Pardon, File #9173, California State Archives; *People v. Witt*, 170 Cal. 104 (1915); *People v. Oxnam*, 170 Cal. 211 (1915); *Oakland Tribune*, December 22–25 1914, January 12–14, 1915, October 16, 1915, October 18–19, 1915, January 21–22, 1915, April 13, 1915, May 23, 1915, January 6, 1916, January 18, 1916, March 3, 1916; *Galveston Daily News*, December 23, 1914, December 29,

1914, June 24, 1915, July 1, 1915, September 21, 1915; *Mountain Democrat,* July 10, 1915, August 14, 1915; *Woodland Daily Democrat,* September 16, 1915, October 30, 1915, March 3, 1916; *Fresno Republican,* September 17, 1915; *Fort Wayne Sentinel,* November 18, 1915; *Modesto Evening News,* March 2–3, 1916.

KROMPHOLD
Application for Pardon, File #256, California State Archives; *People v. Krומphold,* 172 Cal. 512 (1916); *Woodland Daily Democrat,* September 7–8, 1915; *Modesto Evening News,* September 10, 1915, September 1, 1916; *Oakland Tribune,* October 22, 1915, May 3, 1916, September 1, 1916.

SCHOON
Application for Pardon, File #461, California State Archives; *People v. Schoon,* 177 Cal. 678 (1918); *Oakland Tribune,* February 5, 1917, February 20, 1917, April 28, 1917; *Bakersfield Californian,* February 6, 1917; *Modesto Evening News,* July 12, 1918.

NEGRETE
Application for Pardon, File #381, California State Archives; *People v. Negrete,* 178 Cal. 802 (1918); *Oakland Tribune,* January 26–27 1918, September 15, 1918, October 19, 1918, November 29, 1918; *Mountain Democrat,* February 9, 1918.

SHORTRIDGE
Application for Pardon, File #462, California State Archives; *People v. Shortridge,* 179 Cal. 507 (1918); *Modesto Evening News,* May 7, 1918, May 14, 1918, May 2, 1919; *Oakland Tribune,* February 18, 1919; *Mountain Democrat,* May 10, 1919.

TYREN
Application for Pardon, File #508, California State Archives; *People v. Tyren,* 179 Cal. 575 (1919); *Ogden Examiner,* May 8, 1918; *Lodi Sentinel,* May 18, 1918; *Modesto Evening News,* February 13, 1919; *Oakland Tribune,* May 23, 1919.

CLIFTON
Application for Pardon, File #8905, California State Archives; *People v. Clifton,* 186 Cal. 143 (1921); *Oakland Tribune,* July 9, 1920, October 21, 1921; *Fresno Morning Republican,* October 3, 1921.

BISQUERE
Application for Pardon, File #33, California State Archives; *Modesto Evening News,* January 26, 1923; *Reno Evening Gazette,* January 26, 1923.

DONNELLY
Application for Pardon, File #135, California State Archives; *People v. Donnelly,* 190 Cal. 57 (1922); *Oakland Tribune,* November 14, 1921, February 23, 1922; *Modesto Evening News,* March 21, 1922; *Reno Evening Gazette,* February 23, 1922.

KELS
Application for Pardon, File #8477, California State Archives; *Fresno Bee,* September 13, 1923, October 2–3, 1923, October 5, 1923, October 16, 1923,

November 3, 1923, December 5–6, 1923, December 15, 1923; *Modesto Evening News*; September 13, 1923, September 15, 1923, October 2, 1923, October 4, 1923, October 6, 1923, October 8, 1923, October 10, 1923, October 22, 1923, November 13–14, 1923, December 17–19, 1923, December 25–27, 1923, December 31, 1923, January 3–4, 1924, January 12, 1924, January 15, 1924, February 28, 1924, March 22, 1924, March 29, 1924; *Woodland Daily Democrat*; September 29, 1923, October 1, 1923, October 4–5, 1923, October 25, 1923, November 10, 1923, January 4, 1924, January 18, 1924; *Reno Evening Gazette*, September 29, 1923, January 5, 1924; *Nevada State Journal*, October 2, 1923, October 10, 1923, October 13, 1923, October 28, 1923, December 16–17, 1923, January 4, 1924, January 6, 1924, March 30, 1924; *Lodi Sentinel*, October 2, 1923, October 4, 1923, October 6, 1923, October 9–10, 1923, October 12, 1923, October 20, 1923, October 27, 1923, November 15, 1923, November 20, 1923, December 22, 1923, January 3, 1924, January 5, 1924, January 8, 1924; *Oakland Tribune*, October 3–6, 1923, December 13, 1923, December 15, 1923, December 19, 1923, December 22, 1923, January 2, 1924, January 7, 1924, January 14, 1924, March 22, 1924.

SLISCOVITCH

Application for Pardon, File # 473, California State Archives; *People v. Sliscovitch*, 193 Cal. 544 (1924); *Modesto Evening News*, November 23, 1922, August 22, 1924; *Woodland Daily Democrat*, May 12, 1923; *Reno Evening Gazette*, September 22, 1923, September 26, 1923; *Oakland Tribune*, August 22, 1924; *Billings Gazette*, August 22, 1924.

MATHEW/SINUEL

Application for Pardon, File #619, California State Archives; *People v. Matthew*, 68 Cal. App. 95 (1924); *Fresno Bee*, November 3, 1923; *Nevada State Journal*, November 4, 1923, November 7, 1923; *Oakland Tribune*, December 24, 1923, January 13, 1924; *Modesto Evening News*, December 12, 1924.

GEREGAC

Application for Pardon, File #594, California State Archives; *People v. Ferdinand*, 194 Cal. 555 (1924); *Modesto Evening News*, November 9, 1923, November 27, 1923, January 27, 1924, January 28, 1924, January 14, 1925; *Oxnard Daily*, November 27, 1923, January 16, 1925; *Fresno Bee*, November 30, 1923; *Nevada State Journal*, January 29, 1924, July 29, 1924, January 16, 1915; *Sheboygan Press-Telegram*, February 1, 1924; *The Fresno Bee*, February 7, 1924; *Daily Independent* (Pennsylvania) February 7, 1924.

MONTIJO

Application for Pardon, File #632, California State Archives, *People v. Perry*, 195, Cal. 623 (1925); *Oxnard Daily Courier*, February 21, 1924; *Nevada State Journal*, February 21, 1924, February 24, 1924; *Chillicothe Constitution*, February 23, 1924; *Oakland Tribune*, February 27, 1924, May 2, 1925, July 9, 1925; *Fresno Bee*, March 14, 1924, July 10, 1925; *Modesto Evening News*, May 29–30, 1924.

CONNELLY
Application for Pardon, File #94, California State Archives; *People v. Connelly*, 195, Cal. 584 (1925); *Woodland Daily Democrat*, February 7, 1922; *Modesto Evening News*, February 13, 1922; *Mountain Democrat*, February 18, 1922; *Oakland Tribune*, May 31, 1922, June 2, 1924, March 16, 1925, July 23, 1925; *Nevada State Journal*, June 13, 1924, July 23, 1925; *Billings Gazette*, June 18, 1924; *Gridley Herald*, June 28, 1924, July 30, 1924; *Fresno Bee*, July 26, 1924; *Hayward Review*, July 25, 1925.

BOLLINGER
Application for Pardon, File # 32, California State Archives; *People v. Bollinger*, 196 Cal. 191 (1925); *Gridley Herald*, May 31, 1924, June 28, 1924; *Woodland Daily Democrat*, June 27, 1924, August 7, 1924; *Oakland Tribune*, June 27, 1924, July 16, 1924, August 3, 1924, October 9, 1924; *Modesto Evening News*, June 27, 1924; *Independent* (Montana), October 22, 1925; *Zanesville Signal*, January 3, 1926; *Sterling Daily Gazette*, June 17, 1926.

SLOPER
Application for Pardon, File #460, California State Archives; *People v. Sloper*, 198 Cal. 238 (1926); *Billings Gazette*, February 6, 1924; *Fresno Bee*, February 21, 1924, April 10, 1925, September 11, 1925, November 14, 1925, November 16, 1925, February 22, 1926, February 26–27, 1926, April 2, 1926, April 16, 1926, June 23–24, 1926; *Oakland Tribune*, April 10, 1925, June 1, 1925, June 13, 1925, June 20, 1925, September 11, 1925, February 23, 1926, April 1, 1926, April 9, 1926, April 13, 1926, April 29, 1926, June 22, 1926, June 26, 1926; *Reno Evening Gazette*, September 8, 1925, April 25, 1926; *San Mateo Times*, June 25, 1926; Nevada State Journal, June 26, 1926.

PEEVIA
Fresno Bee, June 8, 1926, August 26–27, 1926; *Nevada State Journal*, June 10, 1926; *Reno Evening Gazette*, August 26, 1926; *Oakland Tribune*, August 27, 1926; *Modesto Evening News*, August 28, 1926.

ARNOLD/SAYER
Application for Pardon, File #570, California State Archives; *People v. Arnold*, 199 Cal. 471 (1926); *Woodland Daily Democrat*, November 6–9 1924, November 21, 1924, February 2, 1925, February 20, 1925, March 5, 1925, January 27, 1926, January 27–29, 1927, February 1, 1927, February 4, 1927; *Oakland Tribune*, November 6–7, 1926, February 1, 1925, May 15, 1925, September 20, 1925, November 13, 1926, December 26, 1926, January 27, 1927, February 2–4, 1927; *Modesto Evening News*, January 13, 1927, January 27–29, 1927, February 4–6, 1927; *San Mateo Times*, January 26, 1927, February 5, 1927; *Fresno Bee*, January 29, 1927, February 6, 1927; *Ogden Standard-Examiner*, January 30, 1927, February 5, 1927.

SHANNON

Application for Pardon, File #464, California State Archives; *People v. Shannon*, 203 Cal. 139 (1928); *Fresno Bee*, January 6, 1927, February 19, 1927, March 17, 1927, March 23–24, 1927, April 8, 1927; *Reno Evening Gazette*, January 6, 1927, January 8, 1927; *Oakland Tribune*, January 6, 1927 January 8, 1927 January 11, 1927, February 8–9, 1927, February 14, 1927, April 1, 1926, May 1, 1928, May 4, 1928; *San Mateo Times*, January 7–8, 1927, January 13, 1927; *Modesto Evening News*, January 8–9, 1927, January 14, 1927, January 19, 1927, February 10, 1927; *Woodland Daily Democrat*, January 8, 1927, February 10, 1927, May 10, 1928; *Nevada State Journal*, January 9, 1927 February 1, 1927, February 8, 1927; *Salt Lake Tribune*, February 10–11, 1927; *Modesto News Herald*, March 22, 1927, March 24, 1927, March 29, 1927, May 3, 1928; *Ogden Standard-Examiner*, January 30, 1928.

KURYLA

Application for Pardon, File #253, California State Archives; *Woodland Daily Democrat*, November 14, 1928, January 24, 1929; *Mountain Democrat*, November 23, 1928; *Modesto Evening News*, January 25, 1929; *Oakland Tribune*, January 25, 1929; *Reno Evening Gazette*, January 25, 1929.

RANDOLPH

Fresno Bee, November 27, 1928, November 29–30, 1928, December 7, 1928, February 7–8, 1929; *Modesto News Herald*, November 28, 1928; *San Antonio Express*, December 4, 1928.

ROWLAND

Application for Pardon, File #439, California State Archives; *People v. Rowland*, 207 Cal. 312 (1929); *Fresno Bee*, October 15, 1928; *Woodland Daily Democrat*, October 20, 1928; *Modesto News Herald*, November 27–28, 1928; *Oakland Tribune*, September 27, 1928.

STOKES/BROWN/GREGG/BURKE/CROSBY

Application for Pardon, File #575, California State Archives; *People v. Brown*, 207 Cal. 172 (1929); *Reno Evening Gazette*, September 26, 1924; *Oakland Tribune*, November 11, 1924, November 24–29, 1927, December 1, 1927, December 5, 1927, January 5, 1928, February 7–8 1928, February 15–16, 1928, February 29, 1928, April 11, 1928, May 15, 1928, June 8, 1928, June 6, 1929, June 27, 1929, October 24, 1929, January 10, 1930, January 12, 1930, January 16, 1930, March 20, 1931, December 3, 1941, February 18, 1947; *Evening State Journal and Lincoln Daily News*, November 24, 1927; *Fresno Bee*, November 25, 1927, November 27, 1927, December 7, 1927, February 16, 1928, May 23, 1928, July 29, 1929, December 31, 1929, January 1, 1930, January 3, 1930, January 10, 1930, January 17, 1930, November 28, 1930; *Burlington Daily Times*, November 25, 1927; *Woodland Daily Democrat*, November 26, 1927, December 9, 1927, February 15, 1928, February 21, 1928, January 17, 1930, January 9, 1931; *Modesto News Herald*,

November 27, 1927, February 8, 1928, February 23–24, 1928, February 28, 1928, May 29, 1928, March 11, 1930; *San Mateo Times*, November 28, 1927, November 30, 1927, January 26, 1928, April 13, 1928, April 23, 1928, January 3, 1930, January 9–10, 1930, January 17, 1930. February 20, 1931; *Pennsylvania Derrick*, November 29, 1928; *Gridley Herald*, March 17, 1928; *Charleston Gazette*, May 31, 1928, January 18, 1930; *Cumberland Evening Times*, January 3, 1930; *Ukiah Republican Press*, January 8, 1930; *Denton Record-Chronicle*, January 31, 1930; *Vidette Messenger*, January 25, 1932; Jim Brown, *Images of America: Folsom Prison*, San Francisco, Arcadia Publishing, 2008.

Boss/Davis
Application for Pardon, File #576, California State Archives; *People v. Boss*, 210 Cal. 245 (1930); *Woodland Daily Democrat*, November 19, 1929, November 26, 1929, November 30, 1929, December 2, 1929, December 4, 1929, December 6, 1929, December 11, 1929, January 11, 1930, January 14, 1930, December 2, 1930, December 4, 1930; *Oakland Tribune*, December 6, 1929, December 17, 1929, January 9, 1930, December 5, 1930; *Centralia Daily Chronicle*, January 7, 1930; *Fresno Bee*, January 11, 1930, June 29, 1930, September 11, 1930, December 5, 1930; *Helena Independent*, January 12, 1930; *San Mateo Times*, November 25, 1930; *Modesto News Herald*, December 5, 1930; *Ukiah Republican Press*, December 10, 1930.

Mott
Application for Pardon, File #347, California State Archives, *People v. Mott*, 211 Cal. 744 (1931); *Oakland Tribune*, February 19–20, 1930, July 17, 1931; *Woodland Daily Democrat*, February 19, 1930; Fresno Bee, February 19, 1930, July 17, 1931; *San Mateo Times*, July 16, 1931; *Modesto News Herald*, July 17, 1931.

McCabe
Department of Corrections, Folsom Inmate Case File #432, California State Archives; *People v. McCabe*, 212 Cal. 70 (1931); *Fresno Bee*, June 24, 1931; *Hayward Daily Review*, July 24, 1931.

Hudson/O'Neill
Application for Pardon, File 604, California State Archives; *County of Los Angeles v. Industrial Accident Commission*, 123 Cal. App. 12 (1932); *Oakland Tribune*, December 23, 1930, August 6, 1931; *Fresno Bee*, December 23, 1930, August 6, 1931, September 30, 1931; *Salt Lake Tribune*, February 16, 1931; *San Mateo Times*, October 2, 1931.

Burkhart
Application for Pardon, File #19, California State Archives; *People v. Burkhart*, 211 Cal. 726 (1931); *Modesto News Herald*, March 25, 1930, July 21, 1930, July 1, 1931, September 23, 1931, October 21, 1931, November 17, 1931; *Fresno Bee*, March 25, 1930, March 30, 1930, March 15, 1931, December 3, 1931, December 11, 1931, January 13, 1932; *Oakland Tribune*, July 19, 1930, March 14, 1931, June 2, 1931, January 15, 1932, January 28–29, 1932; *Billings Gazette*, July 19, 1930; *San Mateo Times*, January 15, 1932.

WALKER

Application for Pardon, File #550. California State Archives; *Fresno Bee*, November 14, 1931, November 18, 1931, December 11, 1931, January 4, 1932, January 5–6, 1932, January 8, 1932, March 20, 1932, July 21, 1932, August 4, 1932, August 19, 1932; *Modesto News Herald*, November 14, 1931, March 16–18, 1932; *Oakland Tribune*, March 14, 1932; *Van Nuys News*, April 7, 1932.

FARRINGTON

Application for Pardon, File #174, California State Archives; *People v. Farrington*, 213 Cal. 459 (1931); *Fresno Bee*, April 29, 1930, January 30, 1931, December 6, 1931, January 17, 1933, February 26, 1933, March 3, 1933, March 20, 1933, March 25, 1933; *San Mateo Times*, April 29, 1930, December 2, 1932, March 1, 1933; *Woodland Daily Democrat*, April 30, 1930, June 18, 1930; *Modesto News Herald*, April 30, 1930, June 4, 1930, September 6, 1930, January 17, 1933, March 1, 1933, March 24, 1933; *Oakland Tribune*, June 15, 1930, June 19, 1930, June 27, 1930, September 3, 1930, September 5, 1930, September 11, 1930, September 22, 1930, January 14, 1931, August 26, 1931, April 12, 1932, November 11, 1932, January 16, 1933, February 26, 1933, March 3, 1933, March 10, 1933.

FLEMING

Application for Pardon, File #177, California State Archives; *People v. Fleming*, 218 Cal. 300 (1933); *Fresno Bee*, May 23, 1932, January 17, 1933; *Nevada State Journal*, May 23, 1932; *Bakersfield Californian*, May 23, 1932; *Oakland Tribune*, September 18, 1933, November 17, 1933.

VILLION

Application for Pardon, File #9681, California State Archives; *San Mateo Times*, September 21, 1932, May 1, 1933, August 26, 1933, November 14, 1933, December 1, 1933; *Oakland Tribune*, October 21, 1932, June 14, 1933; *Modesto News Herald*, October 4, 1933.

JOHNSON

People v. Johnson, 219 Cal. 72 (1933); *Oakland Tribune*, June 9, 1932, June 11–12, 1932, January 16, 1933; *Salt Lake Tribune*, October 11, 1932, October 21, 1932; *Fresno Bee*, January 17, 1933; *Modesto News Herald*, November 4, 1933; *San Mateo Times*, January 17, 1934, January 19, 1934.

D. HARRIS

Application for Pardon, File # 213, California State Archives; *People v. Harris*, 219 Cal. 727 (1934); *Daily Helena Independent* (Montana), December 6, 1932; *Woodland Daily Democrat*, December 6, 1932, February 10, 1933; *Modesto News Herald*, January 17, 1933; *Oakland Tribune*, January 17, 1933, January 23–24 1933, February 1, 1933, February 7, 1933, June 9, 1933, June 27–28, 1933, August 5, 1933; *Fresno Bee*, February 7, 1933, April 19, 1933, June 10, 1933, June 22, 1933, June 26, 1933, July 6, 1934; *San Mateo Times*, May 29, 1934; Personal communication with Jeanine Hamner via email, October 10, 2009, October 14, 2009, December 3–4, 2009.

LEWIS

Department of Corrections Inmate Case File, California State Archives; *People v. Lewis*, 220 Cal. 510 (1934); *San Mateo Times*, February 6, 1933, August 3, 1933; *Hayward Daily Review*, May 1, 1933.

NOBLES

Application for Pardon, File #376, California State Archives; *People v. Nobles*, 215 Cal. 466 (1932); *Woodland Daily Democrat*, July 14, 1931; *San Mateo Times*, December 2, 1932, December 12, 1932; *Oakland Tribune*, January 31, 1933, April 6, 1933, May 29, 1933, January 16, 1934, April 16, 1934; *Fresno Bee Republican*, August 13, 1933, September 20, 1933; *Modesto News Herald*, September 16, 1933, November 23, 1934.

LAMI

Application for Pardon, File #307, California State Archives; *People v. Lami*, 1 Cal. 2d 497 (1934); *Woodland Daily Democrat*, April 3, 1933, October 28, 1933; *Oakland Tribune*, December 22, 1934, December 30, 1934, January 11, 1935; *Salt Lake Tribune*, January 12, 1935.

BIEBER

Application for Pardon, File #9792, California State Archives; *Fresno Bee*, November 19–24 1934, January 24, 1935, February 1, 1935; *Modesto Bee and News Herald*, November 20, 1934, November 23, 1934; *Oakland Tribune*, November 20, 1934, November 24, 1934.

MCQUATE

Application for Pardon, File #369, California State Archives; *People v. McQuate*, 2 Cal. 2d 227 (1934); *Hayward Daily Review*, October 16, 1933; *Fresno Bee Republican*, October 16, 1933, May 28, 1934, June 7, 1934; *Mansfield News*, October 16, 1933; *Modesto Bee and News Herald*, October 16, 1933, December 31, 1934, May 24, 1935.

BERMIJO

Application for Pardon, File #49, California State Archives; *People v. Bermijo*, 2 Cal. 2d 270 (1935); *Woodland Daily Democrat*, October 17, 1933; *Oakland Tribune*, January 22, 1934; *Modesto News Herald*, May 31, 1935.

LUTZ

Application for Pardon, File #11967, California State Archives; *Modesto News Herald*, March 21, 1935, June 6, 1935, June 22, 1935; *Fresno Bee Republican*, March 21, 1935, June 20, 1935; *Nevada State Journal*, March 21, 1935; *Oakland Tribune*, March 22, 1935.

GARCIA

People v. Garcia, 2 Cal. 2d 673 (1935); *Fresno Bee*, October 7, 1933, October 9, 1933, July 5, 1935; *San Mateo Times*, October 7, 1933; *Woodland Daily Democrat* December 29, 1933; *Oakland Tribune*, March 23, 1935, July 9–10, 1935.

HALL

Application for Pardon, File #211, California State Archives; *People v. Hall*, 220 Cal. 166 (1934); *Chronology of Folsom Prison, 1858–1943*, author unknown; *Oakland Tribune*, March 9–11, 1933, September 27, 1934; March 9–10, 1935, March 13, 1936, March 20, 1936, March 27–28, 1936; *Centralia Daily Chronicle*, March 9, 1933; *Modesto News Herald*, March 11, 1933, March 14, 1933, April 11, 1933, August 5, 1935, August 8, 1935, November 8, 1935, March 27, 1936; *Salt Lake Tribune*, March 12, 1933; *Fresno Bee*, April 13, 1933, August 5, 1935, March 9–10, 1936, March 19, 1936, March 25–26, 1936, March 28, 1936; *Woodland Daily Democrat*, August 7, 1935, October 3, 1935, December 19, 1935, March 9, 1936, March 12, 1936, March 17, 1936, March 27, 1936, March 31, 1936; *Ukiah Republican Press*, April 8, 1936.

KIMBALL

Application for Pardon, File #266, California State Archives; *People v. Kimball*, 5 Cal. 2d 608 (1936); *Modesto Bee and News Herald*, August 19–20, 1935, August 22–23, 1935, August 25, 1935, September 3, 193, September 24–26, 1935; *Fresno Bee Republican*, August 19, 1935, August 21, 1935, August 23–24 1935, August 26, 1935, August 28, 1935, September 28, 1935, October 1–2, 1935, October 4, 1935, October 9, 1935, October 15, 1935, May 21–22, 1936; *Oakland Tribune*, August 21, 1935, August 23–24, 1935, May 22, 1936; *Reno Evening Gazette*, August 22, 1935; *Woodland Daily Democrat*, August 22, 1935, August 26, 1935, September 6, 1935, December 24, 1935; *Daily Capital News*, August 23, 1935.

STONE

Application for Pardon, File #9886, California State Archives; *People v. Stone*, 6 Cal. 2d 62 (1936); *Fresno Bee*, November 25–27, 1935, November 29, 1935, December 11, 1935, December 18, 1935, January 7, 1936, January 22–25, 1936, January 27–31, 1936, February 7, 1936, April 19–20, 1936, May 12, 1936, May 22, 1936, June 9, 1936, June 11–12, 1936; *Oakland Tribune*, November 25–28, 1935, December 1, 1935, December 3, 1935, January 23–24, 1936, January 28, 1936, June 12, 1936; *Modesto Bee and News Herald*, November 26, 1935, November 29–30, 1935, December 3, 1935, January 24, 1936, January 26, 1936, January 28, 1936; *Woodland Daily Democrat*, November 26, 1935, January 24–25, 1936.

BERRYMAN

Application for Pardon, File #9882, California State Archives; *People v. Berryman*, 6 Cal. 2d 331 (1936); *Modesto Bee and News Herald*, July 9, 1935, May 10, 1936; *Oakland Tribune*, July 9, 1935, September 6, 1935, August 13, 1936; *Woodland*

Daily Democrat, July 10, 1935, September 5, 1935; *Fresno Bee Republican*, May 5, 1936, May 8, 193, August 14, 1936.

JAMES

Application for Pardon, File #9883, California State Archives, *People v. James*, 6 Cal. 2d 226 (1936); *Modesto Bee and News Herald*, July 5, 1936, August 15, 1936; *Oakland Tribune*, July 6, 1936; *Fresno Bee Republican*, June 13, 1936.

DALE

Application for Pardon, File #9881, California State Archives; *People, v. Dale*, 7 Cal. 2d 156 (1936); *Modesto Bee and News Herald*, September 9, 1935, January 8, 1936, March 11, 1936; *Fresno Bee Republican*, September 9, 1935, October 16, 1936; *Oakland Tribune*, September 13, 1935; *Evening Independent*, January 8, 1936.

McGUIRE

Application for Pardon, File #9553, California State Archives; *People v. McGuire*, 9 Cal. 2d 399 (1937); *San Mateo Times*, December 22, 1936; *Woodland Daily Democrat*, December 22, 1936; *Oakland Tribune*, December 22, 1936; *Fresno Bee Republican*, December 22, 1936, August 15, 1937, December 3, 1937; *Modesto Bee and News Herald*, September 30, 1937.

Index

Acknowledgments

I'd like to thank the family members and descendants of the executed men, the guards, and the victims for sharing with me information regarding their ancestors. Special thanks to Sandy Kattleman, Janis Gaye, Jeanine Hamner, Shelly Gaw, Laurie Robinson, Shannon Speight, Patty Jackson, James Cotter, Glo Wellman, Donna Weaver, John Ackerman, and Henry Buchanan. Thank you also to Tom Ryan for providing me with a letter from Warden James A. Johnston detailing the act of hanging. I'd also like to thank Larry Kopp and my grandparents, Stan and Marlene Strohl, for providing information on the origin of the mug shots and documents that instigated this journey.

I owe a debt of gratitude to the Folsom Prison museum crew: Jim Brown, Dennis Sexton, and Julie Davis. To you, I say: I could have stayed all day talking with all of you that afternoon at the museum. Your expertise and knowledge is invaluable and I can't thank you enough for taking the time to dig up information for me. Thank you, too, for putting in so much effort to preserve the history of this remarkable prison. I'd like to thank Folsom Prison Public Information Officer Lieutenant Paul Baker and Correctional Officer Hamblen for taking the time from their busy schedules to take me on a three-hour tour of the prison. It was an amazing opportunity that I won't soon forget.

Thank you, Mom, for not making me tour the prison by myself. And kudos to you for not backing out, even after hearing the "hostage policy." You can officially say that you survived Folsom Prison.

Thank you to the staff at the State Archives in Sacramento, who put up with my endless requests for documents and for allowing me to camp out in the research room for hours and hours each day.

Thank you to Reverend Frank Espegren and the staff of St. John's Lutheran Church in Sacramento for letting me nose around the bell tower, where the murder of Margaret Milling occurred.

I could not have written this book without the Raintree Writers, my critique group: Kenneth A. Harmon, Patricia Stoltey, Laura Powers, and past members Brian Kaufman, Bev Marquart, and Carolyn Yalin. (An extra thank you to Laura Powers, who took on the task of line-by-line editing.) I could and I can always count on everyone's support, advice, and honesty. I'm honored to be part of such a talented group of writers.

Thank you, Scott Moore of Scomo Design for designing a beautiful cover and taking beer and gift cards as payment.

My gratitude to the Northern Colorado Writers and its director, Kerrie Flanagan, is immeasurable. Thank you for the support and knowledge through this crazy endeavor called writing.

Finally, I am forever grateful to my husband, Curtis, and our son, Connor, whose undying love and support made this book possible. Speaking to the both you: I must apologize, however, for making you put up with discussions of executions at the dinner table, and for not knowing just how dangerous touring the prison really was. It probably won't happen again. I love you both.

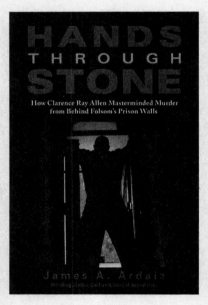